D1191209

THUCYDIDES
AND THE WORLD WAR

THUCYDIDES
AND THE WORLD WAR

MARTIN CLASSICAL LECTURES
VOLUME XII

BY

LOUIS E. LORD
Professor of Classics, Emeritus, Oberlin College
Chairman of the Managing Committee, American
School of Classical Studies at Athens

NEW YORK / RUSSELL & RUSSELL

THE MARTIN CLASSICAL LECTURES
Volume XII

The Martin Foundation, on which these lectures
are delivered, was established by his many friends
in honor of Charles Beebe Martin, for forty-five
years a teacher of classical literature and classical
art in Oberlin College.

PREFACE

THIS volume is not the series of Martin Lectures as they were delivered in 1943. Not even an Oberlin audience would have listened to eight lectures. But since I was writing about Thucydides, it seemed worth while to offer a book which not only dealt with the announced subject, *Thucydides, the First Modern Historian,* but also covered in a more general way the whole subject of the *History.* The first and last chapters are substantially two of the lectures as they were delivered. I have added to them the second and third chapters, which I hope may give the reader unacquainted with Thucydides something of a background, and also a rather full summary of Thucydides' great work in chapters IV, V and VI. This rather extended outline of the *History* serves two purposes: it gives briefly the facts of the Peloponnesian War as Thucydides relates them, and it gives me an opportunity to point out some of those features which make his work so memorable.

In the Bibliography I have listed only a few of the German works on Thucydides; nor can I recommend even these. I strongly distrust the soundness of conclusions as to style, method and date of composition arrived at by such critical methods. Scholars who approach literary works without a sense of humor or proportion, who have no knowledge of the psychology of non-Teutonic peoples, are likely to arrive at conclusions that are ridiculously unsound. Even as distinguished a historian as Eduard Meyer explained the

PREFACE

phrase "red-blooded Americans" as a description of
those Americans who have in their veins blood of the
American Indians. The dreary decades of Homeric
criticism have borne such dry fruits! Just so, all the
elaborate arguments for the fragmentary composition
of the history of Thucydides put forth by Schwartz,
Pohlenz and Schadewaldt have been refuted at vast
labor by Grosskinski and Patzner and finally dismissed
by Finley. After sixty years of German-inspired argument we are just where we started.

While I was greatly flattered by the invitation to
give these lectures on the Charles Beebe Martin Foundation, and while I wish to offer my sincere thanks to
the Committee for extending this invitation to me, I
realize that these lectures are not in the same class
with the eleven fine scholarly volumes which have preceded this one. My only consolation is that Thucydides, like *Hamlet,* cannot be spoiled.

To Professor Frederick B. Artz, of Oberlin College, I am indebted for many helpful and constructive
suggestions; to Professor J. W. Swain, of the University of Illinois, for wholesome restraint in mitigating
my words of appreciation for the "new historians"; to
Dr. George Karo, for that ultimate act of friendship,
reading my proofs; and to Mrs. C. S. Hartman for
eradicating many an error while presiding like Argus
over the making of the book. But by far the greatest
help and the most useful criticism have come from my
wife, who has lived and suffered, not silently, in the
atmosphere of this book for more than a year.

LOUIS E. LORD

Oberlin College
December, 1943

TABLE OF CONTENTS

CHAPTER   PAGE

   I.   THUCYDIDES AND THE WRITING OF HISTORY   1

  II.   THUCYDIDES' ATHENS - - - - - - -   35

 III.   THE SETTING - - - - - - - - - -   49

 IV.   THUCYDIDES' NARRATIVE. I, 431-429 B.C.   65

  V.   THUCYDIDES' NARRATIVE. II, 429-421 B.C.   99

 VI.   THUCYDIDES' NARRATIVE. III, 421-404 B.C.   129

VII.   THE *History* - - - - - - - - - -   171
            ATTITUDE TOWARD SCIENCE - - - - -   173
            ECONOMICS - - - - - - - - - -   179
            DIGRESSIONS - - - - - - - - - -   185
            THUCYDIDES' STYLE - - - - - - -   191
            CHARACTER SKETCHES - - - - - -   200
            THE MIND OF THUCYDIDES - - - -   209
            CONCLUSION - - - - - - - - -   216

VIII.   THUCYDIDES AND THE WORLD WAR - - -   221

NOTES - - - - - - - - - - - - - - - - -   251

BIBLIOGRAPHY - - - - - - - - - - - - -   271

INDICES - - - - - - - - - - - - - - -   277

MAP - - - - - - - - - - - - - Back Cover

I
THUCYDIDES
AND THE WRITING OF HISTORY

IF HE who desires to have before his eyes a true picture of the events which have happened, and of the like events which may be expected to happen.hereafter in the order of human things, shall pronounce what I have written to be useful, then I shall be satisfied. My history is an everlasting possession, not a prize composition which is heard and forgotten."

This is Thucydides' own statement of his purpose in writing the *History of the Peloponnesian War* and his assured conviction of his success. Everyone except H. G. Wells knows that that conviction was correct. Thucydides' purpose was twofold: first, to write an account of a world war that should have accuracy as its ideal; and second, to write a history that future generations might use as a guide to foretell what would happen under similar conditions in other conflicts.

One of the objects of this series of lectures is to examine the *History* of Thucydides with this second purpose in mind to see if the parallels between the world war of the fifth century B. C. and the world war of the twentieth century A. D. are close enough so that we may safely predicate upon the results of the former what will take place in the case of the latter. Since, however, Thucydides has so long been regarded as one of the great historians of the world, it will be profitable to consider the problem of historical writing and what constitutes greatness in a historian.

To the ancient historian the writing of history was no problem at all. Except in the case of Thucydides and Polybius the writer followed the Roman dictum that history is written for the purpose of the reader's enjoyment and not to illustrate or prove a thesis—*ad narrandum non ad probandum.*

Herodotus, Thucydides' great predecessor, wrote his history

> to the end that neither the deeds of men may be forgotten by lapse of time, nor the works great and marvellous, which have been produced some by Hellenes and some by Barbarians, may lose their renown; and especially that the causes may be remembered for which these waged war with one another.

His history is the first and one of the greatest histories of civilization. It touches on a myriad of valuable and interesting subjects—folklore, religion, geography, social customs, ethnic relations, military operations; in fact, it covers the whole field of ancient thought and activity. Herodotus says that no Egyptian, man or woman, will kiss a Greek on the lips. You will search Thucydides' *History* in vain for any valuable information of that type.

Xenophon, who is usually classed as the third eminent Greek historian, is a journalist rather than a historian. He is at best a good war correspondent. Macaulay holds no high opinion of him. He says of him, "The credulity of Xenophon is the credulity of an old woman."

Among Roman historians Caesar is unique. That clear, incisive brain of his makes him quite as preeminent among historians as among statesmen or generals. It is true he learned how to write as he went along. No ancient work is disfigured as are the opening books of his *Gallic War* with such large doses

of indigestible indirect discourse. This he gradually learned to avoid. By the time he had written
the account of four campaigns, a centurion was able to
say two sentences directly, and the history of the seventh year of his war in Gaul is notable for several long
speeches delivered in direct and telling language.

The other two Roman historians whose works have
survived and are notable are Livy and Tacitus. Livy
wrote a complete history of Rome in 142 books. He
was led to take up the writing of history by a desire to
forget, for the time being, the present unhappy state
of the Roman world. Like most thoughtful men he
recognized the futility of the life of his own generation. (Mark Twain says that any man who is a pessimist before he is forty knows too much, and any man
who is not a pessimist after he is forty knows too
little.) Livy says,

> My reward is the privilege of turning away from
> the sight of the evils which our age has beheld for so
> many years, for so long at least as I am devoting my
> entire attention to those earlier times. . . . . Our times
> are those in which we can endure neither our vices nor
> the cure for them.

The reaction of Tacitus, who wrote three generations later, at the end of the first century A. D., was
not to turn away from the evils of his time, which he
thoroughly understood. He portrays them with a
power of concentrated hatred that no other historian
has ever equalled. Following, perhaps consciously,
the condensed style of Thucydides, he outdid his predecessor and all later writers in conciseness and brevity.
He wrote the history of Rome as though he were
inditing a series of telegrams. I shall take one of the

closing chapters of his biography of Agricola to illustrate his method of interpreting history.

Julius Agricola was a distinguished administrator
and a trusted servant of the Emperor Domitian. He
completed the conquest of Britain by subduing the
Scots, a feat which has not since been duplicated. He
returned to Rome, where he died. This is Tacitus'
account of his death. (The facts are printed in ordinary type, Tacitus' interpretive matter in italics.)

> The end of his life brought mourning to us, melan-
> choly to his friends, solicitude even to the bystander
> and those who knew him not; the great public itself
> and this busy, preoccupied city came repeatedly to his
> doors, and talked of him in public gatherings and pri-
> vate circles. No one, on hearing of Agricola's death,
> was glad, nor—at once—forgetful. *Commiseration
> was enhanced by the persistent rumour that he had been
> put out of the way by poison. I have no evidence on
> which to venture an assertion.*
>
> *However it be,* throughout his illness came the chief
> freedmen and the confidential physicians of the Palace
> with a regularity unusual in a prince who visits by
> deputy, *whether this was interest or espionage.*
>
> When the end came, every flicker of the failing life,
> *it was well known,* was chronicled by relays of runners,
> *and no one believed that men so grasp at news in order
> to regret the hearing. Yet in* his face *he paraded the
> semblance of a* sorrowing heart; *his hate was now no
> longer anxious and it was his temperament to hide joy
> more easily than fear. It was well ascertained that* on
> reading the will of Agricola, which named Domitian
> co-heir with the best of wives, the most dutiful of
> daughters, he exulted *as in a verdict of honourable ac-
> quittal. So blinded, so perverted was his intelligence
> by unremitting flattery that he did not see that it is the
> bad prince who is made heir by good fathers.*

Only a glance is needed to see what Tacitus has

done. The facts in Tacitus' own account are these: Agricola's death was a sorrow to his friends and won a sympathetic notice even from the casual man in the street. Domitian sent his most intimate friends and his personal physicians to Agricola's bedside. During the last days of Agricola's illness the physicians' bulletins were brought to the palace by relays of couriers. Domitian showed personal grief at the news of Agricola's death and was much pleased by a complimentary mention in his will.

The facts taken from Tacitus' own account would lead one to believe that Domitian was a benevolent patron of Agricola. It is only when we have the facts interpreted, as they are by Tacitus, in the light of motives behind the facts, that the true picture of Domitian's relations with Agricola appear. Tacitus' interpretation must not be dismissed as mere hateful prejudice. He had lived "in silence" through the tyranny of Domitian and he knew how to pierce the hollow shell of hypocrisy that surrounded even the most trivial act of pseudo-friendliness. It is worth while continually to remember, as Macaulay says, that "facts are the dross of history."

In the opening chapter of his *Histories,* Tacitus affirms that one who professes impartially to tell the absolute truth must speak without affection and without hatred (*neque amore et sine odio*). Two pages later he speaks thus of two prominent characters of Galba's court, "Titus Vinius and Cornelius Laco, the former the most despicable of mankind (*deterrimus mortalium*), the latter the laziest (*ignavissimus*)."

None of these great historians really pretended to be impartial nor, on the other hand, does any in my

judgment pervert the truth. Each intended to tell
the story of the events he was narrating in a truthful
but entertaining fashion. These historians were interested in three things: recording events, interpreting
them and producing literature.

The coming of Christianity and the dominance of
historical narrative by writers of the type of Eusebius
and Saint Augustine changed the character of history. History became what Santayana called the
"Christian epic." Events were interpreted in the
light of how they affected the extension of His Kingdom.

The Renaissance put an end to the "Christian epic"
for a short time. History was again secularized, and
such works as the histories of Machiavelli and Guicciardini show a tremendous change of outlook. Traces,
however, of theocratic historical writing did remain,
for some of the Italians of the Renaissance discussed
whether or not it was proper for a historian to relate
treasons and crimes. Their objection to this, however, was more stylistic than ethical. Crimes and
treasons appeared unsuitable to the grand style which
they felt history should maintain. The Protestant
Reformation and the Catholic Reaction gave the ec-
clesiastical interpretation of history a new lease of life,
extending its waning influence for two more centuries.

The three centuries from 1450 to 1750 saw the crea-
tion, literally, of a new heaven and a new earth. The
discoveries of Columbus, Magellan, da Gama and
other daring adventurers, the science of Copernicus
and Galileo, of Bacon, Leibniz and Newton, set on
fire the imagination of mankind. Dogma gave way to
reason, and history was rewritten by the rationalists

Voltaire, Montesquieu, Hume and the rest. Montesquieu emphasizes the relation between national characteristics and physical environment. Voltaire emphasizes the reality and permanence of national characteristics. His *Age of Louis XIV* and his *Essays on Manners* are really the beginnings of the history of civilization.

Hume, adopting the point of view of a cultured and impartial skeptic, wrote a *History of England from the Invasion of Julius Caesar to the Revolution of 1688.* It was conceived in the very best insular spirit and might have been entitled *Britain in a Vacuum* and sung to the tune of "Britain's a Tight Little Island." The very fact, however, that Hume's vision was limited by the English Channel and the Hebrides did enable him to write the first critical account of the futile attempt of the Scots to govern the English, usually known as the Great Civil War. The writers of this period too often felt that history was based upon a catastrophic foundation. Great events were controlled by the acts of single individuals or were the result of chance.

Romanticism was a predictable reaction from Rationalism. It was the controlling force in the historical writers of the first half of the nineteenth century. Romanticism is a dominant force in such historians as Carlyle and Froude. They were under the spell of popular writers like Chateaubriand and Scott and like them tried to evoke a living and colorful picture of the past. The career of nations, in the opinion of these writers, is controlled by a miraculous force, a *Weltgeist.* Hegel gave in his *Philosophy of History* a theological turn to the Romantic tendency. It was his idea that religion was the moving and unifying factor in the development of the human race. Judaism personified duty; Confucianism, order; Buddhism, patience; Christianity, love; and because there was no other national virtue left for Mohammedanism, it personified justice. He saw in history a great epic process, a continuing struggle toward freedom.

Romanticism was accompanied by a century of nationalistic historical writers, 1800-1900. Race and national characteristics are exploited. Droysen, Ranke and Treitschke represent this school in Germany, Michelet in France, and Froude and Macaulay in England.

During the first half of this period access to new source material and the application of more rigorous critical standards produced a notable improvement in the writing of history. But over the latter half of this period spreads the foggy gloom of the so-called scientific historian. The word "scientist" first occurs in 1840. It was an ominous date in the writing of history.

In the latter half of the nineteenth century science became almost universally dominant. So many discoveries were made and such a remarkable advance in knowledge resulted that men began to feel that the application of the scientific method should be universal. The naive credulity of this period is displayed in its faith in the universal efficacy of the scientific method and patent medicines, a faith equally well justified in both instances. Accordingly, those who professed all subjects sought to make sciences of them. The world was filled with a plethora of sciences and professors thereof. Natural history became the sciences of zoology and biology, natural philosophy became the science of physics. Psychology, economics, politics, sociology and even history all became sciences.

Psychology became a science only by refusing to consider those problems which cannot be measured by physical instruments. The subjects of telepathy, of second sight and foreknowledge have all been neglected because they are not amenable to strict scientific control. In regard to foreknowledge the psychologists have taken the position that prophecy is so rare a gift that it has been necessary to ration it, that some way the Jews have secured a priority, and it is, therefore, none of our business.

The results for history were particularly unfortunate. There arose a bevy of so-called scientific historians, who collected and catalogued endless facts, who had no sense of proportion and no sense of values, who, instead of desiring to interpret facts and to write literature, scorned philosophy and literature. They thought that to write history it was only necessary to produce a conglomeration of unrelated and preferably uninteresting facts expressed in ungraceful and often unintelligible language. Writers like Gibbon and Macaulay were stigmatized because they were interesting. The irritating fact that they were still read was regarded as a proof of public gullibility and lack of discrimination. Gibbon, it seems, had labored under the impression that the form in which he expressed his thought was important. An examination of Gibbon's revision of his own work revealed the horrible fact that he had been concerned not so much with the rectification of errors as with the improvement of style, alteration of phrases, changes of assonance and greater attention to the details of his periods. On this effort to achieve eloquent expression scientific historians looked with scorn. Theodore Roosevelt, himself a writer as well as a maker of history, remarks, "Many learned people seem to feel that the quality of readableness in a book is one which warrants suspicion. Indeed, not a few learned people seem to feel that the fact that a book is interesting is proof that it is shallow." Also, in the name of science all moral values were ignored. Booth's assassination of Lincoln was just a fact, a conflict of two egoisms. Mr. Roosevelt reminds the historian, "It is no proof of impartiality to treat wickedness and goodness as on the same level."

As history became a so-called science, it first fell under the domination of economic historians. This group felt that history was controlled by economic forces and by economic forces only. Personality had nothing whatever to do with it. The war between the States was merely a struggle between the agricultural life of the South and the industrial life of the North. It was caused by the manufacture of shoes at Lynn, Massachusetts, and the extraction of sorghum at New Orleans. The righteous wrath of Garrison and the Abolitionists had nothing to do with the war. Its roots lay deeply hidden in the secret resentment cherished by the small New England farmer against the baronial magnificence of the Southern planter. The results were in no way influenced by Lincoln's long-suffering patience and Lee's high devotion.

The economic historian would have described the death of Agricola thus: In the year 93 A. D. the importation of grain from Egypt fell from three-tenths of a liter per capita for the city of Rome and vicinity to three-sixteenths of a liter. The result was a mild famine which was not greatly mitigated by the fact that the rainfall in the Po Valley was three millimeters greater in July of that year than it had been in June three hundred years before. (Footnote: During this year there died an unimportant ex-governor of Britain by the name of Julius Agricola.)

The reign of the economic historian was disputed by the geographical historian. These writers reduced history to a sort of foreordained Calvinism. That is, it was foreordained not by God but by scenery. The mountains and creeks of a people's environment controlled their destiny. Desires and motives that actuate human beings did not exist. Motives were merely rationalized desires. The people of a country did not do what they wanted to do but what the drainage of their vicinity prescribed. This school of writing produced some brilliant works, such as H. H. Powers' volume on *The Things Men Fight For*. It would be difficult to write an account of the close of Agricola's life in the language of a geographical historian. For in such an account the conqueror of Scotland would sink to a position so small that even a footnote would be beyond his deserts.

Geographically viewed, the conquest of Britain, however, would be told after this fashion. The Romans, following the river courses, were led to the Atlantic seaboard. They were allured by the music of the waves and the tin of Cornwall to embark on voyages of discovery and conquest. Landing in Britain, they were resisted by natives who painted their bodies blue and who had gravitated to their eastern coast, following the course of their principal, albeit small, river. Individuals took part on either side in the ensuing struggle, but their names are either unknown or unimportant. The usual law that islands are subservient to the adjacent coast was again demonstrated to be true by the Roman domination of Britain, a domination that rests on geographical-ethnic laws and, therefore, is destined to be permanent.

Geographical history was challenged by the sociological writing of history. According to the sociologists, every social fact has its *raison d'être* in the development of society, and so the cause of every institution must be sought in the social need which it was intended to supply. For instance, the social privileges enjoyed by the *ancien régime* were the result of services rendered by that regime at its origin. This doctrine was developed especially by the German historians who conceived that Germany had a special call (*Beruf*) to greatness, a historical destiny which Wotan and Providence demanded that she fulfill.

The sociologist boldly proclaims his unique qualification to write history by asserting that none but a sociologist can understand and explain the decline and fall of the Roman Empire. And since they are too busy to do so, we must continue to be ignorant of why Rome fell till they get time to tell us. Where the historian is interested in quality, individuality and uniqueness, the sociologist is interested in quantity, generalization, mass movements and repetition. Needless to say, in the mind of the sociologist there is no question as to which is the more important set of interests.

In the sociological history of the Roman Empire, Agricola's death would appear in this guise: In the closing decade of the first century A. D. class and vocational consciousness were quite highly developed. The freedmen and physicians of the imperial household began to feel the dignity of their station and were considerably irked by some of the assignments on which the Emperor employed them. They particularly objected to his practice of using them as his deputies in the payment of official calls. They regarded this as an aspersion on their class *mores*. A particular instance of this irritating practice occurred in connection with the last illness and death of an ex-governor of Britain in the year 93.

But the sociological interpretation of history had to defend itself against the psychological interpretation. According to the psychological writers of history, both the economic and the sociological interpretations of history are futile, because in the writing of history one is dealing with individuals or groups of individuals, and without a knowledge of the psychological background of the herd no explanation of mass motives can be understood. This was good news for the readers of history. Now at last persons and not things became important. And the psychological historians did discover some interesting facts. The persistence of Puritanism in New England was made possible by the participation of the leading men in the slave trade. John Hancock's bitter opposition to tyranny arose from the fact that he was a smuggler. Southern chivalry was merely a collective compensation for sexual looseness, racial intermixture and maltreatment of the Negroes.

The death of Agricola now appears in this form. The Emperor Domitian, a naturally exacerbated type of introvert, had developed a malignant form of jeal-

ousy-psychosis.   This led him to a crafty secretion
of all the eventualities resulting from his motor re-
flexes and, in particular, a concealment of his polemis-
tic reaction to the extrovert Julius Agricola. The immediately resultant inimical action was the insertion of
a quarter of a pound of Paris green into Julius Agricola's tea, causing gastronomic reactions fatal to the
interior mechanism of the late Agricola. Date: 93
A. D.

Scientific history, thus having run through the gam-
ut of economics, geography, sociology and psychology, was apparently about to return to a sensible basis,
but into this welter of historians, each asserting that
his own interpretation was the only correct one, Freud-
ianism reared its hideous head.   It remarked sarcastically, "Human motives, you said, are the main-
spring of history?   Yes, true, but the motives of any
individual can only be understood by examining his
early life, nay, even the prenatal influences that were
brought to bear upon him when he was yet unborn. Are
you aware of this fact," asks the Freudian, "that
Rhodes and Kipling loved the British Empire because of a mother transference?   Take the early history of our country.   Hamilton was an extrovert because he saw little of his father and was made much
of by his mother. He, therefore, stood for order,
whereas Jefferson stood for freedom and liberty. He
was an introvert.   He had an anti-authoritative complex caused by his dislike of a domineering father,
who died when Jefferson was young.   Nearly all the
early history of our country's development can be accounted for by these elementary facts.   Are you aware
that P. T. Barnum was a symbol of compensatory Pu-

ritanism?   And that Lincoln was a product of cyclo-
themia induced by a mother attachment and rebellion
against his father?"   Now, considering the fact that
Lincoln's mother died when he was extremely young
and that he was reared by his stepmother, it seems
that to really understand history one must consider
carefully the prenatal influence of stepmothers.

A Freudian's account of Agricola's death might
have run something like this: Nothing is known of the
Emperor Domitian's mother, but, from the fact that
he was crafty, cruel and an inveterate liar, it may be in-
ferred, with confidence, that she was lovely, kind and
deeply religious.   The Emperor's unsocial characteristics can only be explained as a violent reaction against
such unfortunate mother attributes. His jealous hatred of her virtues became a permanent neurosis which,
by metastasis to detestation of the virtues of his min-
isters, led him in the year 93 to poison secretly the
ex-governor of Britain.

It must be admitted, however, that recent historical
writing does owe to the scientific historians a more
critical attitude toward historical evidence. Further,
the avidity with which the scientific historians collected all sorts of facts led to the amassing of huge
amounts of material.   In an unsuccessful attempt to
digest this amorphous mass, certain categories were
cast aside. After all, even a scientific-economic-socio-
logical-psychological historian could not use all this
material.   Snooping around the hopper into which
historians were pouring all sorts of unrelated facts,
wheat and chaff, in an indiscriminate stream, in the
fond hope that in some way or other the grinding
could produce flour, harassed students discovered a

series of discarded data. These unused facts proved
to be related to the development of art, religion, medicine, philosophy etc. From these there arose histories of art, histories of medicine and so on; and,
most useful of all, histories of thought. It has been
pointed out, quite correctly, that personal motives and
ideals are often illusive and are subjects of an honest
difference of opinion, but that a man's thought can be
accurately obtained from his writing. It is impossible
to know, for instance, very much about Plato's life.
About his thought much is known. Histories of
thought and courses in the history of thought (such as
Professor Artz has been giving at Oberlin for a number of years) are becoming increasingly common and
are extremely valuable.

With the turn of the century there arose what was
called by its disciples the "new history." This origi-
nated in Germany and France and was later imported,
duty free, to America. The apostles of this school in
America were a group of teachers and students of
history at Columbia University. They wrote what
they termed the "new history." They were not overcome by modesty. They affirmed:

> It is not unfair to designate the current political
> historiography as an incomplete and melodramatic ex-
> pression of a superficial and distorted view of human
> society and social evolution." "The old history is to
> the new history as alchemy is to chemistry." "It is
> restricted to the ascertainment and literary exposition
> of episodes and anecdotes drawn from the lives of fig-
> ures in politics of the past." Macaulay's picture of
> England in 1685 is remarkable, but "any careful and
> conscientious writer who brings together all that is
> known of the manners, customs, institutions and ideals

of any age will give the reader a more accurate, comprehensive and intelligible picture of the past than is furnished by the most consummate genius of political and episodical historiography.

This new history professed to have conferred upon the world three great contributions to historical writing: first, to have given an account of more types of activity; second, to have taken into account prehistoric ages; third, to have conceived modern history as a world history. The new historians were willing also to point out in what way a history of the past could benefit the future:

> The chief way in which history can aid the future is by revealing those elements in our civilization which are unquestionably primitive, anachronistic, and obstructive, and by making clear those forces and factors in our culture which have been most productive in performing the necessary function of removing these primitive barriers to more rapid progress.

Just so; but what are primitive and anachronistic elements? Monogamous marriage and a respect for truth are at least two anachronistic elements in our culture. Is the New History's gift to the future to be the discovery of a force that will enable us to "remove these primitive barriers" and to exchange what we have for what we have not with the greatest possible speed under the impression that any change is progress? Well, for the last ten years we have seen just such a force at work. It is called Nazism.

A knowledge of the collective psychology of a period is said by these new historians to be

> . . . . necessary to explain this development, and the task of the historian is to discuss, evaluate, and set forth

the chief factors that create and shape a collective view
of life and determine the nature of the group struggle
for existence and improvement.

Progress, they complain, is limited by an undue respect for the wisdom of the ages.   All progress has
been made in spite of and against such wisdom.   This
respect is due to our long animal ancestry before we
were human beings.   This ancestry accounts for our
strange deference to authority and our unbelievable
conservatism.

> Conservatism is partially a savage and primitive
> trait and partly a sort of collective neurosis through
> which mechanism the guardians of the existing order
> seek to avoid facing the dynamic social relations of the
> present day."   "The end of man is to keep ourselves,
> body and soul, and our environment, physical, social,
> and industrial, always at the tip-top of condition—it
> is the only true divine power that ever was or will be."
> "Historians from the time of Tacitus to Kingsley in-
> sisted on passing moral judgment on their characters."
> "But we [the new historians] do not know enough to
> make ethical judgments.   When we know what the
> good life is, it will be so complicated a process that we
> shall not understand it."

A member of this guild of new historians selected
himself to write a volume assessing the guilt of the
first World War.   If any event in history has been the
result of a peculiar psychological attitude on the part
of a particular nation, certainly that was true of this
war.   The psychological attitude of the German people, the bellicose bluster of their Kaiser, in fact the
whole mental attitude of the Central European group,
was ripe for an aggressive war, yet this impartial, so-
cially conscious, supercilious new historian turned up

with no psychological analysis of groups or nations, placed no onus for the disaster on the military clique in Germany and Austria but presented his reader with a group of seven individuals, whom he names, who were directly responsible for the war.   He further states, on the authority of the German ambassador, that Sir Edward Grey was a liar.   So much for the new historian.

From this brief and rather unsympathetic survey of the history of history it is quite clear that history is a thing much like the elephant examined by a group of six blind men in the old Hindu fable.   The blind men, you remember, approached the animal from different points and as they touched flank, tusk, trunk, leg, ear and tail, they reported that the elephant was very much like a wall, a spear, a snake, a tree, a fan and a rope.

Is history, then, nothing but a "fable that men have agreed upon," "an hypothesis to account for the existence of things as they are"?   Dr. Johnson says: "The historian tells either what is false or what is true: in the former case, he is no historian; in the latter, he has no opportunity for displaying his abilities, for truth is one and all who tell the truth must tell it alike." And Tolstoy says that "modern history is like a deaf man answering questions which no one has asked him."

Aristotle thought the historian's task inferior to the poet's:

> The distinction between historian and poet is not in the one writing prose and the other verse—it consists really in this—that the one describes the thing that has been and the other a kind of thing that might be. Hence poetry is something more philosophic and of

greater import than history, since its statements are of the nature of universals whereas those of history are singulars.

Ranke's famous boast was that he would write history exactly as it happened (*wie es eigentlich gewesen*). It was later pointed out that the historian's real task was rather to show not what exactly had happened but how it had developed (*wie es eigentlich geworden*). The emphasis has now shifted one point further. We should be told not what happened, nor how it developed, but why it so developed (*warum es eigentlich geworden*).

First, then, causes are the most important object of the historian's research.

Broadly interpreted, history should be a record of everything that has happened. This is, however, quite clearly impossible. The events of the last week in a single village, if completely chronicled, would fill more volumes than all the libraries of the world could contain. At this rate history would be "complete and unknowable." Limits of time and space require, on the other hand, that it should be "knowable and incomplete." And this in spite of the fact that scientific historians tell us that all facts must be presented because elimination of some facts involves choice, and choice is a process which is subjective and, therefore, unscientific.

Even collecting material for a small portion of history often swamps a historian. Shortly after he received his master's degree from Harvard in 1896, Mr. Nelson Gay settled in Rome with the intention of writing a history of the Italian *Risorgimento*. He began collecting material. When he died in 1932 he was still collecting material. He had assembled the finest library in the world on his particular subject. He had written many valuable reviews and a few articles. He had served countless historians who were writing on the *Risorgimento,* but his task remained incomplete.

Perhaps the writing of the history of any extended period should be entrusted to a group of scholars. The now impressive series of Cambridge Histories is an example of this. Sir Herbert Fisher's brilliant one-volume *History of Europe* is not an exception to this tendency. He has covered with apparently equal facility all periods in the long course of Europe's history, but lack of space has prevented him from dealing fully with the controversial matter of any period.

Secondly, then, it must be true that, with the increased facilities for gathering information, future historians will increasingly be inclined to confine themselves to specialized branches or single periods.

In the third place, it is clear that history can never become an exact science in the sense that the physical sciences are exact. A physical science depends for its conclusions on experiments that can be repeated and verified by different scientists. Thus the truth of any physical law or chemical reaction can be verified an infinite number of times by an infinite number of people. Geology alone of the physical sciences is at a disadvantage here. Just when the geologist has computed the length of time elapsed since the glacial period by the recession of the gorge of the Niagara River during known historical times, the Niagara Falls will, quite inconsiderately, bite off in a couple of weeks more of the gorge than has been eroded in the last century and vitiate the conclusion of the geologist by a small matter of a couple of million years. It has been noted that the Mississippi River, by cutting off its bends, is constantly shortening its course, and that the distance between Cairo and New Orleans, which is now 973 miles, was 1,250 miles 176 years ago. So Mark Twain has pointed out the fact that on the basis of these undoubted statistics (a shrinkage of one and two-thirds miles a year) the distance from Cairo to New Orleans in the Silurian period was 1,300,000 miles and that 608 years hence it will be only two miles. And seven hundred years from now New Orleans will have passed Cairo on its way upstream. "There is," he adds, "something fascinating about Science. One gets such wholesale returns of conjecture out of such a trifling investment of fact."

History, however, dealing as it does with persons and motives, can never be an exact science. The fall of Rome did not take place in a laboratory. Personalities and motives are intangible and illusory. When one contemplates the tangled web of motives which underlies some of our simplest actions, he is appalled at the presumption of the historian who could tell us what conflicting emotions tore the heart of Elizabeth when she abandoned Essex to his fate or signed the death warrant of Mary. Yet he who would be a historian worthy of the name must try to do just this. For history, if it is to have life at all, if it is not to be a dead and dreary waste, history, like man, must live not by bread alone, nor by statistics, nor dates, nor facts, but by every word that proceedeth out of the mouth of its characters and by every hidden motive from which their actions spring. As Droysen says,

"Historical criticism can never reach the historical fact for this is a complex of acts of the human will. These acts have been performed and are gone. There remain of them only traces and memories."

It follows then that history must deal chiefly with personalities. It is impossible to see how any serious reader can believe that history is not largely controlled by the accident of personality. Yet this was Tolstoy's belief, and he was nothing if not serious. If Emperor Frederick III had not had a cancer of the throat, if he had lived to the advanced age of his father, William I, or his son, William II, would Germany have been armed and eager for war in 1914? The death of Lincoln must have deeply affected the reconstruction period of our own history. Charles Sumner and Thaddeus Stevens might have been able to thwart him in his efforts to "bind up the nation's wounds," but no one can doubt that he would have been able to mitigate or more probably eliminate the horrors of the carpetbag era. Can anyone read the history of the settlement that followed our first World War without believing that the conflicting personalities of Wilson and Lodge wrecked the hopes of the permanent peace that humanity had a right to expect at the close of that struggle? Would we have had as favorable an outlook in this second World War without Churchill at the head of the government in England? Would we have entered as promptly into the struggle, or been as well prepared, if Hamilton Fish, instead of Roosevelt, had been in the White House?

Prince von Bülow in his *Memoirs* has some instructive remarks to make about Germany's relation to Russia. He says that the strained relations existing between Russia and Germany just before 1914 were largely due to the unfriendly attitude of Lambsdorff, Russian Minister of War. This unsympathetic attitude on Lambsdorff's part was caused by the fact that the Kaiser had refused to confer upon him the Order of the Black Eagle when he retired from his position as Ambassador to Germany. Von Bülow strenuously urged the Kaiser to confer this honor, but the Kaiser stubbornly refused to "throw away his highest decoration." Von Bülow certainly had an unusual opportunity to study history in the making, and his judgment coincided with that of the Austrian historian, Heinrich Friedjung, who says that "history is not an exact science chiefly because it deals with the riddle of personality at every turn."

To believe that history can be written objectively is a palpable illusion. Thinking men from Euripides to Eduard Meyer know this. Euripides says, "Physical science alone is a calm investigation of unchanging facts," and Eduard Meyer adds, "The limits of what is to be considered of historical importance and found worthy of record are of a purely subjective nature." Every historian must tell his tale by a selection of facts. He cannot use them all. But in the very act of selection he is making his interpretation of history. The murder of Caesar was a political event, and the moment a historian decides to include that in his narrative, he has thereby decided to write political history.

Neither can the greatest type of historian be impartial, for "a mind devoid of all prepossession is likely to be devoid of all other mental furniture." The impartial historian may have no friends, as Lord Acton, "that great mute student," as Churchill calls him, says.

But the reason for this friendless condition is not so much that he has not flattered or praised anyone as because an impartial historian is so impersonal that he could no more radiate friendship than could a telephone pole. Polybius, the Greek historian of the Punic Wars, says:

> Directly a man assumes the moral attitude of a historian he ought to forget all considerations such as love of one's friends, hatred of one's enemies. . . . he must sometimes praise enemies and blame friends, for as a living creature is rendered useless if deprived of his eyes, so if you take truth from history, what is left is but an unprofitable tale.

And yet Polybius, for all his careful work, produced a history that was very little read. He takes the greatest of pains with his narrative, but he fails to arouse the slightest interest. Gildersleeve says, "He is scrupulous in the avoidance of hiatus but there is one hiatus which he cannot escape—the yawn on the face of his reader." If impartiality is demanded from historians, it is, as Jebb remarks, "judicial impartiality which is not neutrality." What Edmund Burke said of representatives in Parliament is equally true of historians, "They owe to the public not only their knowledge but their judgment."

History cannot be written impartially, as can botany, and the reason is quite clear. An author can approach the life of the cabbage quite objectively. He has no conception of the voluptuous thrill that a cabbage feels when it sinks its roots into well fertilized earth. He, therefore, can lay aside all prejudice and describe the life of a cabbage "without love and without hatred." If a common cabbage were to write botany, the account would be filled with prejudice of color, scorn for the inferior red cabbage, race prejudice against such foreign interlopers as the Chinese cabbage and scorn for debased cabbage substitutes like Brussels sprouts. A cabbage, however, could write an impartial history of human events, and the nearer a historian's mental processes approach those of a cabbage, the nearer he may approach impartiality in historical writing.

Macaulay has already been quoted as saying that "facts are the dross of history." And that is eminently true. For it matters little except for purposes of the card catalogue whether C. J. Caesar was born in 102 B. C. or whether, as Chase and Stewart quaintly put it, "he was born, by common consent, in 100 B. C." It matters greatly what were Caesar's intentions, his purposes and his ideals. No writer can accurately describe the work of a great personality like Caesar or William of Orange or Cromwell unless he has made himself so thoroughly a part of the age of which he writes that he is virtually one of the participants in the events narrated. And no one with imagination can become a part of any historical era without becoming a partisan of one side or the other in the inevitable turmoil of human strife.

And this necessary partiality has been a characteristic of all great historians. We have seen how partial Tacitus was. Gibbon's *Decline and Fall* began to appear in the same year that saw the birth of the Declaration of Independence. His work is still an authority for the periods which he covered, yet no one would accuse Gibbon of impartiality. He says of John XXIII, ". . . . the most scandalous charges were suppressed; the vicar of Christ was only accused of piracy, murder, rape, sodomy and incest. . . . . ." Scarcely an impartial way in which to write about the Pope. Motley, also, did not write *sine odio* when he was describing Philip II of Spain, and Macaulay is scarcely sympathetic in the picture he draws of the Tories. Yet for all the scorn that the new historians heap upon Macaulay, he was one of the great writers of history. Lord Acton heard Stubbs agree with Creighton and heard Mommsen agree with Harnack that the world's greatest historian was Macaulay. James W. Thompson, who was President of the American Historical Association in 1941, regards Gibbon as entitled to this distinction.

Among the various types of history it will always be true, in spite of the lament of the economic historian, that political history will have a larger place in the interest of mankind than any other type of history. There is much truth in Churchill's statement:

> Battles are the principal milestones in secular history. Modern opinion resents this uninspiring truth, and historians often treat the decisions of the field as incidents in the drama of politics and diplomacy. But great battles, won or lost, change the entire course of events, create new standards of values, new moods, new atmospheres in armies and in nations to which all must conform.

As Theodore Roosevelt says,

> The tense epic of the Gettysburg fight, the larger epic of the whole Civil War, when truthfully and vividly portrayed, will always have, and ought always to have, an attraction and interest that can not be roused by the description of the same number of hours or years of ordinary existence. There are supreme moments in

which intensity and not duration is the all-important element.

And this is what Justice Cardozo means when he says, "The picture can not be painted if the significant and insignificant are given equal prominence." The interest in such events as the overthrow of Napoleon or the defeat of the Persians at Salamis will always bulk larger in the consciousness of mankind than an investigation on the "Beginnings of the Manufacture of the Mousetrap." The potato crop in Maine may be a fascinating and important economic subject, but long after it has been harvested, eaten and forgotten, men's minds will dwell with sympathy and interest on the tragedy of the Inca and the marvelous adventures of Clive.

And because political history will always be the dominant type of history, the great historians will be men of affairs, men who, as Aeneas modestly says of himself, have been a great part of the actions of their times. Montaigne says, "The only good histories are those written by men who had command in the events they describe." And the man who has himself taken part in the making of history is likely to be the best judge of the value of historical evidence. He will know how much, or rather how little, importance is to be attributed to partisan speeches and party platforms. He will have a better idea of the actual influence of blocs and lobbies. He will be more likely to estimate, with accuracy, hidden forces and concealed deals. For the historian must be a man of keen insight and of mature judgment. It is just this intimate knowledge of practical politics and personal acquaintance with politicians that has enabled Free-

man to write so well of *Lee* and *Lee's Lieutenants,*
and Haskell to write so illuminating a life of Cicero.

Of course, it is not universally true that the great
historians are themselves great historical personages.
Though Gibbon was a member of the House of Commons, and Mommsen was a member of the Prussian
Diet and for one term, until he absentmindedly in-
sulted Bismarck, a member of the German Reichstag,
they were not men of large political experience. On
the other hand, Tacitus was Proconsul of Asia, the
highest office he could hold under the Empire, Macaulay was a member of the House of Commons, of
the Supreme Council of India, and Secretary of State
for War in the British Cabinet. Motley was Minister
of the United States to the Netherlands. Prescott was
Minister to Spain. And Churchill, Premier of Britain
in the present war, drew from his forty years of political experience the insight and knowledge of affairs
that have made him the great biographer of his great
ancestor, Marlborough.

To sum up then: in my opinion, the great historian
will deal with a limited period of time or a special
subject; he will deal not merely with events but will
search for their causes; he will set before us personalities, not philosophic abstractions; his personalities
will be living creatures, and he will acquaint us with
their motives; he will strive to be impartial but in this
he is foredoomed to fail, and in his failure he will
make us feel that the cause which he is driven to es-
pouse is the cause of justice and is our cause as well
as his; and if he has elected to write political history,
he will himself be a political figure of some importance.

How far does Thucydides fulfill these requirements?
Thucydides limited himself strictly—perhaps too
strictly—to the twenty-seven-year Peloponnesian
War, not the events that occurred during the twenty-
seven years of the war, but to the war and the war
alone. "Thucydides, an Athenian, wrote the history
of the war in which the Peloponnesians and the Athenians fought against one another."

Thucydides dealt with causes and not with symptoms. "The real though unavowed cause I believe to
have been the growth of the Athenian power . . . . but
the reasons publicly alleged on either side were as follows." He indulges in few extended character sketches, and it is true that in general we know his personalities only as soldiers. (Theramenes is to him a
"good speaker and a sagacious man"; he was com-
monly known as a "good dresser," Theramenes the
Dude.) Yet with all his reserve he makes us see
with remarkable clarity the resourceful Themistocles,
the Olympian Pericles, the devout Nicias, the brilliant and unstable Alcibiades, the energetic Brasidas,
the capable Demosthenes, the shifty Perdiccas, and
the ward boss Cleon. He always deals with motives.
Nicias favored peace, for "he hoped to leave behind
him to other ages the name of a man who in all his life
had never brought disaster on the city." The motive
which caused the Spartans to request the Athenians
not to rebuild their city walls, which the Persians had
destroyed, was the distrust which their allied cities
felt of the growing Athenian power; the reasons which
they alleged for the request were quite another matter. Though he, Thucydides, more than any other
great historian, gives the impression of disinterested

detachment, his account is vitally alive, and it will be shown that he is far from impartial. His history is a political history, perhaps too strictly political, and he himself, as Montaigne would require, "had command in the events he describes." He was Admiral of the Fleet.

One of the most remarkable features of the *History*, and one seldom mentioned, is the fact that it is contemporary history. Tacitus and Ranke might be mentioned as notable contemporary historians, but most historians of distinction have dealt with the past —Livy, Mommsen, Gibbon, Macaulay. The events of which they write have receded from view until their true perspective may be observed. It is almost impossible to see recent things as they are. No good history of the World War of 1914-1918 has yet been written. Only now are we at last able to lay aside sectional prejudice and see our own Civil War clearly. That Thucydides could do this in the midst of the most cruel civil war in history is proof of his pre-eminence. He is certainly the greatest, as he is the first, contemporary historian.

But simply to have satisfied all these categorical requirements is not sufficient to make Thucydides a great historian. Such a conclusion would indeed degrade history to a science. Thucydides was a great historian because he was a great man, a profound thinker. From the first sentence, "Thucydides, an Athenian, wrote the history of the war . . . . " to the incomplete close of the narrative in the twenty-first year of the war, there is scarcely a page that does not contain some keen observation, some profound judgment. ". . . . war is not an affair of arms, but of money which gives to arms their use. . . ." "For by war peace is assured, but to remain at peace when you should go to war may be often very dangerous." "And, as in the arts, so also in politics, the new must always prevail over the old." ". . . . simplicity . . . . so large an element in a noble nature." ". . . . revenge . . . . is not always successful because it is just." "For the love of honour alone is ever young, and not riches, as some say, but honour is the delight of men when they are old and useless." In no ancient author, except perhaps Aristotle, is the reader so soon and so continuously impressed by the fact that he is in the presence of a spacious intellect, that he is listening to the words of a great man of action who is also a profound student of human character and an incisive judge of men.

On February 27, 1835, Lord Macaulay finished reading Thucydides' *History*. Before he closed the volume he wrote on its final page, "This day I finished Thucydides after reading him with inexpressible interest and admiration. He is the greatest historian that ever lived."

II
THUCYDIDES' ATHENS

OF THUCYDIDES' life very little is known beyond what he himself tells us in his history and the inferences which may be made from what he says. The date of his birth cannot be definitely fixed, but it must have been about 460 B.C. His father's name was Olorus, and since Thucydides had connections in Thasos and Thrace, it is a reasonable supposition that this Olorus was descended from that Olorus, one of the kinglets in the district of the Hellespont, whose daughter Miltiades married. It seems probable, therefore, that Thucydides was related to the great family of Miltiades and Cimon.

Thucydides had large interests in Thasos and on the neighboring coast. Perhaps it was owing to these interests that, when he was elected general in 424, he was assigned with a squadron of the fleet to guard that area. He was here on this island, the most beautiful of all the islands in the north Aegean, when Brasidas, the Spartan, made his descent upon Amphipolis.

Thasos, with its delicately rounded, forest-clad hills, presents a sharp contrast to the ruggedness of its neighbor, Samothrace. From its beautiful harbor the white town looks north toward the shore of the Aegean, where lies Philippi. But the beauties of nature were far from the thoughts of Thucydides on that summer morning in 424 when word came to him that Brasidas the Spartan was at the gates of Amphipolis.

This city on the Strymon was Athens' most important outpost in Chalcidice. With all possible speed

Thucydides set his squadron in motion, but in spite of his best efforts, when at evening the triremes swept into the harbor of Eion, he knew that he had arrived too late. Brasidas had offered the inhabitants of Amphipolis easy terms, and they had capitulated. Thucydides seized Eion and thus blocked Amphipolis' access to the sea, but that was not enough. The angry Athenian assembly, charging Thucydides with having guarded his own property in Thrace at the expense of the state, passed a decree of banishment. For twenty years Thucydides did not set foot in Athens.

When he did return, Athens had fallen, and the city was at the mercy of the Spartans. He must have died soon after, probably shortly before 400 B. C. He was less than sixty years old.

When Thucydides was born Athens was at the height of her power. He lived to see her humiliation. He was ten years younger than Socrates, twenty-five years younger than Euripides. His birth coincided almost exactly (and this is perhaps significant) with the birth of Hippocrates, the great physician of Cos. Anaxagoras came to Athens about the time of Thucydides' birth, and Thucydides may have remembered his prosecution in 450 and his flight. He would scarcely have remembered the death of Aeschylus when it was reported from Sicily. When Thucydides was a youngster, the Parthenon was begun, and Phidias' gold and ivory statue of Athena was dedicated when he was in his early twenties. Shortly before he was elected general he witnessed the performance of Sophocles' *Oedipus Tyrannus,* and the year of his generalship was made notable by the performance of Aristophanes' *Knights.* Sophocles and Euripides died only three or four years before Thucydides, and Socrates' condemnation and death followed soon after.

Thucydides' life thus corresponded almost exactly with the literary careers of Sophocles, Euripides and Aristophanes. His banishment from Athens, however, from 424 to 404, prevented his intimate acquaintance with the later work of Sophocles and Euripides; of Aristophanes' plays he saw only the first four, including the now extant *Acharnians* and *Knights*.

How much he could learn of the literary activity of Athens while he was in exile we do not know. Of his travels, even, we are ignorant. He tells us that he associated "with the Peloponnesians quite as much as with the Athenians, because of my exile." His contempt for the architectural poverty of Sparta sounds like the comment of one who had personally experienced the hospitality of that loathsome place, and his knowledge of the topography of Acarnania suggests autopsy. He was familiar with Plataea but apparently he had not visited Pylos and Sphacteria. It is certain that he visited Syracuse.

Here Euripides was very popular, and Thucydides, whose scientific proclivities caused him to be attracted by Euripides' skepticism, doubtless heard much talk of his heterodox plays. He may even have seen some of them produced. At Abdera, too, in Thrace, this poet's provocative plays were so popular that people went about the streets humming the choruses. A sort of madness inspired by him, a Euripiditis, had seized the place. And it is not improbable that Thucydides may have felt his influence here, though "influence" is hardly the term to apply to the historian in his maturity. That masterful intelligence dispersed rather than absorbed influence.

At the time of his banishment Thucydides must have been about thirty-five years old. His passion for the accurate statement of facts, his determination to distinguish ultimate causes from superficial phenomena, his interest in a rational interpretation of nature, these things he acquired from his association with the Periclean circle and took with him into exile. It is doubtful if the intellectual life of Athens after 424 had much effect on his attitude toward history.

And life at Athens after the war began, that is, after Thucydides' thirtieth birthday, was not what it had been in the great years of expansion after the Persian War. During much of the time the entire population of Attica was crowded into the inadequate space within the fortifications. Disease and discomfort made life hard. Unlike the citizens of most Greek communities, the Athenians had not dwelt in crowded walled cities but had lived in villages in the open country. This made the cramped conditions they were forced to submit to in Athens all the harder to bear. Little of this appears in Sophocles. His serenity was undisturbed, and he stood aloof from the conflict between the older and the younger generations. In Hades (according to Aristophanes) he refused to contest the tragic throne with Aeschylus—he left that to Euripides. Sophocles was "gentle [εὔκηλος] here as he was there."

But in Euripides the tumultuous unrest of the times is all too evident, and Aristophanes' comedies are full of the hardships of war and praise of peace. He and his countrymen can laugh at their privations as the

English enjoy their cartoons of bombed London, but the long protracted strain wore down their spirits. What shall it profit a nation if it gain the whole world and lose its own soul? There might be an answer to that question, but Athens had lost the whole world and its soul to boot. The Athens of 424-404, the Athens Thucydides left behind him, was not the Athens of Pericles' Funeral Oration.

> And we have not forgotten to provide for our weary spirits many relaxations from toil; we have regular games and sacrifices throughout the year; our homes are beautiful and elegant; and the delight which we daily feel in all these things helps to banish melancholy. Because of the greatness of our city the fruits of the whole earth flow in upon us; so that we enjoy the goods of other countries as freely as of our own.

No amount of speculation on the influence of geography on human behavior and no amount of study devoted to the Mendelian law of heredity can account for the violently inquisitive proclivities of the ancient Greeks. "For all the Athenians and strangers which were there spent their time in nothing else but to tell or to hear some new thing." Why should "observing the heavens" mean such different things to the Jew, the Greek and the Roman? "To observe the heavens" meant to the Hebrew an awed contemplation of God's greatness. "The Heavens declare the glory of God and the firmament showeth His handiwork." "To observe the heavens" to a Roman meant practical political chicanery. The magistrate who, like Bibulus, retired to his house "to observe the heavens" meant that he hoped to find and was determined to observe ill omens that would prevent elections and render void

all laws that might be passed by an energetic colleague. It was better than appealing to the Supreme
Court to declare a law unconstitutional, for the decision depended on the eyesight of one prejudiced official and not on the judicial opinions of "nine old men."
But "to observe the heavens" to a Greek meant an inquiry into the laws that governed the movements of
the sun, the moon and the planets. It meant the beginning of astronomy. His curiosity was insatiable.
The command, "Be still and know that I am God,"
would have produced anything but silence in a Greek
community.

This curiosity led the Greeks, principally the Ionian
philosophers, to speculate on the nature of the universe and the causes of natural phenomena. This immediately led to a rationalistic explanation of events
that had hitherto been regarded as the result of divine intervention. The gods were losing ground. It
was just a little old-fashioned to believe in the super-
natural. One must find an underlying physical cause.
Even the orthodox Herodotus was affected. It was
said that the diver Skyllias leaped into the sea at Aphetae and did not come up until he broke water at Artemisium, a matter of ten miles. Herodotus says, "Let
it be stated as my opinion that on this occasion he
arrived at Artemisium in a boat." Hippocrates
taught that there was no such thing as a "sacred disease." All diseases are alike due to natural causes and
yield to specific remedies. Thucydides ignores all
superstition except as it affects the action of men.

But about the time of Thucydides' birth a reaction
took place against Ionic philosophy; or, to put it more
accurately, the emphasis shifted from a search into the

secret of the physical universe to a search for the laws that govern man's action. Not the universe but the individual was now the subject of speculation. Men sought to discover not "What is knowledge?" but "Is knowledge possible?"

This emphasis on man naturally led to speculation on man's relation to God and to his fellow men; sociological problems came to the fore. Socrates, Cicero says, brought philosophy down from heaven to dwell among men.

But there was another reaction against the Ionian philosophers, a reaction among the devout and conservative majority against this prying into holy secrets, this atheism. And as the war went on and disaster drew nearer, the people of Athens became more devoted to religion, as people always do in times of disaster and discouragement.

There arose then a sharp cleavage between the conservative elements in the state, such devout persons as the favorite general Nicias, along with such devotees of the "good old times" as Aristophanes and what might be termed the advanced thinkers like Euripides, Socrates and the Sophists in general.

Sophocles seems to have been mildly attracted by those speculative thinkers who devoted themselves to the study of man's capabilities.

> Wonders are many and none is more wonderful than man; the power that crosses the white sea, driven by the stormy southwind, making a path under surges that threaten to engulf him. . . . . And speech, and wind-swift thought, and all the moods that mould a state hath he taught himself. . . . .

Those who believe that Thucydides was greatly influenced by Hippocrates' style of reasoning and writing could find here also in Sophocles a trace of that healer's influence. For Sophocles goes on, "Only against Death shall he call for aid in vain; but from baffling maladies he hath devised escapes." The only difficulty is that Hippocrates was eighteen years old when this was written. In his youth Sophocles may have been attracted by metaphysical speculation, though the passage quoted above is slight evidence of the fact. What is certain is that his life and his writing were both devoted to a reasoned and serene conservatism. At the end it was not the march of man's achievements that held his admiration, but the gifts of his own native city.

> And a thing there is such as I know not by fame on Asian ground, or as ever born in the great Dorian isle of Pelops,—a growth unconquered, self-renewing, a terror to the spears of the foemen, a growth which mightily flourishes in this land,—the gray-leafed olive, nurturer of children. . . . . And another praise have I to tell for this city of our mother, the gift of a great god, a glory of the land most high; the might of horses, the might of young horses, the might of the sea.

The olive that fed the people, the steeds of the young horsemen that still swing in procession down the Parthenon frieze, the oars that sped Athens' triremes, these are the pride of Sophocles' old age.

But Euripides was tormented by the riddle of the universe and many other questions. He was not deeply interested in the drama—it was rather the problems of human action that vexed him, and he used the drama for their exposition for lack of a better literary form. And this was unfortunate for the drama. He was a thinker, not a playwright. Sir Richard Jebb says, in effect, that Euripides should have written the drama as Sophocles did or else he should have sat down and kept still. But the questions his plays raise will not down. They cry for solution, and so Aristophanes, the conservative, inveighs against the new education of the Sophists and the new poetry of Euripides. In his view young men are being taught to be disrespectful of their elders, to question the worship of the gods; the youth themselves are degenerate, corrupted by luxury, soft, poor descendants of "the men who at Marathon fought"; the music of Euripides' choral odes is jazz. He has degraded the glorious heroes of the past. It is the endless conflict of the older against the younger generation. "Surely ye are the people and wisdom shall die with you."

Pericles died before this conflict reached its height, before the war had had its deadening effect on the populace. His sympathies were with the philosophers. He was criticized because of his brain trust. Anaxagoras, his friend, was condemned to death for his heretical teaching; Pericles was only able to help him escape. Damonides, a professor of music, another of his advisers, was banished, and men found fault with Pericles for allowing the professor of philosophy, Protagoras, to draw up for him the constitution of the colony the Athenians founded at Thurii in southern Italy.

Thucydides was undoubtedly of this circle. His admiration for Pericles was profound, and the whole spirit of his *History* is the spirit of scientific skepticism. What his fate would have been had he remained at Athens during the whole war is uncertain.

The temper of the people was certainly against all those who failed to be orthodox in their views; the number of trials and convictions for blasphemy shows that. Perhaps it was better, after all, that Thucydides should have spent the best twenty years of his life in Hellas instead of in Athens.

For though the Athenian people from 424 to 404 were distinctly conservative, though the forces of Aristophanes and the conservatives dominated the law courts and convicted the "atheists," though Anaxagoras was expelled and Socrates put to death, the new generation had accepted the new education, and to them the heroes of Marathon were really "musty old Japhets." Sophocles won the prizes at Athens, but it was Euripides' verses that freed the Athenians from the Sicilian prisons. Phidias might rear his gold and ivory statue of Athena in her sanctuary and might depict the birth of the goddess on the Parthenon's eastern pediment with all the religious reverence and devotion of the older generation. But the Hermes who sits so casually on his chair in the eastern frieze, holding his knee in his clasped hands and jauntily swinging his foot, is a god of the new generation. Ancient custom and belief were giving way to reason and skepticism. The new wine was bursting the old bottles.

We can imagine only dimly what were Thucydides' thoughts when he returned to Athens after her defeat. The glorious buildings on the Acropolis, which both he and Pericles foresaw would gain immortality for Athens, were still there. Indeed, a new graceful Ionic temple had risen beside the Parthenon. But the navy and the merchantmen that once crowded the harbor were gone, the strong walls of the Piraeus were overthrown, and the long walls whose building was perhaps his earliest memory were lying in the dust. Athens, shorn of all her subjects and her allies, lay defenseless, and the "fruits of the whole earth" no longer flowed in upon an imperial city. And bitterest of all for him to bear was the knowledge that all this was brought to pass by the folly of his own countrymen. As for him, he could leave to future generations a record of this disaster that might save other states from making the same fatal mistakes that had ruined Athens. For posterity his *History* should sound a warning against the greed of politicians, the selfishness of factions and the suicide of civil strife; for posterity his *History* should be "an everlasting possession."

III
THE SETTING

IN 490 B.C. at Marathon, in 480 at Salamis and in 479 at Plataea the encroachments of the King of Persia on the Greek world were arrested. The defeat of the great Persian Empire at the hands of the independent cities of Greece and the Islands was one of the great surprises of history. Perhaps nothing so unexpected has occurred in the two thousand years since, except the defeat of the Russian colossus by the small Empire of Japan in 1905.

The Greeks owed their success primarily to the farsighted statesmanship of the Athenian Themistocles and to the superiority of the Greek foot soldiers. Themistocles was the brains of the combination which for a short time held together the Greek cities in their one period of voluntary cooperation. He induced the Athenian democracy to forgo selfish pleasure and to devote the state revenue not to the support of the citizens in WPA projects (that came later) but to the building of a navy. The strength of the Athenian Navy, which was the backbone of the fleet that operated against Xerxes, was the great contribution which Themistocles made to the freedom of Greece. His ability won from Thucydides the highest praise.

The land forces of Greece were led by Sparta. She furnished the largest number and the best troops. It was the valor of these troops and the superiority of their arms over those used by the Persians which enabled Pausanias, the commander of the Spartans at Plataea, to gain the final victory that drove the Persians out of Greece. Of this achievement Herodotus says, "The most famous victory of all those about which we have any knowledge was gained by Pausanias"; such praise as this he does not accord to any other leader in the Persian wars.

The final victory of the Greeks over the Persian fleet and the Persian army at Mycale in 479 relieved Greece for the moment from the threat of invasion. But no man could tell when the Persians would reassemble their vast forces and collect themselves for another effort to subjugate the free Greek cities. Organized resistance seemed necessary. For a short time it appeared that the Spartans would take the lead in this organization against the Persian King, but the inertness of their character prevented that. Moreover, their insufferable insolence and their veniality made them hated by all the city states which they tried to administer. Rejected and disgusted, they withdrew and left the field to Athens.

Driven by their constant fear of another Persian invasion, the free cities, under the leadership of Athens, formed a league, the Confederacy of Delos. This league consisted of Athens and the other cities. The exact number is unknown, it varied from time to time; but there were at least 260. These cities were located along the eastern coast of Greece, throughout the islands that dot the Aegean Sea and down the coast of Asia Minor. They were free and independent states, paying tribute and allegiance to no superior.

They entered the Confederacy voluntarily under the condition that each state was to furnish yearly for the common defense a certain number of ships. But since some of the states were too small to equip even a single trireme, it was arranged that they might pay a fixed

amount of money into the common treasury. This
money would be employed by Athens to build the
ships. Other states, large enough to equip one or
more ships, found it more convenient to pay the money than to construct and maintain the boats. This
number increased as the years passed, and before long
only the large islands, Lesbos, Chios and Samos, contributed actual ships.

Thus the Confederacy embraced all the cities of this
large region stretching from the Island of Rhodes on
the southeast along the coast of Asia Minor, to Byzantium (Istanbul) and Chalcedon on the Bosporos,
as well as those lying at the north end of the Aegean
Sea, a large group on the Chalcidian peninsulas, Euboea and the Cyclades. "All" is not strictly correct, for
there were a few cities that did not join.

Among these was Carystus, a city on the southern
end of Euboea, the large island lying along the east
coast of Attica. It seemed illogical to the Athenians
that Carystus should not be a member. All the other
cities of Euboea made their contributions to this worthy project; why should Carystus be exempt? The
answer naturally was that it should not, and the next
step was to compel it by force to join the League.

When the Confederacy was formed, nothing was
said about the possibility of withdrawal. It is probable that this was an intentional omission. The Confederacy at first was a haphazard, loose arrangement,
and it seems likely that no one expected it to last indefinitely. Once formed, however, its advantages
were so clear, especially to the Athenians, that the
question of withdrawal, when raised by Naxos, the

largest of the Cyclades, was answered in the negative by those who controlled the Confederacy, as was the proposal of the eleven southern states to withdraw from the Federal Union in 1861. Naxos was subdued by force and compelled to remain in the Confederacy and to continue its contributions. The next year the same thing happened to the great Island of Thasos, the largest island in the northern group. These two precedents made it clear that no member could withdraw from the Confederacy unless it could make good its withdrawal by successful resistance.

The treasury of the League, into which was paid annually about one-half million dollars, was kept in the little sacred Island of Delos, deposited there in the temple of Apollo. The Athenians, however, began to feel that so large an amount of money could not be safely left in so unprotected a situation; the Phoenician fleet might possibly seize this money before the Athenians could intervene. Accordingly, they moved the treasury to Athens and deposited it in the new temple erected to their patron goddess, Athena. The Parthenon became the safety deposit vault of the Confederacy of Delos, which now was more exactly the Athenian Empire.

The Greek cities were now arranged in three classes, with Athens in control. First there were Lesbos, Chios and Samos, the three independent islands, each supporting a small navy and paying no tribute to Athens; second, something over two hundred cities, each of which contributed money annually but managed its own affairs; and third, cities like Carystus and Naxos, after its reduction, which were subject to Athens. These paid a tribute.

Payment of this contribution or tribute or tax, by whatever name it was called (the Greeks called it a φόρος), was distasteful to the free Greek cities. They had begun by making a voluntary contribution for protection against a potential invasion. They now found themselves, twenty-five years after the last battle with Persia, still paying this contribution to avert an invasion which was no longer a threat and, as the Persian monarchy lost its driving power, was not even a vague danger. Naturally they asked the question, "What are we getting out of this?"

They were further irked by the fact that at the call of Athens they were subject to military service, either as foot soldiers, in campaigns which brought them nothing and Athens everything, or as rowers in the fleet. Further, legal questions involving crime had to be referred to Athens for decision. It was infinitely hurtful to the pride of the Greek in Paros who had beaten up his neighbor over some personal dispute to be put to the expense and trouble of going to Athens to explain before an inquisitive Attic jury just why he had felt it necessary to operate on the anatomy of his neighbor.

A still further limitation was imposed on these free Greek cities by their membership in the League. They were forced to maintain a democratic, as opposed to an aristocratic, constitution. This, too, was irksome to the Oligarchs, who were excluded from power as long as their city was a member of the Confederacy. Just as every well regulated community in Britain today contains its Conservatives and Liberals, and every hamlet in America its Democrats and Republicans, so every Greek city contained two parties, a Democratic and an Oligarchic faction.   These parties were maintained in the Greek cities with an intensity of conviction that would be the envy of every New-Dealing Democrat.   Aristotle has been given a great deal of credit for pointing out that man is a political animal. Considering the fact that he dealt with Greeks, this observation lacks fundamental profundity.   When a Greek community the size of the modern town of Pylos, with a population of 2,180, can produce twenty-three candidates for the office of mayor, to discover the fact that man is a political animal certainly does not qualify the author of the remark for the title of "the master of them that know."

These Greek communities were intensely proud of their freedom.   Even a second-rate author like Xenophon can become eloquent over it.   He says, "You [Greeks] bow the knee to no man but to the gods alone."   Independence and the right to "liquidate" political opponents were the two most important phases of the Greeks' desire for life, liberty and the pursuit of happiness.

The removal of the treasury from Delos to Athens was the final step in converting this voluntarily contributing galaxy of Greek states to an empire controlled and managed by and for the people of Athens.   And it was a proud empire.   Through the Bosporos and the Dardanelles, controlled by Athens' cities, came the grain from the rich fields of Russia to feed the people of Athens.   Across the Aegean from Ephesus, Miletus and Rhodes came the products of the East, to be sold in Athens' markets.   Through the Aegean, past the fair islands dotted with white cities subject to Athens, sailed the Athenian merchant vessels carrying the manufactures of Athens to be sold to their subject states. At the western end of the Gulf of Corinth was the allied city of Naupactus, Athens' Gibraltar, assuring the Athenian merchant safety on his western voyage from the marauding rival, Corinth.

It is not necessary, and this is not the place, to enlarge on what all this wealth pouring in upon Athens meant. It meant the Age of Pericles, with all the beauty, art and literature that have come down to us to enrich our civilization.

The energy of this imperial city may be judged by the achievements of a single year. In 459 B. C. the Athenians defeated a Peloponnesian fleet off the Island of Aegina and began the successful siege of the town. Aegina was, after Corinth, their most active commercial rival. They occupied Megara, the pestiferous Doric town near the east side of the Isthmus of Corinth, and when the Corinthians tried to expel them they were defeated by an emergency army of Athenian old men and boys. They manned and equipped a fleet of two hundred vessels, which sailed to Egypt, went up the Nile and took the royal Egyptian city of Thebes. Two years later they defeated the Boeotians, their neighbors on the north, and mastered all their cities except Thebes.

It is true that the gains of this remarkable year were soon lost. The great squadron which had first been so successful in Egypt was defeated five years later and largely destroyed. Athens was forced to abandon Boeotia and to give up Megara. But as compensation for this, all of Euboea was conquered and its supplies were at the disposal of the Athenians, and Samos, one of the three independent members of the League, which had revolted, was conquered and reduced to the rank of a dependency.

When the Peloponnesian War opened Athens was, therefore, mistress of this naval empire, having associated with her only two very subordinate states, Lesbos and Chios. She had appropriated the funds of the Confederacy to beautify herself. In the Parthenon there was a reserve treasure of six million dollars. The income from the League was spent on the beautification of Athens, and this was done deliberately. Thucydides (not the historian) had tried to make the Athenians feel that this was an illegal use of the money. The question had been put to a public vote, and Thucydides had been driven into exile. There can be little question that by modern standards Thucydides was right, but the glories of the age of Athenian greatness could not have been achieved if his policy had been followed. There will be few who will regret the choice which Athens made.

Opposed to Athens were the Lacedaemonians and their allies. The superiority of the Spartans on land was unquestioned. Several times during the war that followed this superiority was challenged, and the challenger invariably lost.

The Spartan state is still an anomaly. Sparta was an armed camp in which the men lived in barracks from the time they came to manhood until they were sixty. They ate in a common mess hall and visited their families only surreptitiously. At the head of the state were two kings, who were controlled by a board of nine men, the Ephors, who acted as the King's executive council, advisors and supervisors. Legislation was reduced to a minimum. It was handled by a senate, all of whose members were over sixty. Its decisions were ratified or rejected by the assembly without debate.

These Spartan families were supported by a slave class called Helots. In peace the Helots did all the work. In war they accompanied their masters and fought with them in their campaigns. A revolt among the Helots, who far outnumbered the Spartans, was a thing always to be dreaded. To prevent it the Spartans had each year an open season for Helots during which it was lawful and desirable for the Spartans to kill them. Thus the ringleaders were thinned out, and satisfactory living conditions attained. Thucydides mentions one occasion when, as an extra precaution, two thousand of the most energetic and outstanding Helots were promised their freedom and then secretly murdered.

Frugality was cultivated among the Lacedaemonians by using for money iron instead of gold, silver and bronze. Hoarding was thus discouraged, for even a small fortune would clutter up the house and overflow into the back yard. Stealing, if undetected, was honorable, but there were few thefts of money, for it was too cumbersome to conceal on one's person. Even a strong man could not carry off more than thirty cents' worth. The result was that a Spartan, unaccustomed to handling gold and silver coin, was so dazzled by metallic glitter whenever he got beyond the boundaries of his country that his allegiance was purchased not by the highest but by the first bidder.

All luxuries were denied the Spartans, even the luxury of speech. In its earlier and purer form Fascism imitated this practice. In the town hall at Mantua the three Fascist beatitudes blazoned on the wall were: *Saluto Romano; Brevi Visite; Non Sputare Sul Pavimento.* The two contributions that the Lacedaemonians have made to modern civilization are the inspiring example of Spartan courage and the too little heeded example of laconic speech.

Sparta's military pre-eminence made her the natural head of a land league opposing the maritime empire of Athens. In this league were the other states of the Peloponnesus, with the important exception of Argos. The Argives took no part in the first phase of the Peloponnesian War because they were inhibited by a thirty-year truce which they had signed with their more powerful rival.

In the north of Greece the Lacedaemonians had as important allies the people of Boeotia, the district just northwest of Athens, with the city of Thebes as its center. Corinth was an anomalous member of the league. It, like Athens, was a maritime commercial city, and the economic rivalry and the jealousy between Corinth and Athens played a large part in animating and continuing the Peloponnesian War. In 431 B. C., then, these two rivals faced each other, Sparta, the head of a confederacy, and Athens, the mistress of an empire.

It will be convenient to outline in the briefest possible way the course of the Peloponnesian War before we turn to Thucydides' account of that struggle.

The war began with a quarrel between Corcyra (Corfu) and its colony Epidamnus (Dyrrhachium, Durazzo). Corcyra appealed to Athens for assistance in subjugating her colony. Epidamnus appealed to Corinth, and Corinth appealed to Sparta and its allies. The allies decided for war.

The strategy of Pericles, who directed the Athenian state, was as follows: All the inhabitants of Attica were to be brought into the fortified area included in Athens and the harbor city, Piraeus. These two cities, lying six miles from each other, were strongly fortified and connected by two long walls. The people were to be supported by grain brought from overseas in Athens' ships. No land battle of importance was to be undertaken, but the territory of the enemy was to be raided and his commerce destroyed. Eventually he would be worn out.

The war falls into three periods. The first phase lasted from 431 B. C. to 421 B. C. The fighting was limited to the coast of the Peloponnesus, northwestern Greece (Aetolia and Acarnania) and the northwestern Aegean. It was largely a naval war, though important land operations were also undertaken. The leading Athenian figures are Phormio, Demosthenes, Nicias and Cleon. On the Peloponnesian side Brasidas dominates the scene. Pericles' policy was followed, with some important exceptions, and was justified by the results. The first round went to Athens.

The second phase of the war covered the years of the so-called Peace of Nicias, 421 B. C.-414 B. C. It was a peace in which there was no peace. Fighting went constantly on. Nicias, Athens' most timorous general and most devout citizen, negotiated this peace. It was satisfactory to Athens and Sparta, for Sparta had consulted only her own advantage, sacrificing the interests of her allies in the same barefaced way in which the English Tories abandoned their allies in concluding the Peace of Utrecht. Sparta was unwilling or unable to enforce the terms of the peace, hence fighting continued.   Corinth, dissatisfied, naturally, with the way in which she had been sold out by Sparta, endeavored to form, in alliance with Argos (whose thirty-year truce with Sparta had expired) a new league without the Lacedaemonians.   Boeotia refused to join, and the league collapsed.   Athens, under the leadership of Alcibiades, now tried, with Argos, to organize another confederacy.   Elis and Mantinea cooperated, but the quadruple alliance was wrecked by Sparta and Tegea at the Battle of Mantinea.   The Spartan foot soldier, even if ill led, was still the best fighting man in Greece.   The engagements in this phase of the war were mostly on land and in the Peloponnesus.   They centered around Argos.   Alcibiades emerges, a figure potent for good and ill.   Spartan prestige is renewed.   The second round goes—on points—to Sparta.

The third phase of the war lasted from 414 B. C. to 404 B. C.   While the peace was still nominally in force Athens began her expedition against Syracuse. The Athenians had conceived the idea of subduing Sicily and thus erecting in the west an empire as great as their empire in the east. In this effort to subdue Syracuse the Athenians lost two magnificent armies and navies.   It was a blow that would have ruined any other state, and her allies thought it had ruined Athens.

Athens broke the peace in 414, and war was formally resumed. The theater was the Aegean and its eastern coast.   The new factor was Persia.

Persia took the side of Sparta.   All of the eastern coast of the Aegean was lost to Athens, except Samos, Lesbos, Cos and Halicarnassus.   Revolution broke

out in Athens itself. An oligarchical government of
four hundred was set up, only to be overthrown in favor of a democracy, limited to five thousand. Euboea,
the great bulwark of Athens, revolted, and still Athens fought on. They won a naval victory in 410 at
Cyzicus, and the Spartans offered peace. The Athenians refused. They were defeated at Notium in 407
and still fought on. They won a great victory in 406
at the Arginusae Islands, and then in the next year
their whole navy was caught at Aegospotami, in the
Hellespont, and destroyed. The next summer, 404,
overcome by starvation, Athens capitulated, and the
Spartans, though urged by the Corinthians and Thebans to destroy the city utterly, as Athens had done to
its victims, displayed an unexpected magnanimity and
spared Athens because of her former services to the
cause of Hellenic freedom. The final decision was
a knockout by Sparta in the third round.

IV
THUCYDIDES' NARRATIVE

I. From the Beginning of the War to the Death of
Pericles—431-429 B. C.

BY SURVEYING the early history of Greece in the first twenty chapters of his work, Thucydides proves that this is the greatest war ever waged. If these twenty chapters alone of his narrative had survived, Thucydides would still have deserved to rank as a very great historian, for nowhere in ancient historical writing does such an account of early civilization exist. No historian until the latter half of the nineteenth century conceived the possibility of such a summary of early Greek times. Here is no common mythology or tale of legendary deed, but a reasoned account, based upon scientific observation, of what early history must have been. It will be useful to give briefly an idea of this remarkable document.

The earliest Greek civilization was largely nomadic. The best lands most often changed hands as a result of conquest. The soil of Attica being poor, that peninsula did not suffer from war so much as the richer lands of Thessaly and Boeotia to the north. The Trojan War was a historical event, not a sun myth, and Minos, King of Crete, was a real person whose empire, maintained by a fleet, extended over a large part of the Aegean. The correctness of these statements of Thucydides has only been verified in the twentieth century. The scientific historians of the nineteenth century would have laughed them to scorn.

The earliest inhabitants of the Aegean Islands were largely Carians, not Greeks, as is proved by the contents of the graves opened at Delos during the Peloponnesian War. This is the earliest case where historical fact is proved by archaeological research. Piracy was a recognized and honorable vocation, as is shown by the fact that the inquiry, so common in Homer, as to whether a man's business is commerce or piracy, is a commonplace question, not an insult. The unsettled character of early Greek civilization is clear, for only recently at Athens have men given up the custom of wearing arms as a matter of everyday dress, a custom which still prevailed in many of the backward parts of Greece.

Thucydides is sometimes blamed for neglecting economic facts. Yet, in these opening chapters, the dependence of civilization upon money is constantly emphasized. "The cause of the inferiority [of early times] was not so much the want of men as the want of money. . . . Poverty was the real reason why the achievements of former ages were insignificant. . . ." The older cities were not located on the coast because of the fear of piracy. They were inland, where they were better protected. There was no collective action among the states of Greece before the Trojan War, and Thucydides' proof of this again shows his keen insight. For nowhere in the Homeric poems is "Hellenes" used as a term for Greeks in general, and, conversely, there are no "barbarians" in Homer because, of course, the world had not yet been divided into two classes, Greeks and barbarians.

Agamemnon was able to lead the Greek chieftains in the Trojan War not because they had bound themselves by oath to avenge the rape of Helen, but because he was the most powerful of all the Greek kings, and the others joined him because they feared to offend him. Thucydides determines the size of the armament employed in the Trojan War exactly as a modern scientific historian would:

> For it numbered, as he tells us, twelve hundred ships, those of the Boeotians carrying one hundred and twenty men each, those of Philoctetes fifty; and by these numbers he may be presumed to indicate the largest and the smallest ships; else why in the catalogue is nothing said about the size of any others? That the crews were all fighting men as well as rowers he clearly implies when speaking of the ships of Philoctetes; for he tells us that all the oarsmen were likewise archers. And it is not to be supposed that many who were not sailors would accompany the expedition, except the kings and principal officers; for the troops had to cross the sea, bringing with them the materials of war, in vessels without decks, built after the old piratical fashion. Now if we take a mean between the crews, the invading forces will appear not to have been very numerous when we remember that they were drawn from the whole of Hellas.

And the Trojan War lasted for ten years instead of a single campaign because of the limited resources of the assailants:

> .... the invading army was limited, by the difficulty of obtaining supplies, to such a number as might be expected to live on the country in which they were to fight. After their arrival at Troy, when they had won a battle (as they clearly did, for otherwise they could not have fortified their camp), even then they appear not to have used the whole of their force, but to have been driven by want of provisions to the cultivation of the Chersonese and to pillage. And in consequence of this dispersion of their forces, the Trojans were enabled to hold out against them during the whole ten years, being always a match for those who remained on the spot. Whereas if the besieging army had brought abundant supplies, and, instead of betaking themselves

to agriculture or pillage, had carried on the war persistently with all their forces, they would easily have been masters of the field and have taken the city; since, even divided as they were, and with only a part of their army available at any one time, they held their ground. Or, again, they might have regularly invested Troy, and the place would have been captured in less time and with less trouble.

Thucydides gives the date for the Dorian invasion, a date which many modern historians accept, the date for the naval development of Samos, for the first naval battle among the Greeks, the reasons for the wealth of Corinth (where he becomes a geographical historian), a brief and convincing account of the development of navies. He shows that Sparta's supremacy was due to the excellence and stability of her constitution, which prevented factional strife. He speaks of the difficulty of ascertaining the truth about past history, giving a concrete illustration of the falsity of tradition by showing that the belief common at Athens about the tyrannicides, Harmodius and Aristogeiton, is incorrect.

He points out the danger of trusting rumor and estimating the importance of an ancient city by the size of its remains, illustrating this by the priceless contrast between Sparta and Athens:

Suppose the city of Sparta to be deserted, and nothing left but the temples and the ground-plan, distant ages would be very unwilling to believe that the power of the Lacedaemonians was at all equal to their fame. And yet they own two-fifths of the Peloponnesus, and are acknowledged leaders of the whole, as well as of numerous allies in the rest of Hellas. But their city is not built continuously, and has no splendid temples or other edifices; it rather resembles a straggling village like the ancient towns of Hellas, and would therefore make a poor show. Whereas, if the same fate befell the Athenians, the ruins of Athens would strike the eye, and we should infer their power to have been twice as great as it really is.

To have written those sentences twenty-five hundred years ago would alone constitute a valid claim to greatness. For today the visitor at Sparta sees of the ancient town only the slightest traces, a single foundation of what may have been an important tomb or a small temple, a theater of the Roman epoch, the pitiful ruins of three temples to Artemis and the tiers of seats where sadistic onlookers watched torture inflicted on Spartan boys. The traveler today finds his only consolation for visiting the site of that great city in wandering beside the banks of the lovely Eurotas, where Helen used to run races with the maidens of her age, and in looking aloft at the towering range of Mount Taygetus.

Thucydides closes this summary of early Greek history by noting that the Persian Wars (which were undoubtedly memorable) were determined by four battles, two on land and two on sea:

> But the Peloponnesian War was a protracted struggle, and attended by calamities such as Hellas had never known within a like period of time. Never were so many cities captured and depopulated—some by Barbarians, others by Hellenes themselves fighting against one another; and several of them after their capture were repeopled by strangers. Never were exile and slaughter more frequent, whether in the war or brought about by civil strife. And traditions which had often been current before, but rarely verified by fact, were now no longer doubted. For there were earthquakes unparalleled in their extent and fury, and

eclipses of the sun more numerous than are recorded to
have happened in any former age; there were also in
some places great droughts causing famines, and lastly
the plague which did immense harm and destroyed
numbers of the people.   All these calamities fell upon
Hellas simultaneously with the war, which began when
the Athenians and Peloponnesians violated the thirty
years' truce concluded by them after the recapture of
Euboea.

Thucydides also states his own method of historiography at this point and later amplifies it by speaking
of his exile:

As to the speeches which were made either before or
during the war, it was hard for me, and for others who
reported them to me, to recollect the exact words.   I
have therefore put into the mouth of each speaker the
sentiments proper to the occasion, expressed as I
thought he would be likely to express them, while at
the same time I endeavored, as nearly as I could, to give
the general purport of what was actually said.   Of
the events of the war I have not ventured to speak
from any chance information, nor according to any
notion of my own; I have described nothing but what
I either saw myself, or learned from others of whom
I made the most careful and particular enquiry.   The
task was a laborious one, because eye-witnesses of the
same occurrences gave different accounts of them, as
they remembered or were interested in the actions of
one side or the other.

        .   .   .   .

For I well remember how, from the beginning to the
end of the war, there was a common and often-repeated saying that it was to last thrice nine years.   I lived
through the whole of it, being of mature years and
judgment, and I took great pains to make out the exact
truth.   For twenty years I was banished from my
country after I held the command at Amphipolis, and

associating with both sides, with the Peloponnesians quite as much as with the Athenians, because of my exile, I was thus enabled to watch quietly the course of events.

Having thus sketched the history of Greece to the outbreak of the Peloponnesian War, Thucydides sets forth succinctly what he believes to be the deeper cause of the struggle. This statement should not be overlooked nor discounted because of its brevity. Thucydides does not go into the details of exports and imports, shore duties and excise taxes, discriminations in citizenship and limitation of trade, those tedious underlying economic causes which he might have exploited at great length. He is writing a history of the war and therefore rightly takes it for granted that economic facts underlay the jealousy which the Lacedaemonians felt for the splendid Athenian empire. He simply says,

> The real though unavowed cause I believe to have been the growth of the Athenian power, which terrified the Lacedaemonians and forced them into war; but the reasons publicly alleged on either side were as follows.

After this masterly introduction Thucydides devotes the rest of the first book to events preceding the actual outbreak of hostilities. He begins by picturing the situation in Epidamnus (modern Durazzo), where the Democratic party was in power. The alternation of power between Democrats and Oligarchs in these Greek cities corresponds roughly to the alternation of party government in Great Britain. But when the Oligarchs were in power in Greece, the Democrats were not only out of office but, if they valued their lives, they were out of the city. Instead of retiring to country estates to wait for a change of heart on the part of the electorate, they retired precipitately to some neighboring city, or when, as in the case of Epidamnus, there was no neighboring city, they removed their persons and movable effects to the neighboring barbarians, with whom they dwelt until, through intrigue or foreign support, they could again return to power and drive their Oligarchic opponents into exile.

When the scene opens in Thucydides' *History,* the Democrats were in power in Epidamnus.   The Oligarchs, from their lairs in the barbarian country, appealed to Corcyra, the mother city, to reinstate them. Corcyra refused to do so, the Democratic element in Corcyra being in power at the time.   They then appealed to Corinth, which was the mother city of Corcyra and stood in the position of grandmother to Epidamnus.   The Corinthians, who had long been jealous of their daughter city, which had shown too much insulting independence, offered to aid the Oligarchs and sent warnings to Corcyra.   Corcyra offered to submit the matter to arbitration. The Corinthians refused and sent a small squadron to attack Corcyra. The Corcyraeans defeated this squadron and on the same day captured Epidamnus, to which the Corinthians had sent a supporting squadron.

Emboldened by this double success, the Corcyraeans proceeded to devastate all the colonies of Corinth lying about the mouth of the Corinthian Gulf.   They also descended upon the shipbuilding yards in Cyllene, which had furnished some of the Corinthian ships, and sacked the place.

Corinth at once began preparations to chastise her unruly, overgrown daughter.   Seeing that the matter was to become serious, Corcyra appealed for help to Athens and offered to join the Athenian Empire, from which she had up to this time held aloof. The Corinthians also sent an embassy to Athens to state their side of the case. It was in a certain sense an appeal of both parties to arbitration. In the speeches of the two envoys, which he gives in full, Thucydides outlines with great clarity the issues which were placed before the sovereign Athenian assembly. The Corinthians appealed to precedent and justice, the Corcyraeans to expediency. The Corinthians urged their right, a well recognized one, of a founding city to control, within limitations, the actions of its colonies.

None of this is denied by the Corcyraeans. They say simply that their navy is stronger than the Corinthians', that war is imminent, that Athens will need their support, and further that all commerce going to Sicily and the west passes by their city and that for such commerce Athens needs their protection.

At first the Athenians were inclined to favor the claims of the Corinthians, supported by custom and justice. At a second assembly, however, they went over to the side of expediency. Thucydides emphasizes this change of mind because it was the first of several similar cases where expediency was allowed to sway the scales against justice. He states very plainly the reason for the decision: "For they knew that in any case the war with Peloponnesus was inevitable, and they had no mind to let Corcyra and her navy fall into the hands of the Corinthians."

The scene now shifts to the northwest Aegean, where again the Corinthians came into contact with the Athenians.

In the region called Chalcidice three peninsulas jut out toward the southeast like three fingers of a hand. The northernmost ends in the great mountain of Athos, where burned one of the signal fires which flashed to Greece the news of the fall of Troy and where now are situated the famous Greek monasteries. On the isthmus that connects the westernmost of these three promontories with the mainland was Potidaea, a colony of Corinth but at this time a member of the Athenian Empire. The Athenians, fearing that Potidaea was too much in sympathy with Corinth, ordered the Potidaeans to tear down their walls. The Potidaeans sent an embassy to Sparta seeking aid, and the Spartans promised to invade Attica if Athens attacked Potidaea. This would, of course, be in contravention of the treaty between Athens and Sparta, but since the Spartans failed to make good their promise, Thucydides does not regard this as a violation of the treaty. Potidaea revolted and was closely invested by the Athenians.

At this point Thucydides leaves the story of the Potidaeans, in accordance with the strict chronological order of his narrative, and the fate of the city is not related until Book II, Chapter 70. Potidaea eventually surrendered, the inhabitants were allowed unusually easy terms, for the lives of the men were spared, and they were allowed to leave the city, each with one garment and the women with two. The siege was expensive. It cost Athens about two million dollars.

Thucydides returns to the dispute between Athens and Corinth. A meeting of the Lacedaemonian allies was called at Sparta. Here the Corinthians stated their grievances against Athens.

It happened that there was an Athenian embassy at Sparta at the time. The ambassadors were invited to hear the discussion and also to speak. The Athenians reminded the assembled Peloponnesian envoys of the services which Athens had rendered to Hellas in the Persian invasion. They argued that the victory of Salamis was the decisive victory and that that had been brought about by the Athenians, who furnished "the greatest number of ships, the ablest general, the most devoted patriotism." Their empire had been the natural result of the inefficiency of the Lacedaemonians. They admit frankly their own unpopularity but argue that the Lacedaemonians, if they had chosen to retain their power over the Greek cities, would have been even more deeply hated. ". . . . if you, and not we, had persevered in the command of the allies long enough to be hated, you would have been quite as intolerable to them as we are. . . ." And for the first time Thucydides states the heartless principle that might makes right, which governs the Athenians' actions all through his *History*. ". . . . the world has ever held that the weaker must be kept down by the stronger. . . . . Did justice ever deter any one from taking by force whatever he could?"

The Athenian envoys meet the criticism brought against them for compelling their allied cities to bring their cases of law to Athens for decision by saying that they should be praised for this moderation, whereas they might have decided these cases in their allied cities at their own pleasure and arbitrarily. "Mankind resent injustice more than violence, because the one seems to be an unfair advantage taken by an equal, the other is the irresistible force of a superior."

The Athenian envoys closed their case by urging the Lacedaemonians not to go to war at the instigation of the Corinthians, and they offered to submit the whole matter to arbitration.

The Lacedaemonians now adjourned the conference and debated the matter in private. Up rose their aged king, Archidamus. He counseled moderation. He spoke of the power of the Athenians on the sea. Here we may well think that Thucydides is giving his own reasons and not the reasons of a Spartan. "To what do we trust? . . . . To our money? . . . . we have none in a common treasury, and we are never willing to contribute out of our private means. . . . . For if we can neither defeat them at sea, nor deprive them of the revenues by which their navy is maintained, we shall get the worst of it. . . . . Charges brought by cities or persons against one another can be satisfactorily arranged; but when a great confederacy, in order to satisfy private grudges, undertakes a war of which no man can foresee the issue, it is not easy to terminate it with honour. . . . . war is not an affair of arms, but of money which gives to arms their use, and which is needed above all things when a continental is fighting against a maritime power. . . . ."

This good advice of Archidamus might have been effective had it not been that Sthenelaidas, who was one of the Spartan ephors, the executive committee of the state, was determined on war. His speech smacks of the Spartan laconic directness. He says, "I do not know what the long speeches of the Athenians mean . . . . If they behaved well in the Persian War and are now behaving badly to us they ought to be punished twice over, because they were once good men and have become bad. . . . . Wherefore, Lacedaemonians, prepare for war as the honour of Sparta demands." That closed the debate, and a large majority voted to break the treaty. And again Thucydides, having brought his narrative to this point, emphasizes the economic background of the war. "In arriving at this decision . . . . the Lacedaemonians were influenced, not so much by the speeches of their allies, as by the fear of the Athenians and of their increasing power. For they saw the greater part of Hellas already subject to them."

With this remark Thucydides begins his account of the way in which the Athenians had acquired this commanding power. He devotes the last thirty chapters of Book I to the history of the fifty years which elapsed between the end of the Persian Wars and the outbreak of the Peloponnesian War in 431.

Professor Finley has pointed out that the digressions in Thucydides are usually introduced to support some statement which he had made. Thus the account of early Greece with which the narrative begins proves Thucydides' statement that the Peloponnesian War was the greatest war that had occurred. The following digression is introduced to prove his statement that the Athenian Empire was a great power, increasingly threatening to Sparta. It also proves that the Athenians were right in charging the Spartans with incompetence and veniality. It may also be worth while to point out, as Thucydides does, that ". . . . the intervening portion of history has been omitted by all of them [the previous historians], with the exception of Hellanicus; and he, where he has touched upon it in his Attic history, is very brief, and inaccurate in his chronology."

Thucydides' account of these fifty years begins with the story of Themistocles' clever device for outwitting the Spartans and rebuilding the Athenian walls, an intentional contrast to the account of the debate preceding the outbreak of war, in which the Spartans had thwarted the Athenians. He brings as proof of the haste with which these Themistoclean walls were built about the city the observation that one can still see pieces of columns and sculpture built into these walls. He traces the splendid deeds of Cimon, the growth of the Athenian Empire, the revolt and reduction of Naxos. The rebellion of the Helots at Sparta, the subjugation of Aegina, the proud expedition to Egypt, the loss of Boeotia to Athens by the defeats at Tanagra and Coronea, the revolt and subjugation of Samos, the conquest of Aegina and the final subjugation of Euboea are all briefly described.

Returning to his narrative, Thucydides again reiterates what he believes to be the real cause of the war.

> They [the Lacedaemonians] had never been of a temper prompt to take the field unless they were compelled. . . . But the Athenians were growing too great to be ignored and were laying hands on their allies. They could now bear it no longer: they made up their minds that they must put out all their strength and overthrow the Athenian power by force of arms. And therefore they commenced the Peloponnesian War.

Here Thucydides also states his considered opinion that the Spartans were responsible for beginning the war.

The Spartans had voted to go to war, but before

hostilities were actually begun they called a second conference, at which all their allies were represented. The majority voted for war.

This assembly took place in 432 B.C., and in the interval of nearly a year before hostilities began the Spartans sent embassies to Athens, making various demands. The first was that Athens should expel the "curse of the goddess." This was a reference to an old scandal in Athenian history which concerned the family of Pericles. The demand was, in effect, an order to the Athenians to exile their leading statesman. Of course the demand was refused, as the Spartans had expected.

The Athenians countered, however, by demanding that the Spartans cleanse themselves by expelling the "curse of the Brazen House." The temple of Athena of the Brazen House at Sparta had been defiled by the seizure and execution of the Spartan general, Pausanias. Thucydides again avails himself of the opportunity to enhance the interest of his narrative by relating in a digression the disastrous careers of both Pausanias and Themistocles.

Pausanias had been the Spartan hero of the Persian Wars. He had won the glorious victory of Plataea, which had elicited from Herodotus his most enthusiastic encomium. Pausanias yielded to the usual Spartan vices, overweening pride and veniality. He had become unbearable to the cities subject to Sparta, and dangerous to the Spartans themselves. He had adopted the dress and manner of a Persian viceroy and maintained a regal court. Finally he became a traitor to his city. He was seized and executed.

Themistocles, whom Thucydides regards as the

greatest man of his age and on whom he bestows more praise than on anyone save Pericles, had a scarcely more happy fate. He was banished from his native city on suspicion of peculation. He was hounded out of Argos by the Spartans, chased through barbarian territory, twice narrowly escaping the Spartan soldiers sent to arrest him, once by the eloquence of his appeal as a suppliant to a barbarian prince and once by threats, overawing the captain of the boat in which he was escaping. By his arts of persuasion he secured permission to settle in the territory of the Great King of Persia, whose power he had broken at Salamis, and there in a foreign land he died, in great affluence but in exile. His bones were brought home and buried secretly in Piraeus, beside the sea which he had made an Athenian lake.

"Such was the end," remarks Thucydides with his characteristic restraint, "of Pausanias the Lacedaemonian, and Themistocles the Athenian, the two most famous Hellenes of their day."

Having postponed the climax of his narrative by this interesting digression, Thucydides resumes the story.

After this exchange of polite insults the Spartans put aside their subterfuges and demanded flatly that the Athenians revoke the decree by which they had forbidden Megara, a city only fourteen miles west of Athens but a member of the Peloponnesian League, the privilege of doing business in the markets of the Athenian Empire, and that they raise the siege of Potidaea. Finally, when this was refused, came an embassy with the blunt demand that the Athenian Empire be dissolved. "The Lacedaemonians desire to

maintain peace; and peace there may be, if you will restore independence to the Hellenes."

The Athenian assembly met to debate the question.
The issue was now fairly before them. The assembly
was divided. Some argued in favor of war, and some
argued for the appeasement of Sparta by revocation
of the Megarian decree. And now Pericles, Thucydides' hero, is introduced briefly to us.

Pericles, the son of Xanthippus, was the first man
of his day at Athens and the greatest orator and statesman. He spoke against appeasement. He pointed
out that the treaty with the Lacedaemonians provided
for the arbitration of disputes, but this arbitration the
Spartans had refused; that the Spartan demands for
the relief of Potidaea and Aegina and the rescinding
of the decree against Megara were but the beginnings
of trouble; that appeasement, like blackmail, knew
no end; that the Athenian Empire was strong; that
money was necessary, above all things: "Now wars are
supported out of accumulated wealth, and not out of
forced contributions"; that the government of Athens
allowed them to make quick decisions by referring
matters to their assembly, whereas the Peloponnesian
Confederacy, made up of many races, could never act
with unity or speed. It is interesting to note here that
a democracy is spoken of as capable of quick action
(the U. S. Senate had not yet invented the filibuster to
paralyze democratic action) and also that Pericles an-
ticipates Napoleon's famous saying, "Give me a coali-
tion to fight against."

Pericles then proposed briefly his plan of campaign.
The Athenians were to withdraw into their city and
Piraeus and there, protected by their long walls and

the fortifications of the two cities, they were to allow their country to be ravaged. They were not to engage in a land battle with the Spartans, who could undoubtedly put into the field an invincible army, but were to be supported by the tribute from their empire and wear down the Lacedaemonian Confederacy by cutting off its supplies at sea, destroying its commerce and harrying its coast. The Athenian assembly followed Pericles' advice and voted to inform the Lacedaemonians "that they would do nothing upon compulsion, but were ready to settle their differences by arbitration upon fair terms according to their treaty."

"These," says Thucydides in summation, "were the causes of offence alleged on either side before the war began."

Thus closes the first book of Thucydides' *History*. With consummate art he has not only set before us the ultimate and immediate causes of the Peloponnesian War, but by his skillful use of digression he has sketched the early history of Greece up to the Persian Wars, the fifty years that intervened between that war and the Peloponnesian War, the careers of the two greatest of the Greeks, Pausanias and Themistocles, the two series of incidents that were immediately provocative of the Peloponnesian War (the dispute between Corinth and Corcyra, and the siege of Potidaea, supported by Corinth against Athens), the two meetings of the Peloponnesian League at which war was decided upon, the subsequent negotiations between Athens and Sparta, and the final summing up of the situation in the masterly words of Pericles and his statement of policy for the campaign.

Quite incidentally, apparently, Thucydides has also

placed before us the irreconcilable conflict of ideals
(or ideologies) that divided the Athenian assembly at
the beginning of the war and that was to continue to
divide it and ultimately to wreck Athens: the conflict between justice and expediency, between right-
eousness and realism. Realism and the "Wave of the
Future" had won in the debate about the alliance with
Corcyra, expediency had outweighed justice. It was
not the last time the Athenians were to make this fatal choice.

At the beginning of the second book Thucydides
announces the method upon which his narrative is arranged. The campaigns are to be detailed by "sum-
mers and winters" and following "the order of
events." To this method he strictly adheres throughout his *History*. It has obvious disadvantages because
he not only relates the events of a particular summer
before he passes to the succeeding winter, but the
events of each summer follow each other in the order
in which they occur. This means the breaking up of
a narrative, sometimes into several sections. For instance, the campaign against Potidaea begins in Book
I, Chapters 56 to 66, is continued in Book II, Chapter 58, and completed in Book II, Chapter 70. The
departure of the first Athenian expedition against the
Peloponnesus is described in Book II, Chapters 23
to 25. In Chapter 26 the beginning of the Athenian
expedition against the Locrians is described. In Chapter 30 the narrative of the Peloponnesian expedition
is continued, and in Chapter 32 the author returns to
the Locrian expedition which he had left at Chapter
26. The fortunes of the city of Plataea are told in
Book II, Chapters 2 to 6 and 71 to 78; in Book III,

Chapters 20 to 24 and 52 to 68. This interlacing of subjects leads to a certain feeling of disconnection and interruption of interest as the narrative proceeds, but it does preserve what Thucydides evidently thought of greater value, an exact chronological sequence.

The account of the war begins with an impressive passage in which the date of the opening of the war is fixed to the exact hour by a series of facts that sound like the long roll of a drum beating the call to quarters:

> For fourteen years the thirty years' peace which was concluded after the recovery of Euboea remained unbroken. But in the fifteenth year, when Chrysis the high-priestess of Argos was in the forty-eighth year of her priesthood, Aenesias being Ephor at Sparta, and at Athens Pythodorus having two months of his archonship to run, in the sixth month after the engagement at Potidaea and at the beginning of spring, about the first watch of the night an armed force of somewhat more than three hundred Thebans entered Plataea, a city of Boeotia, which was an ally of Athens, ...

At the close of every campaign after the first year the time is marked by a recurrent sentence which echoes through the narrative like the tolling of a solemn bell. "So ended the —— year in the Peloponnesian War of which Thucydides wrote the history."

The war opened (March, 431 B. C.) with a treacherous attack by the Thebans on Plataea, the little city within the Boeotian border that had so gallantly sent one thousand hoplites, the only assistance which the Athenians received in their first great battle against the Persian king at Marathon. It was an event of which the Plataeans were justly proud, and which they never forgot, a service which at the last they vainly hoped would save them from massacre.

The Thebans, with the connivance of some traitors, introduced a small force into the city by night. The larger force was following from Thebes to make good the conquest of the city. At first the Plataeans, taken by surprise, had no thoughts of resistance, but when they discovered how small was the invading party, they attacked it. The invaders became confused in the dark and rainy night, tried to escape, mistook the door into a building for the city gate and were caught like rats in a trap. They were forced to surrender. The supporting forces from Thebes which had expected to arrive in the night were delayed by the rain and only arrived after their comrades had surrendered. When the facts were disclosed to them by a herald, they were constrained to retire by the promise (they said) that their captured compatriots would be released. They said also that the Plataeans took an oath to this effect. Both of these statements the Plataeans denied, and as soon as the Thebans had retreated from their territory, they straightway put their prisoners to death. This treacherous attack on Plataea was, as Thucydides says, "a glaring violation" of the thirty-year truce. It brought both sides to active warfare.

The general feeling throughout Greece, as Thucydides takes pains to state, was distinctly hostile to Athens. The rule of the imperial city was very unpopular.

As the general war is about to begin, Thucydides adds one of his rare anecdotes. Archidamus, the aged Spartan king, sent a herald to Athens, still hoping to avert the war.   The herald was not even allowed to enter the city and was escorted to the frontier under guard so that he might not communicate with anyone. When he arrived at the Athenian frontier, he turned to his Athenian escort and with all the brevity of Spartan speech, and with the solemnity of a prophet, announced, "This day will be to the Hellenes the beginning of great sorrows."

Here Thucydides digresses on the ease and happiness of the life of the Attic citizens and gives a short account of the early history of Athens.   The crowding of this agrarian population into the city occasioned considerable hardship and much heartburn.   The people were naturally disinclined to move.

> They were depressed at the thought of forsaking their homes and the temples which had come down to them from their fathers and were the abiding memorials of their early constitution.   They were going to change their manner of life, and in leaving their villages were in fact each of them going into exile.

Arriving in the city, they occupied whatever place they could find.   They invaded the temples and shrines, except such as could be securely closed against them.   They settled between the long walls and all about the Piraeus.

> Many also established themselves in the turrets of the walls, or in any other place which they could find; for the city could not contain them when they first came in.

Meanwhile the Spartan army appeared and began to ravage the fields.   The Athenians would have been glad to go out and fight them and would have done so, if it had not been for Pericles' restraining influence.

The excitement in the city was universal; the people were furious with Pericles, and, forgetting all his previous warnings, they abused him for not leading them to battle, as their general should, and laid all their miseries to his charge.

The Athenians now dispatched their first expedition to harry the Peloponnesus. Each year the same thing occurred. The Peloponnesians sent an army to ravage Attica, and then Athens sent a naval expedition to attack the Peloponnesian coasts. In the third year of the war the annual invasion of Attica was postponed in favor of the siege of Plataea, and in the sixth year of the war the Spartans refrained from invading Attica because they were terrified by a series of earthquakes.

During the first expedition which Athens sent to the Peloponnesus the Athenian nemesis appeared on the Spartan side in the person of Brasidas. He "happened to be in those parts" when the Athenians attacked Methone, and saved that city by energetically collecting a few troops and throwing himself into the citadel. For this act he was the first general in the war to be publicly thanked by Sparta. He was to be thanked many times subsequently by the Spartans, and cursed by the Athenians.

At the end of the year there occurred a solemn ceremony at Athens. It was customary each year, at the close of the campaign, to hold a public funeral in honor of those who had fallen in the service of their country. The bones of the dead were conveyed to the place of burial, and a single pall served as a memorial for all those whose bodies had been missing. A public oration was delivered by some eminent citizen.

It was Pericles who spoke for the dead who died
in the first year of the Peloponnesian War. His
oration is given in full by Thucydides, who doubtless
heard it. Whether or not the oration as we have it
is the work of Pericles or the work of Thucydides or,
as is most probable, a combination of what Thucydides could remember and what he added of his own,
the result is one of the noblest funeral orations ever
spoken. In fact, the oration overshadows the occasion, for comparatively few Athenians had fallen in
this first campaign. The oration is, rather, a tribute
to all those who fell during the war. It is a defense
and a glorification of the Athens of Pericles. It is
the funeral oration of Athens herself.

Pericles begins by speaking of the glorious ancestry
of the Athenians, briefly, for the tale would be long
and it was already familiar. But the reasons for
Athens' greatness are fully described. Athens is a
democracy in which the poor and rich alike are re-
warded for their services, for ".... poverty is not a bar,
but a man may benefit his country whatever be the ob-
scurity of his condition." It is a democracy in which
respect for law is the governing principle. ".... we are
prevented from doing wrong by respect for authority
and for the laws, having an especial regard to those
which are ordained for the protection of the injured
as well as to those unwritten laws which bring upon
the transgressor of them the reprobation of the general sentiment."

The democracy is imperial and into the imperial
city of Athens flows tribute from all her empire, and
the lives of the citizens are thereby enriched. Athens
by the very character of her citizens is more than a

match for all her enemies, but the valor of her citizens is the result rather of their own characteristics than of any laborious exercise such as is maintained in Sparta. The Athenian citizen is a man of fine feeling and aesthetic appreciation—

"For we are lovers of the beautiful, yet simple in our tastes, and we cultivate the mind without loss of manliness." An Athenian citizen must take his part in the service of his city. "We alone regard a man who takes no interest in public affairs, not as a harmless, but as a useless character. . . . Athens is the school of Hellas. . . ." And the memory of Athens' greatness will be immortal. "And we shall assuredly not be without witnesses; there are mighty monuments of our power which will make us the wonder of this and of succeeding ages; we shall not need the praises of Homer or of any other panegyrist. . . ."

To such a city the citizens naturally give their allegiance and their lives. In the hour of trial, these men who have died did not shrink.

> They resigned to hope their unknown chance of happiness; but in the face of death they resolved to rely upon themselves alone. And when the moment came they were minded to resist and suffer, rather than to fly and save their lives; they ran away from the word of dishonour, but on the battle-field their feet stood fast, and in an instant, at the height of their fortune, they passed away from the scene, not of their fear, but of their glory.

And the sacrifice of their lives will not have been forgotten. "For the whole earth is the sepulchre of famous men; not only are they commemorated by columns and inscriptions in their own country, but in foreign lands there dwells also an unwritten memorial of them, graven not on stone but in the hearts of men." And those who have lost sons or fathers or husbands will be comforted by the glory of those who are gone. "For the love of honour alone is ever young, and not riches, as some say, but honour is the delight of men when they are old and useless." With Pericles' funeral address Thucydides closes his account of the first year of the Peloponnesian War.

As if to make more brilliant, by contrast, the illumination of Athens in the Periclean age, Thucydides introduces immediately his description of a terrible plague which visited Athens in the second summer of the war. Whether this scourge was identical with the Black Death which swept over Europe in 1354, or what the nature of the disease was, is still a matter of discussion among physicians.

Thucydides, having in mind, as always, that his history is to be of use in future generations in interpreting phenomena and in avoiding the mistakes of the past, has given a remarkably vivid and accurate account of the symptoms of this disease and the usually fatal course of the malady. Modern physicians have been baffled in their attempt to identify the plague, not because Thucydides' description has been incomplete or inaccurate but because a disease, after it has been prevalent for a number of years, builds up an immunity against itself in the human body, and the symptoms and the course of the disease become so modified that it is difficult to recognize the original disease from its later manifestations. Smallpox, which was such a terrible scourge in Europe in the eighteenth century, from which so many persons, even among the wealthy class, died, has now become a comparatively mild disease, even where it is not prevented by inoculation.

Thucydides' description of the plague has become the model for all descriptions of a similar nature. Lucretius models his description of the plague in the sixth book of his *De Rerum Natura* on this passage of Thucydides, and Defoe uses it in his description of the great plague which decimated London. Thucydides himself suffered from the malady and was one of the few to recover.

But it is not so much the description of the physical sufferings which attended the plague that arouses the horror of the reader as it is the analysis of the psychological effect which the plague produced on the crowded population of Athens and Piraeus:

> There were other and worse forms of lawlessness which the plague introduced at Athens. Men who had hitherto concealed what they took pleasure in, now grew bolder. For, seeing the sudden change,—how the rich died in a moment, and those who had nothing immediately inherited their property,—they reflected that life and riches were alike transitory, and they resolved to enjoy themselves while they could, and to think only of pleasure. Who would be willing to sacrifice himself to the law of honour when he knew not whether he would ever live to be held in honour? The pleasure of the moment and any sort of thing which conduced to it took the place both of honour and of expediency. No fear of Gods or law of man deterred a criminal. Those who saw all perishing alike, thought that the worship or neglect of the Gods made no difference. For offences against human law no punishment was to be feared; no one would live long enough to be called to account. Already a far heavier sentence had

been passed and was hanging over a man's head; before
that fell, why should he not take a little pleasure?

The wretched population of the crowded city, dis-
heartened by the loss of their property and terrified by
the ravages of the plague, turned on Pericles in their
anger, and for a short time he lost control of the Athenian government.   Overtures of peace were made to
Sparta, but were promptly rejected. Pericles was de-
prived of his office as general and fined, in spite of a
sturdy speech in which he defended the policy which he
had laid out at the beginning of the war. He put the
matter to the Athenians bluntly:

> And do not imagine that you are fighting about a simple
> issue, freedom or slavery; you have an empire to lose,
> and there is the danger to which the hatred of your
> imperial rule has exposed you.   Neither can you resign
> your power, if, at this crisis, any timorous or inactive
> spirit is for thus playing the honest man. For by this
> time your empire has become a tyranny which in the
> opinion of mankind may have been unjustly gained,
> but which cannot be safely surrendered.

The popular indignation soon passed, and the people, who for so long had depended on Pericles, again
elected him general and again trusted the entire conduct of their affairs to him.

Some modern historians have been inclined to doubt
the wisdom of Pericles' policy. Thucydides never did.
He believed that, had the Athenians been willing to
follow it consistently, Athens would have been victorious, and his view is, in my opinion, correct. Pericles had foreseen the war long before it came. He had
descried "war swooping down upon them from the

Peloponnesus," and it may be, as has been suggested, that he was glad to have the inevitable war come when it did, because he realized that he and he alone could guide the Athenians to victory. He foresaw every contingency which might happen, even foresaw that the Spartans might seize and fortify permanently some outpost in Attica. He had provided against all the eventualities of a long war, all except one—his own death. He lived through two and a half years of the war, and his death was the first of many misfortunes which tipped the scales in favor of Sparta.

The Peloponnesian War is the most heartbreaking war in history. The sympathies of all mankind are with Athens in spite of her tyrannical treatment of her allies. It may well be, as Pericles said, that Athens' treatment of them was justified, for they received at her hands more than they gave. And, in any case, no one can doubt that Thucydides is correct in saying that the Spartan leadership would have been much more tyrannical than that of Athens. The sympathies of mankind and the interests of humanity demanded an Athenian victory, and that victory was thwarted only by a long series of seemingly chance occurrences. No other great war has been decided by such a series of accidents. The overthrow of Carthage at the hands of Rome was not due to the accident of Hasdrubal's death at the Metaurus. That defeat undoubtedly shortened the war, but the sturdy resistance of the Roman burghers and the steadfast loyalty of the Roman allies guaranteed ultimate success. Napoleon's downfall was due to no chance occurrence but to the wasting ulcer of the Spanish campaign and the terrible losses in Russia. The defeat of France in the War of the Spanish Succession was due to the genius of Marl-borough and not to a series of accidental blunders on the part of the French. The collapse of the empire that Charles XII of Sweden had built has no signifi-cance because, as Churchill says, Charles XII was "historically a monstrous irrelevancy."

But in the Peloponnesian War one can put his finger on almost a dozen places and say, "If I could but change this event, the whole course of Greek history might be altered." If the plague had not swept Ath-ens, if Pericles had not died, if a wise successor to Peri-cles had made peace after Sphacteria, if Alcibiades had not been removed from command in the Sicilian expedition, if the moon had not been eclipsed on that August night in 413, if Alcibiades had had more judg-ment and less brilliance, if the admirals had not been executed after Arginusae, if the Spartans had not hap-pened to have Brasidas in their number, if Gylippus had been prevented from entering Syracuse, if the ad-miral in command at Aegospotami had been willing to take Alcibiades' advice, if Nicias had been more of a man and less of a priest; and there are many more in-complete conditions whose favorable conclusions might have meant a victory for Athens and an even greater age of artistic development to follow the age of Pericles.

Thucydides was well aware of "the uncertainty of fortune, which may strike anyone, however innocent." He comes back to this theme again and again. "A man may regulate his own desires, but he is not the dis-penser of fortune. . . ." "Realise, while there is time, the inscrutable nature of war; and how when pro-tracted it generally ends in becoming a mere matter of chance, over which neither of us can have any control, the event being equally unknown and equally hazardous to both." These are the words of the prudent Archidamus, and we may be sure that Thucydides wrote them with the bitter knowledge of all the disasters that the Goddess of Chance had heaped on Athens. To this Goddess no successful appeal might be made. To her the wretched Melians appeal, and the Athenians answer them with death. To her the upright Nicias appeals in the hour of his disaster at Syracuse, and to him the Syracusans return the same answer—death.

Thucydides bestows upon Pericles the finest epitaph which his restrained temperament allows him to award, and then he justifies Pericles' policy and shows how it would inevitably have been successful if it had been followed.

> And yet after they [the Athenians] had lost in the Sicilian expedition the greater part of their fleet and army, and were now distracted by revolution, still they held out three years not only against their former enemies, but against the Sicilians who had combined with them, and against most of their own allies who had risen in revolt. Even when Cyrus the son of the King joined in the war and supplied the Peloponnesian fleet with money, they continued to resist, and were at last overthrown, not by their enemies, but by themselves and their own internal dissensions. So that at the time Pericles was more than justified in the conviction at which his foresight had arrived, that the Athenians would win an easy victory over the unaided forces of the Peloponnesians.

As Pericles lay dying, his friends gathered about his couch and spoke of the great things he had done for the state. The dying statesman roused himself and said, "and yet none of you has mentioned the thing of which I am most proud." When they asked him what it was, he said, "Because of me, no living Athenian has ever put on mourning." Perhaps better than anything else, that is the measure of the greatness of Periclean Athens—its humanity.

V

THUCYDIDES' NARRATIVE

II. From the Death of Pericles to the Peace of Nicias
429-421 B. C.

THE second invasion of Attica (430 B.C.) lasted longer than any of the others, forty days. The war was already beginning to harden men's souls. From the beginning of the war the Spartans had adopted a policy of putting to death all the people whom they captured on the sea, the theory apparently being that anyone on a boat must be either an Athenian or an Athenian sympathizer. The Athenians retaliated by executing some commissioners whom the Spartans were sending to the King of Persia, asking for an alliance. These commissioners had fallen into the hands of the Athenians and were executed by them without trial or without even being allowed to make any statement. The Athenians justified this reprisal for the wholesale slaughter which the Spartans were conducting on the sea, and indeed the Spartan practice was so silly, to say nothing of its cruelty, that the Spartans abandoned it when its inevitable results were pointed out to them.

Meanwhile the siege of Plataea was begun, and during the third summer (429 B. C.) the Spartans devoted themselves to this instead of ravaging Attica. The Athenians had removed from Plataea all but the active defenders and had agreed to send aid, an agreement which they never kept. The Spartans besieged the place with the assistance of the Thebans, and, since the Spartans were notoriously poor at siege operations, the Plataeans had reason to believe they might hold out until they were relieved. The Spartans completely surrounded the city with a wall and tried to reduce it by mining operations. The mines and countermines were extensive, giving some inkling of what this type of warfare might develop into in such sieges as that of Tournai in the eighteenth century. Thwarted in mining operations, the Spartans piled an immense amount of brush between their wall and the city wall and set fire to it. Thucydides speaks of the blaze as the greatest ever created by man. His description is good enough to be that of an eyewitness. The Plataeans were only saved as they had been before, by the intervention of the god of storms, who, instead of creating a wind which would carry the conflagration into the city, produced a downpour which put out the fire.

The Spartans then completely walled in the city and, when they retired for the winter to the Peloponnesus, left a garrison sufficient to man the walls. As food was running low, and as the Plataeans despaired of Athenian help, they determined to escape. With endless care they counted the bricks in the Spartan wall, over and over again, until they knew the exact height of the wall. Scaling ladders of this height were built, and on a dark night a considerable part of the garrison planted these against the wall, overpowered the guards and escaped. They reached Athens safely, but the next summer those who were left were forced to capitulate. They surrendered themselves, and the Spartans pledged that no one should be punished without a trial.

Five commissioners were sent from Sparta, who simply asked each man whether or not he had done anything to assist the Lacedaemonians in the war. To this question there could be but one answer. The

Plataeans made a pitiful plea for mercy and spoke of the great services which they had rendered to Greece at the time of the Persian invasions. The Spartans might have been moved, but the Thebans were there to urge that no mercy be shown to these men whom they so bitterly hated. The Spartans, preferring to sacrifice the lives of the Plataeans rather than the good will of the Thebans, put all the men of the garrison to death and sold the women into slavery. The city was torn down and for a time obliterated from history.

The operations in northwestern Greece were of considerable importance. Phormio was the Athenian admiral in charge, with his base at Naupactus. He distinguished himself by intercepting the considerable Spartan fleet that was on its way north under the charge of its admiral, Cnemus. Phormio fell upon this fleet. He formed his ships in a single column and began circling around the unhappy Peloponnesians. By threatening to ram the enemy he kept forcing them into a smaller and smaller space. When the wind rose their ships became less manageable. Finally, when the whole mass was huddled together in confusion and terror, his fleet turned their prows inward and rammed them from all sides. The admiral with a few ships escaped.

The Lacedaemonians were so incensed that they sent three commissioners to investigate the situation and to give the unhappy admiral advice. The advice which they gave him was certainly good advice but not very helpful. "He was told that he must contrive to fight again and be more successful. . . ." However, the Spartans did make a better showing in the next engagement, for they succeeded in dividing Phormio's fleet into two parts. Most of his ships were driven ashore. Eleven fled to Naupactus. Ten reached the harbor safely, came about and were ready, with their prows pointed offshore, to repel the Spartans. The last ship was coming in, hotly pursued by a Spartan trireme. A merchant ship was lying at anchor near the entrance to the harbor. Past this Phormio's trireme sped. Then, instead of making for the harbor, it bore sharply about, encircled the merchantman and rammed the Spartan ship amidships as it was approaching. The Spartan ship sank with all on board, whereupon the rest of the Spartan fleet backed water. The Athenians, taking heart, came out, routed them and recovered most of the captured boats. The following winter (429 B.C.) Phormio conducted a brilliant expedition against Acarnania. With these exploits to his credit and the Lacedaemonian activity on sea paralyzed on the western coast, he returned to Athens and passes from the narrative of Thucydides without commendation or comment, the most able admiral that Athens produced during the entire war.

The third year of the war (429 B. C.) saw a daring attempt by that un-Spartan Brasidas to attack the Piraeus. He was foiled in this and had to be content with a raid on Salamis. The only importance the event had was to show how unprepared the Athenians were and what an enterprising leader was Brasidas.

In the fourth year of the war (428 B. C.) there occurred the memorable revolt of Mytilene. Not only did the city of Mytilene revolt, but the whole Island of Lesbos, with the exception of Methymna, a city on the northern end of the island, deserted the Atheni-

ans. They appealed to the Spartans for aid, and
the Spartans, as usual, were too late in sending it.
The Athenians were enraged by Mytilene's revolt,
for Lesbos had been one of the two independent members of the Empire, had furnished ships and paid no
tribute. Their treatment, therefore, at the hands of
Athens, had been exceedingly liberal. An expedition
was dispatched, and the inhabitants of Mytilene were
finally forced to capitulate. A delegation of the leading citizens was sent to Athens to secure what mercy
they could. The debate in the Athenian assembly
which follows is notable. Cleon, who comes to the bar
of history condemned alike by Thucydides and Aristophanes, had succeeded Pericles as the most influential citizen of Athens. It is hard to arrive at a just
estimate of his character. He had energy, self-con-
fidence in large quantities, a loud and persistent voice.
He was probably honest as far as money matters went,
for he was never convicted of embezzlement. He was
charged, probably justly, with seeking his own ag-
grandizement, and, though chance gave him a golden
opportunity to serve his country, lack of judgment and
vain pride caused him to cast it away. He is an example of the tendency of democratic government to
throw second-rate men into positions of importance
if not of control. Franklin Pierce and Warren G.
Harding illustrate this in our own government. England seems to have escaped this because her government is so largely in the hands of the great families
trained by tradition (and Eton, Harrow, Oxford and
Cambridge) to rule.

Cleon advocated that all the male citizens of Mytilene be put to death and the women sold into slavery.

The assembly followed his advice and voted the ultimate penalty. A trireme was dispatched with orders to Paches, the general in charge, to carry out the decree. But during the following night a wave of pity swept over the Athenians, and the following day another assembly was held, and the whole matter was debated again. Cleon was the principal speaker in favor of confirming the decree and he minced matters not at all:

> You should remember that your empire is a despotism exercised over unwilling subjects, who are always conspiring against you; they do not obey in return for any kindness which you do them to your own injury, but in so far as you are their masters; they have no love of you, but they are held down by force. . . . . But if, right or wrong, you are resolved to rule, then rightly or wrongly they must be chastised for your good.

Diodotus, an Athenian otherwise unknown, voiced the sentiments of the more merciful party:

> Neither, if perchance there be some degree of excuse for them, would I have you spare them, unless it be clearly for the good of the state. . . . . You are angry with the Mytilenaeans, and the superor justice of his [Cleon's] argument may for the moment attract you; but we are not at law with them, and do not want to be told what is just; we are considering a matter of policy, and desire to know how we can turn them to account. . . . . at present, although a city may actually have revolted, when she becomes conscious of her weakness she will capitulate while still able to defray the cost of the war and to pay tribute for the future; but if we are too severe, will not the citizens make better preparations, and, when besieged, resist to the last, knowing that it is all the same whether they come to terms early or late?

It is interesting to note that Diodotus does not make any plea for mercy. Like Cleon, he appeals to expediency. The people of Mytilene are to be spared not because of any humanitarian feelings or any mercy, but because to spare them is in the end better policy for Athens from a selfish point of view. Still, it is hard to believe that pity, which prompted the Athenians to call the second assembly, did not play a large part in persuading a slight majority of the Athenians to vote that the ultimate penalty was to be inflicted only upon the ringleaders.

It was twenty-four hours since the trireme bearing the death sentence had departed, and it was a question whether the sentence would not be executed before it could be countermanded. A second trireme was dispatched with all speed. The rowers were offered a reward if they arrived in time. They were fed barley mixed with wine and oil while they rowed, and they rowed and slept by turns. What a "purple patch" might have been written about this race across the Aegean for the lives of several thousand human beings! Here, as always, Thucydides displays aloof restraint. He says:

> Fortunately no adverse wind sprang up, and, the first of the two ships sailing in no great hurry on her untoward errand, and the second hastening as I have described, the one did indeed arrive sooner than the other, but not much sooner. Paches had read the decree and was about to put it into execution, when the second appeared and arrested the fate of the city.
> So near was Mytilene to destruction.

The drama was closed by the execution of the delegation from Mytilene which was at Athens and the execution of about one thousand wretched persons in Lesbos.

In the fifth year of the war (427 B. C.) Nicias appears. More will be said of his character later. At present it is enough to characterize him as the Stanley Baldwin of Athens. He led an expedition against Minoa, an islet off the port of Megara, which he took, and there the matter rested. No further action was taken against this little city, which was such a thorn in the flesh of the Athenians.

Meanwhile civil war broke out in Corcyra (Corfu). It is one of the most beautiful of all the Greek cities, situated on an excellent harbor on the east side of the fair island. It was the fabled home of the Phaeacians, and in spite of its terrible history something of the delicate charm of the revered Alcinous and his lovely daughter, Nausicaa, still hovers over the place. It is here that Homer puts into the mouth of Odysseus, centuries before the birth of Christ, the most perfect description of happy married life that literature knows, "There is nothing mightier and nobler than when man and wife are of one heart and mind in a house, a grief to their foes, and to their friends great joy, but their own hearts know it best."

But in the fifth century B.C. this island was torn with the most horrible civil war. Oligarchs and Democrats massacred each other in violation of all human and divine laws. The Democratic party at present had the upper hand. They had caught some of their opponents in the temple of Hera. Fifty of them were persuaded to come out and stand trial. All were condemned to death. The rest of the prisoners refused to come out when they saw what was happening. They hung themselves to trees outside the temple or killed themselves within the sacred enclosure. Having perpetrated this slaughter, the Corcyraeans fell upon each other, and indiscriminate murder was committed throughout the city.

> Every form of death was to be seen ; and everything, and more than everything, that commonly happens in revolutions, happened then. The father slew the son, and the suppliants were torn from the temples and slain near them ; some of them were even walled up in the temple of Dionysus, and there perished. To such extremes of cruelty did revolution go ; and this seemed to be the worst of revolutions, because it was the first.

This murderous outburst in Corcyra was the beginning of similar outrages that swept over all Greece. Thucydides does not give us the details of what happened in other cities. It is quite unnecessary to do so.

The Oligarchs, driven from Corcyra, passed across the strait and occupied a height on the neighboring mainland. Here, two years later, they were attacked by a force consisting of Athenians and Democrats from Corcyra. They retreated to the summit of their fortified position, Mount Istone. Being surrounded, and resistance being hopeless, they surrendered, stipulating, however, that their fate should be decided by the people of Athens. They knew all too well what would happen to them if they fell into the hands of their brethren in Corcyra. One of the clauses in the articles of surrender provided that if the captives attempted to escape, the other conditions were no longer to be valid. The Corcyraeans approached some of the captives, with whom they were, of course, acquainted, and told them that the Athenians were planning to violate their oaths and surrender them to the Courts of Corcyra. They provided a vessel in which the captives might escape. Some of them were foolish enough to be deceived by this ruse, and an attempt to escape was made. They were seized, and the Athenians, declaring that the conditions of the surrender no longer were binding, surrendered them to the Democrats at Corcyra. They were imprisoned in a large building and led forth in bands of twenty. Their hands were tied, and they were forced to pass between files of armed men. When any of the armed men saw a particular enemy passing him, he struck him down. The unhappy prisoners were urged forward with whips. What was going on outside was soon discovered by the Corcyraeans in the building. They refused to come out, whereupon the armed men got upon the roof, tore it off, and began exterminating the prisoners by throwing down tiles and shooting at them with arrows. Thucydides concludes the act:

> Most of them at the same time put an end to their own lives; some thrust into their throats arrows which were shot at them, others strangled themselves with cords taken from beds which they found in the place, or with strips which they tore from their own garments. This went on during the greater part of the night, which had closed upon their sufferings, until in one way or another, either by their own hand or by missiles hurled from above, they all perished. At daybreak the Corcyraeans flung the dead bodies cross-wise on waggons and carried them out of the city. The women who were taken in the fortress on Mount Istone were reduced to slavery. Thus the Corcyraeans in the mountain

were destroyed by the people, and, at least while the
Peloponnesian war lasted, there was an end of the great
sedition; for there was nothing left of the other party
worth mentioning.

If the fifth year of the war was beclouded by the
introduction of Nicias, the sixth (426 B. C.) makes us
acquainted with the greatest general that Athens produced during the war, Demosthenes. He appears with
an Athenian force supporting the Acarnanians in northwest Greece. The Acarnanians had made a descent
upon the Island of Leucas. They had requested that
Demosthenes assist them, but he thought that he would
accomplish a much larger project. He was a general
capable of handling large bodies of soldiers and conducting elaborate campaigns. He now conceived the
idea of conducting an expedition with the assistance
of the Messenians of Naupactus through Aetolia and
Locris, passing north of Parnassus and falling upon
the Phocians and, later on, the Boeotians. It was an
ambitious project and was doomed to utter failure.
Demosthenes and his forces became involved in the
passes of the Aetolian mountains. In their heavy armor
they were no match for the light Aetolian troops, who
withdrew before them while archers harassed them on
all sides. Demosthenes was lucky to get back safely to
Naupactus with a remnant of his forces. These were
dispatched to Athens, but he himself prudently abode
in Naupactus. He knew very well the welcome he
would receive at Athens.

The Aetolians, now flushed with their victory, induced the Lacedaemonians to make a descent upon
Naupactus with their help. The Locrians also added

their puny contingent to this force. Demosthenes seems not to have actually been in Naupactus at the time but, like Brasidas, he "happened to be in those parts." He hastily got together a band of soldiers, threw them into the town and thus forestalled the Lacedaemonians.

And in the next campaign Demosthenes was able to retrieve all of his misfortunes. The Ambraciots, a northern Aetolian tribe, thought that they saw a fine chance to get the better of their old enemy, the Acarnanians, and seize Olpae. They had the assistance of a considerable contingent of Peloponnesian troops, mostly from Mantinea. Demosthenes, with the Acarnanians, captured most of these troops, but a remnant got away into Olpae. A truce was asked by the Lacedaemonians, and Demosthenes, who knew that a large Ambraciot force was coming to the rescue, was anxious to make some accommodation whereby he could be free to act without fear of attack in the rear. So he made a secret agreement with the Peloponnesian forces that they should be allowed to withdraw, an agreement which they were glad to accept.

Demosthenes then faced the Ambraciots. The Acarnanians fell upon the Ambraciots with enthusiasm, routed them, and being lightly armed and knowing the country well, pursued them. The carnage was terrible. In fact, the army was so completely wiped out that a herald from Olpae who arrived next day, when he saw how many of his fellow countrymen had perished, was so overcome with emotion that he departed without even asking for the terms he had come to seek. The slaughter was so considerable that Thucydides does not venture to give the number of those killed:

it "would appear incredible when compared with the size of the city." And he adds significantly:

> Of this I am certain, that if the Acarnanians had been willing to destroy Ambracia as Demosthenes and the Athenians desired, they might have taken it at the first onset. But they were afraid that the Athenians, if they once got possession of the place, would be more troublesome neighbours than the Ambraciots.

In this he was right, for the Acarnanians were of no further service to the Athenians, and, in fact, matters in the northwest of Greece from this time settled down. Athens had been successful in preventing the Peloponnesians from getting any hold in this district, while they themselves did gain the advantage of having a safe passage through these waters on their way to Corcyra and Sicily. Athens had won the war in northwestern Greece.

During the seventh year of the war (425 B. C.) a notable event took place at Pylos. Demosthenes had obtained permission from the Athenian assembly to seize and fortify some place on the Peloponnesian coast from which forays into the enemy country could be conducted. For this purpose he was given a small force and five triremes. With these he proceeded, along with the fleet, which was on its way to Corcyra and to Sicily. When they reached Pylos, on the western coast of the Peloponnesus, they were detained by adverse winds. Pylos is a rocky promontory, uninhabited, which rises four hundred and fifty feet out of the sea. Opposite it, separated by a narrow channel, is the north end of the long, narrow Island of Sphacteria. The southern end of the Island of Sphacteria is separated from the mainland by a channel of considerable width. East of this island opens the considerable Bay of Navarino. It was in this bay in 1827 that Admiral Codington blew the Turkish fleet out of the water, thereby assuring the independence of the Kingdom of Greece. Here the Athenian squadron lay at anchor, weather-bound. Demosthenes asked the admirals to direct their men to help his force fortify the promontory at Pylos. Something of their scornful answer appears in Thucydides' account. He says that Demosthenes was told that there were plenty of desolate promontories on the coast of the Peloponnesus which he might fortify if he wanted to waste the public money. However, as the storm continued and the ships were delayed, the soldiers, for want of something else to do, of their own accord fell to the work, and soon a rough fortification was constructed on the summit of the promontory. This Demosthenes occupied, placed his ships at the foot, protected them by stockades and prepared to carry out his mission of harrying the neighboring country.

The Spartans, who had been ravaging the Attic territory, were alarmed by this report. That the Athenians should be occupying a site on their coast was intolerable. Besides, the grain was not yet ripe in Attica. Unseasonable spring rains were cold and disagreeable, and they wanted to come home. Therefore, after delaying at Attica only about two weeks, they did return. Meanwhile the allied fleet, which had gone north to Corcyra with the idea of helping the Oligarchs, was recalled, and Demosthenes was attacked. As usual, Brasidas was on hand and was a leading spirit in the attack. He recklessly rammed his

ship on the rocks, encouraging his men "Not to be spar-
ing of timber when the enemy had built a fort in their
country; let them wreck their ships and force a landing." He said to the allies that

> .... they should not hesitate at such a moment to make
> a present of their ships to the Lacedaemonians, who
> had done so much for them; they must run aground,
> and somehow or other get to land and take the fort
> and the men in it.

Fortunately for the Athenians, he was wounded and
fell swooning into his ship, dropping overboard his
shield, which the Athenians seized. It was taken to
Athens and for many years was one of the proud trophies exhibited there.

To further the attack upon Pylos the Spartans
landed a detachment of four hundred and twenty on
the Island of Sphacteria. This island is about a mile
and three quarters long, low in the southern end and
rising to a height of about three hundred feet at the
north end, which looks across the narrow passage to
Pylos. On the eastern side of the northern half of
the island the cliffs rise almost sheer out of the sea. At
the middle of the island on the eastern side is a landing,
and almost in the center of the island there is a small
spring. There is no water at the northern end. The
island slopes gently to the west, and along the western
side one can make his way easily except for the ram-
pant growth of thistles and several varieties of bushes,
all equipped with most efficient thorns. The island was
uninhabited. There were no paths, and even where the
terrain was fairly easy, the thorns and brambles made
walking very difficult.

The Spartans were landed on the island apparently to prevent the Athenians from seizing it, but soon after this was done the Athenian squadron which had gone to Corcyra returned. They attacked the Spartans in the bay, defeated them and forced them to beach their ships. The conditions were now reversed, the siege of Pylos had been lifted, and the siege of Sphacteria began.

The Athenians blockaded the island by day, and during the night ships constantly encircled it. The Spartans on the island were soon reduced to short rations. The Athenians were unable to starve them out, for when the weather was bad the patrol could not be effectually maintained on the western side, and the Spartans offered freedom to any of the Helots who would swim across with provisions or get across in boats. The siege dragged on, and nothing was accomplished.

At Athens the anger of the Athenian Assembly arose. Finally in one of the debates Cleon, taunting Nicias with the inefficiency of the operations, said that if he were in command he would bring back the Spartans dead or alive in twenty days. "Very well," said Nicias, "I'll temporarily give up my office as general, go and get them." Whereupon Cleon, seeing his bluff called, began to hedge. The more he hesitated and offered excuses, the more eager the Athenian public became that he should go, and finally, much against his will, he was given charge of the expedition, told he could have what forces he wanted and any colleague he wished to associate with himself. Then for once Thucydides drops his customary aloofness and speaks his mind bluntly:

His vain words moved the Athenians to laughter; nevertheless the wiser sort of men were pleased when they reflected that of two good things they could not fail to obtain one—either there would be an end of Cleon, which they would have greatly preferred, or, if they were disappointed, he would put the Lacedaemonians into their hands.

But Cleon shrewdly chose Demosthenes to help him.

When Cleon arrived at Pylos, a force of Athenians was landed on the island. The brush had been accidentally set on fire, and the Spartans, when the attack began, were no longer able to conceal their position. The Athenians did not come to close grips with them but attacked with arrows and javelins. Step by step the Spartans were forced back through the ashes and over the rough stones until they were driven to the wall at the summit on the north end of the island. Here they stood, partially protected, and it seemed impossible to dislodge them.

Then one of the Messenians who were serving with the Athenians came forward with a project. He said that he and his fellows, who knew the ground, could make their way along the eastern shore of the island at the edge of the water and climb up back of the Spartans at the north end. This proposal was accepted. The Messenians made their way with difficulty over the rocks. So steep were the cliffs that they were concealed from the Spartans above, who were facing the Athenians on the west. When the Messenians came to the difficult climb up the cliff at the northern end, they found just below the top a convenient hollow in which they could gather, unseen by the Spartans, for their final rush. When they appeared at last at the rear of

the Spartans and above them, the Spartans realized
that the game was up.   The Athenians offered to allow them to surrender, and much to the surprise of
everyone the Spartans accepted.   They stipulated that
they should be allowed to consult their friends on the
mainland. They were told, "The Lacedaemonians bid
you act as you think best, but you are not to dishonour
yourselves," whereupon the Spartans surrendered.
Four hundred and twenty had passed over to the
island, and two hundred and ninety-two surrendered
and were taken alive to Athens.   Their surrender was
a surprise and a shock to all of Greece. Thucydides
says:

> Nothing which happened during the war caused great-
> er amazement in Hellas; for it was universally im-
> agined that the Lacedaemonians would never give up
> their arms, either under the pressure of famine or in
> any other extremity, but would fight to the last and
> die sword in hand.   No one would believe that those
> who surrendered were men of the same quality with
> those who perished.

And so Cleon returned to Athens, having actually
made good his boast. The shields of these Spartans
were exhibited in the Stoa Poicile in the Agora at
Athens as one of the trophies most treasured by the
Athenian state.   In 1936 one of these shields, with
the inscription on it,

ΑΘΗΝΑΙΟΙ ΑΠΟ ΛΑΚΕΔΑΙΜ[ΟΝ]ΙΩΝ ΕΚ [ΠΥ]ΛΟ

"The Athenians from the Lacedaemonian [spoils]
from Pylos," was found by Mr. T. Leslie Shear, who
was excavating the Athenian Agora for the American
School of Classical Studies.

The Spartans were utterly shaken. Two hundred and ninety-two Lacedaemonians had surrendered. Of these, one hundred and twenty were Spartans. So small was the Spartan community already that this was a serious loss in number as well as prestige. The disease which was eventually to ruin Sparta was at work. Limitation of citizenship, intermarriage, a decline in birth rate were finally to decimate this hornets' nest to such an extent that the Achaean League one hundred and fifty years later could laugh at the pretensions of the city that was once mistress of Hellas.

In the next year of the war, the eighth (424 B. C.), the Athenians succeeded in seizing the Island of Cythera, which lies off the southern coast of Laconia. With a garrison stationed here, and with Pylos firmly in their hands, they had Sparta between the upper and nether millstones. The Messenians could now take refuge from Spartan tyranny by going to Pylos. The oppressed Helots could run away either to Pylos or to Cythera. Athens was now in the most favorable position to make peace, and the Spartans were exceedingly downhearted. After the capture of their soldiers at Sphacteria they had again and again sent emissaries to Athens, asking for peace, and the Athenians had constantly raised their terms. Pericles' policy had been completely justified. Wise leaders at Athens could now have negotiated a peace which would have left Athens with heightened prestige and in possession of everything that she had had at the beginning of the war. In addition she had captured and held Aegina, one of her most active commercial rivals. She had Corcyra as a powerful if rather independent ally, and her influence was paramount through Acarnania and Ambracia. Cleon was pre-eminently responsible for losing this golden opportunity.

The eighth year of the war (424 B. C.) also saw the elaborate plan evolved by Demosthenes for the subjugation of Boeotia. It required the coordination of three forces. He himself was to attack Boeotia from the west, with his fleet from Naupactus landing at Siphae, a little town in Boeotian territory at the end of the Corinthian Gulf. Hence he was to march overland through Boeotia and join Hippocrates, who was to lead the Athenian force over Parnes and fall upon eastern Boeotia at Delium, a shrine in the territory of Tanagra. On the same day a revolution in favor of Athens was to be accomplished at Chaeronea. Thus Boeotia was to be paralyzed by the occupation of three strategic points. On the west, communication with Corinth was to be cut off by the occupation of Thespiae and Siphae. On the east, access to the sea at Calchis was to be prevented by the occupation of Delium, and on the north the occupation of Chaeronea would block traffic on the great north road which runs west of Lake Copais around the foot of Parnassus. This was the most ambitious effort for the coordination of land forces during the war, and it failed because of treachery and lack of correct timing. Someone betrayed the plot and prevented the rising at Chaeronea. There was also confusion as to the day on which the attack was to be made, and Demosthenes arrived at Siphae a day too early, only to find himself forestalled by the betrayal of the plot. He had to be content with making a demonstration against Sicyon on the south side of the Corinthian Gulf. Hippocrates was left to make an attack, unsupported, on Delium. The Boeotians, freed from any fear of attack in the rear, opposed him in full force. The Athenians lost nearly one thousand men, among them their general, Hippocrates.

Meanwhile Brasidas had been showing his usual energy in a campaign in the northeast. At the beginning of the war the Athenians had formed an alliance with Sitalces, King of the Odrysian Empire in Thrace, an alliance which might have been very significant. With his assistance they intended to attack Perdiccas, King of Macedonia. The Athenians had promised to send a fleet to cooperate with Sitalces in the suppression of all resistance to their empire along the shores of the northwest Aegean. Sitalces raised a considerable force and in the third winter of the war came down to the coast.

The Athenians, however, missed their opportunity simply because they did not send to Sitalces the force which they had promised. He waited in vain for them, and when the force failed to arrive he made peace with Perdiccas, a peace which was cemented by the marriage of Perdiccas' sister and Seuthes, the nephew and heir of Sitalces. Perdiccas now became an ally of Athens.

In the eighth year of the war (424 B. C.), the indefatigable Brasidas turned his attention to this northeastern region. He decided to march across Thessaly, a territory friendly to the Athenians. When an objection was raised by the Thessalian towns, he took a very reasonable attitude, a proceeding quite in keeping with his character. He said that if the Thessalians did not wish him to pass through, he would, of course, give up the attempt, but that he had not heard of any war between the Thessalians and the Spartans and that he hoped that they would allow him to pass through their territory, which he promised to do without harm. Taken off their guard by the very reasonableness of his talk they permitted him to pass. Reaching the coast, he began at once with characteristic energy to prosecute the war by attacking the cities of the Athenian Empire. He constantly offered to set them free, and when some of them showed signs of resistance he said that he would set them free whether they wished it or not. One after another, the towns of the Athenian Empire along the coast were taken over by Brasidas. In every case he showed mercy to the inhabitants, and the story of his mercy spread, and now in the winter of the eighth year of the war he performed a feat which had a far-reaching effect on history.

Amphipolis was an important Athenian city on the Strymon. Toward it Brasidas made his way through the storm of a winter night. Fighting in the winter was not considered a reasonable occupation among the Greeks, who went home to their firesides as soon as the weather became unsettled in the fall, much as in eighteenth-century Europe armies went into winter quarters in the fall, and nothing could be done until the spring. Brasidas, however, made war summer and winter alike, and when he appeared before the gates of Amphipolis the inhabitants were in no position to resist him. Also, he offered very easy terms. The Athenians might remain in the city and enjoy the use of their property or they might depart in five days, taking their possessions with them.

Word was dispatched to Thucydides, who, with a small squadron, was on guard at Thasos. The moment the news came Thucydides sailed for Amphipolis. We can imagine the haste and anxiety with which the sailors sped their ships across the short space of sea. But he arrived too late. When the news of this disaster reached Athens, he was banished. It was known that he had had the privilege of working gold mines in the neighboring district of Thrace, and suspicion was raised that he was protecting his own property and neglecting the interests of the city. For twenty years he was in exile from his country and during this time he wrote the greater part of his *History*. If it is true, as has been said, that the most important thing about the Peloponnesian War was that Thucydides deigned to write its history, then posterity may well rejoice in the failure that Athens punished.

A sentiment for peace had been developing at Athens, and Sparta was already anxious to discontinue hostilities and to recover the prisoners who had been taken at Sphacteria. Accordingly, with the coming of the summer of the ninth year of the war (423 B. C.), the Athenians and the allies made a truce for a year. But meanwhile Brasidas was going on with his conquests in the Chalcidian peninsula. He had already taken the town of Torone on the southernmost of the three projecting peninsulas, and two days after the truce had been signed he was admitted into the adjoining town of Scione. This he refused to give up, claiming that he had captured it before the truce was signed, whereas he had only seized it before he knew that the truce had been signed. However, he held on to it stubbornly, and the Spartan failure to make him disgorge his prey was one of the things that prevented the truce from maturing into a peace.

The close of the truce in the ninth winter of the war found Brasidas engaged in an ineffectual attempt to capture Potidaea. The truce came to an end with the tenth summer of the war (422 B. C.), but no fighting was indulged in until after the Greeks had had their athletic sports at the Pythian Games. War was a serious business, but if the Greeks had to choose between a war and an athletic contest, the athletic contest was given the preference. At the terrible crisis of the Persian Wars, Leonidas was sent off to Thermopylae with only three hundred Spartans, and the rest went to the show at Olympia.

As soon as the truce was at an end Cleon induced the Athenians to send him to Chalcidice to oppose Brasidas. He succeeded in retaking Torone and then made an attack upon Amphipolis. The loss of this colony had been a bitter blow to Athens. Cleon invited Perdiccas to assist him, but Perdiccas found it convenient to be unavoidably delayed. In justice to Cleon it must be admitted that he was a man of energy. He marched swiftly and incompetently upon Amphipolis and almost succeeded in taking it before Brasidas entered the city. When Cleon did, however, see that Brasidas was within, he beat a retreat. Brasidas rushed out in pursuit, and Cleon led the van in a wild flight. He was overtaken and killed. Brasidas in the moment of victory was struck down. His followers carried him into the city, where he died, but not until he knew that he was victorious. In gratitude for his services the inhabitants of Amphipolis gave him a public burial and in his honor yearly celebrated games and offered sacrifices to him as a hero. Seldom have sacrifices been so well deserved.

Perdiccas was now left in alliance with the Athenians, an alliance which he maintained until for genealogical reasons he joined the combination of Argos and Sparta against Athens.   Thucydides says ironically, "He did not, however, immediately desert the Athenians, but he was thinking of deserting, being influenced by the example of the Argives; for he was himself of Argive descent."   In the fifteenth year of the war (417 B. C.) he was blockaded by the Athenians, and the next year his territory suffered from their inroads. Two years later he passed again to the Athenian side and gave them ineffectual assistance in another misguided attempt to recapture Amphipolis.

With the deaths of Cleon and Brasidas peace emerged above the horizon.   Thucydides says of Brasidas and Cleon that they were the two greatest enemies of peace, "the one because the war brought him success and reputation, and the other because he fancied that in quiet times his rogueries would be more transparent and his slanders less credible. . . ." Aristophanes represents them as the two pestles which War is using to pulverize the cities in a huge mortar. From the point of view of Athens the peace should have been concluded immediately after the seizure of Cythera. Since that time the Athenians had suffered a severe reverse at Delium. They had lost Panactum, one of their fortresses near the Boeotian border, and they had been distinctly worsted in their campaigns at Chalcidice.   Their prestige had been dimmed. The Lacedaemonians, on the other hand, were strongly inclined to peace not only because they felt that they must re-

cover their countrymen who had surrendered at Sphacteria, but also because the constant raids which the
Athenians were conducting from that point and from
Cythera were wearing them down, and their Helots
were deserting in large numbers. A still further argument for peace on the Spartan side was that the
thirty-year truce with Argos, their powerful neighbor
on the north, was just about to expire. The cooperation of Argos with the Athenian Empire might well
ruin Spartan supremacy on land.

Accordingly, peace was concluded in the spring at
the close of the tenth winter of the war (421 B. C.).
The peace was a settlement on the basis of *uti possidetis*. Panactum was to be restored to the Athenians,
and in the northwest Aegean Athens was to have back
her long desired colony of Amphipolis and in general
was to have a free hand in reducing her recalcitrant
allies in that region. Certain cities were to be exempt-
ed from any obligations toward Athens except the
payment of the basic tribute as fixed by Aristides.
Athens was to be allowed to retain Nisaea and Minoa
on the Megarean coast. She was to give up Cythera
and Pylos and above all she was to restore those two
hundred and ninety-two Lacedaemonian prisoners.

The peace was a shameful betrayal of Sparta's allies. Corinth had insisted on the declaration of war
and had been most active in bringing the war about.
She had lost heavily. The peace left her shorn of all
her colonies on the western coast of Greece and with
a navy badly crippled. The Boeotians were supposed
to give up Panactum, and also to consent to the resto-
ration of Plataea. It is small wonder that these states
refused to sign the treaty. Besides the Boeotians and

Corinthians and Megareans, the people of Elis also refused to ratify this treaty.

So unstable was the situation, so fraught with the seeds of war, that the Lacedaemonians and Athenians felt that it must be bolstered up with an alliance. Accordingly, an alliance was made between these two states for fifty years.

The policy of Pericles, if that policy meant the demonstration of the invincibility of the Athenian Empire, had been justified. The Athenians could have secured a better peace after the action at Sphacteria, but the present arrangement left Athens in possession of almost everything which she had had at the beginning of the war, and in addition to that her influence was paramount on the coast of western Greece. The road to Sicily and the west was open to her. She had lost comparatively few ships; her empire, in spite of the cracks in the northwest Aegean, was still intact. In a few years the tribute from the empire would have refilled the treasury of Athens, the Propylaea might have been completed, and other public works equally noble might have been undertaken. What the Athenians needed was a third statesman to carry on the tradition of Themistocles and Pericles. A third statesman was at hand, a nephew of the great Pericles, Alcibiades. He might have added to the age of Pericles an age of Alcibiades equally brilliant. With the intellectual endowments of a god and the irresponsible conceit of a buffoon, he ruined Athens.

At this point in his narrative Thucydides pauses to point out the essential unity of the twenty-seven-year struggle between Athens and Sparta. He has no illusions about the peace which had been patched up. He says:

> .... the term "peace" can hardly be applied to a state of things in which neither party gave back or received all the places stipulated ; moreover in the Mantinean and Epidaurian wars and in other matters there were violations of the treaty on both sides . . . .

VI
THUCYDIDES' NARRATIVE
(With Additions by Xenophon)
III. From the Peace of Nicias to the End of the War
421-404 B. C.

THERE were two reasons why the peace broke down. In the first place, Sparta had deliberately sold out the interests of her allies. No peace between her allies which did not include the two most powerful members of the confederation after Sparta, Corinth and Boeotia, could be enduring. In the second place, Sparta either could not or would not fulfill the conditions of the peace. Her general refused, perhaps with the connivance of Sparta, to give up Amphipolis, and the Boeotians destroyed the Athenian fortress of Panactum, which they had captured. The Spartans could have rebuilt it but refused to do so. In retaliation for this the Athenians, though they gave up the prisoners, refused to surrender Pylos, and it remained for years a thorn in the side of the Spartans.

The thirty-year truce between Sparta and Argos was at an end, and during the seven years which followed before the actual resumption of hostilities in the eighteenth year of the war (414 B. C.) the center of interest is the Peloponnesus. Corinth, dissatisfied with the terms of the peace, endeavored to form a new Peloponnesian league in which Argos should replace Sparta. Tegea, however, refused to join this league, and futile negotiations followed. Sparta and Athens were constantly haggling over the implementation of the peace, and Alcibiades was trying to bring about a situation in which Athens and Argos might form an alliance which, with the assistance of the other Peloponnesian states, might crush Sparta. A war ensued between Argos and her neighbor to the north, Epidaurus, in which Athens assisted Argos. The Argives were out-generaled by the Spartans and were apparently saved from annihilation only by a truce which the Spartan king was foolish enough to make. And finally, in the fourteenth year of the war (418 B. C.), a battle occurred near Mantinea in which the Spartans, with the assistance of the Tegeans, utterly defeated the Athenians, the Argives and the Mantineans. Sparta's prestige was again high. They had proved that their land forces, no matter how poor the tactics of their leaders might be, could win a victory in the open field under impossibly bad conditions.

Two years later the Corinthians formally declared war on Athens, a declaration which seemed to have very little effect on the actual state of affairs.

Despite all this turmoil and confused fighting, in which Argos, Corinth, Elis and Mantinea arranged themselves constantly in different combinations, war was not declared between Athens and Sparta. An anomalous condition existed under which the Athenians could fight the Spartans in the open field, apparently without breaking the treaty or even the alliance which existed between them. But when, in the eighteenth year of the war (414 B. C.), the Athenians sent out an expedition by sea which landed marauders on the Spartan territory and wasted the country, the treaty was formally abrogated, and Thucydides, whose judgment in the matter must be final, says:

> The Athenians assisted the Argives with thirty ships. The use which they made of them was a glaring violation of the treaty with the Lacedaemonians. Hitherto they had only gone out on marauding expeditions from Pylos; when they landed, it was not upon the

shores of Laconia, but upon other parts of the Pelo-
ponnese; and they had merely fought as the allies of
the Argives and Mantineans. . . . . Thereby [i.e., by
landing troops on Spartan territory] the Athenians at
last gave the Lacedaemonians a right to complain of
them and completely justified measures of retaliation.

During the sixteenth summer of the war (416 B.
C.) the Athenians made a descent on the volcanic Island of Melos. This island lies southeast from the
coast of Laconia, a hundred miles north of Crete. It
was a Doric island and had been enjoying a boon which
the Greeks regarded as priceless, liberty. The Athenians now determined to make Melos a part of their
empire. Without any provocation they landed upon
the island in force. The inhabitants of Melos, being
Dorians, did not put much confidence in their popular
assembly, so the Athenian leaders, who thought it wise
to address the Melians before they attacked them,
were given an audience only by the magistrates and
the chief men.

Here Thucydides presents a situation dramatically
but by a new method. Instead of set speeches on either side, with the familiar arguments of expediency
against justice, a colloquy is held between a representative of the Melians and one of the Athenian envoys.
It has sometimes been suggested that Thucydides intended to work this dialogue up later into speeches.
That seems doubtful. It is, rather, like two speeches
dovetailed together, in which each argument is answered immediately instead of assembling all of the
arguments on one side and then opposing them by arguments on the other side.

The dialogue is conducted in a highly realistic spirit. The Melian representative at the beginning of the discussion states the alternatives, ".... if the justice of our cause prevail and we therefore refuse to yield, we may expect war; if we are convinced by you, slavery." The Athenian envoy sets out his case in what is probably the most barefaced advocacy of expediency in all Thucydides:

> .... we both know alike that into the discussion of human affairs the question of justice only enters where there is equal power to enforce it, and that the powerful exact what they can, and the weak grant what they must.

The Melian representative makes the only answer which he can, namely, that expediency should prompt the Athenians to be merciful and tolerate independent Greek cities:

> But do you not recognise another danger? For, once more, since you drive us from the plea of justice and press upon us your doctrine of expediency, we must show you what is for our interest, and, if it be for yours also, may hope to convince you :—Will you not be making enemies of all who are now neutrals?

The Melians finally refused to surrender to the Athenians, in these noble words:

> Men of Athens, our resolution is unchanged; and we will not in a moment surrender that liberty which our city, founded seven hundred years ago, still enjoys; we will trust to the good fortune which, by the favour of the Gods, has hitherto preserved us, and for human help to the Lacedaemonians, and endeavor to save ourselves.

To which the Athenians sarcastically replied:

Well, we must say, judging from the decision at which you have arrived, that you are the only men who deem the future to be more certain than the present, and regard things unseen as already realised in your fond anticipation, and that the more you cast yourselves upon the Lacedaemonians and fortune and hope, and trust them, the more complete will be your ruin.

The following winter Melos surrendered, and Thucydides laconically closes the account:

.... the Melians were induced to surrender at discretion. The Athenians thereupon put to death all who were of military age, and made slaves of the women and children. They then colonised the island, sending thither five hundred settlers of their own.

For many years the Athenians had been turning their eyes with longing toward the rich cities in southern Italy and Sicily. Here were many Greek colonies from many cities in the homeland. Now that they held the commanding position in northwestern Greece and controlled, by their domination of Corcyra, the approach to Sicily, nothing was more natural than that they should indulge in the hope of extending their empire to the west. If the cities of Italy and Sicily could be brought into the Athenian Empire, her revenues might easily be doubled, and Athens might become even more powerful than she was now.

Two expeditions had previously been sent to Sicily, the first during the fifth year of the war at the request of the people of Leontini. This had done little, but some of the ships had visited the islands of Aeolus and the troops had landed on the island of Strongyle (Stromboli). Thucydides notes the volcanic nature of this island and its blazing volcano. He is under no illusion as to the reason for the dispatch of this expedition. He gives the economic background for this enterprise and strips the mask from the face of the Athenians. "The Athenians sent the ships, professedly on the ground of relationship, but in reality because they did not wish the Peloponnesians to obtain corn from Sicily."

Again, two years later, a second expedition had been sent out. Demosthenes had accompanied this expedition as far as Pylos, where he had initiated the famous campaign already narrated. Neither of these expeditions had been significant, but they had served to arouse the suspicion of the people of Sicily.

The Sicilians finally held a memorable conference at Gela, where they were addressed by a Syracusan, Hermocrates. His plea was, Sicily for the Sicilians—isolationism, no foreign intervention. He spoke of the Athenians with considerable disrespect and much truth:

> The Athenians are a much more convincing argument of peace than any words of mine can be. . . . . the Athenians do not attack us because we are divided into two races. . . . but because they covet the good things of Sicily which we all share alike.

He concluded:

> We will never again introduce allies from abroad, no, nor pretended mediators. This policy will immediately secure to Sicily two great blessings; she will get rid of the Athenians, and of civil war. And for the future we shall keep the island free and our own, and none will be tempted to attack us.

The Sicilians took the advice of Hermocrates and concluded peace among themselves, and the Athenians sailed home. The generals, who had accomplished nothing, were received with the usual Athenian welcome—two of them were exiled and the third fined.

The Athenians were now, in the seventeenth summer of the war (415 B.C.), about to embark upon their most ambitious and disastrous enterprise, the invasion of Sicily in force and the subjugation of Syracuse. To this Thucydides devotes the greater part of two books, VI and VII. Instead of bringing in the early history of Sicily as he usually does, in a digression in the midst of his narrative, he places it at the beginning of Book VI. He says (what was quite true) that the average Athenian had no conception of the magnitude of this undertaking. Sicily was a vast island, a voyage around which occupied eight days. The population of the island was great, and its cities close to the mainland of Italy, and in any such struggle as this the Greek peoples of the cities of Italy would be involved also. The struggle was in magnitude no less than a second Peloponnesian war.

Thucydides' outline of early Sicilian history is a model for conciseness and completeness.

The excuse for invading Sicily was a plea from the inhabitants of the Elymian town of Egesta (Segesta). On the previous expeditions Athens had used as a pretext the fact that she was assisting Ionian cities against Dorian cities, and though this excuse was merely a specious one, the conflict between the ideals of these two Greek peoples is emphasized all through this account, and it doubtless was a potent factor in aligning the cities of Italy against each other.

The people of Egesta affirmed that they were suffering at the hand of their neighboring city, Selinus.

The people of Selinus appealed to the Syracusans—
Dorians appealing to Dorians. Now apparently there
was danger of a great Dorian uprising in Sicily which
would threaten Athens. Egesta, an Elymian city,
could not appeal to the Athenians on the ground of
consanguinity. They had, however, a stronger appeal: they offered to finance the war. Athenian envoys were sent out to test their enthusiasm for the war
and more especially to examine their financial stand-
ing. The Athenians were entertained in the home of
one wealthy Egestan after another and they marvelled
at the richness of the table service. They were apparently too overcome with the gorgeousness of the food
and wine to notice what later proved to be the truth,
that the plates and goblets were identical, that they
had been collected from all Egesta and the neighboring towns and were being passed on from host to host.
By this device the simple people of Egesta led the
astute Athenians to believe that each home was possessed of elaborate gold and silver services. The
envoys returned enthusiastic, and the sovereign people
of Athens debated in their assembly the expediency
of dispatching an expedition to conquer Syracuse.

This assembly was held early in the seventeenth
summer of the war (415 B.C.). The assembly voted
to undertake the expedition, and three generals were
elected, Alcibiades, Nicias and Lamachus. Five days
after this decision was reached another assembly was
held, at which the question was debated, how many
ships and how much money should be employed? Nicias, whose motto was, "Never put off till tomorrow
what you can just as well do the day after tomorrow,"
attempted to dissuade the Athenians from undertak-

ing the project, considering it ill-advised. He intimated that it had been undertaken largely at the instance of Alcibiades, of whom he disapproved. Nothing loath, Alcibiades took up the argument. He has
often been described as the most significant Athenian
figure in the Peloponnesian War from this time on.
Endowed with everything that a man needed to make
him a leader in Athenian politics, birth, wealth, beauty,
a brilliant intellect, a persuasive tongue, a great capacity for friendship, he lacked the most important and
indispensable gift, the gift of judgment. His brilliance inspired admiration, his openhanded generosity
inspired devotion and love, his intellect commanded
confidence; but in spite of all these things his egotism
and his fatal lack of balance, his utter disregard of the
consequences of his actions, filled the Athenian people
with distrust. Association with Alcibiades was like
malaria, a matter of fever and chills. Aristophanes
says of him, "the city loves him and she hates him and
she longs to have him back." And in the *Frogs* he puts
into the mouth of Aeschylus what apparently was his
own judgment of Alcibiades, "'Twere best to rear no
lion in the state: but having reared 'tis best to humor
him." And there is some reason to think that this was
the purport of a remark of Pericles himself.

At the persuasion of Alcibiades the Athenians voted
ample supplies for the expedition, and preparations
were made. "They virtuously professed that they were
going to assist their own kinsmen and their newly-
acquired allies, but the simple truth was that they
aspired to the empire of Sicily."

Thucydides' narrative of this expedition is remarkable for many things, but in nothing is it more re-

markable than the way in which the historian gives to his readers from the beginning the impression that doom hangs over this enterprise. The first mistake had already been made. The eldest of the generals to whom this expedition was entrusted did not believe in the enterprise. Constitutionally opposed to action, Nicias should never have been placed in a position of authority to execute a command in the wisdom of which he did not believe.

The city was busy with the preparation of this great armament. It was almost ready to set sail when there happened a curious and terrifying portent. One morning when the Athenians arose they found that the statues of Hermes which stood in the streets in front of almost every door throughout the city had all been mutilated. It was further disclosed that some of the gay young men of the city had put on a burlesque of the Eleusinian Mysteries. The celebration of the Mysteries each year at Eleusis was perhaps the most revered of all Greek rites. Only those could be initiated into these Mysteries who were of pure Greek blood and whose lives were blameless. To be one of the *mystai* was to have one's life approved, and those who had been initiated into these rites had a fairer hope both for this life and for the life to come. The rumor of the morning said that Alcibiades and his drunken companions had held a burlesque of the Mysteries in his house and had initiated his favorite steed. It is difficult to conceive of the shock which this news brought to the conservative members of the Athenian state. Perhaps we can get some idea of it if we can imagine a President of the United States or a Chief Justice, convivially disposed, administering the sacred sacrament to a favorite dog. Sober Americans would be no more outraged at this than the Athenians were at the profanation of the Eleusinian Mysteries and the mutilation of the Hermae. Whether Alcibiades was guilty or not of the profanation of the Mysteries, or whether he had a hand in mutilating the Hermae, for this too was sacrilege, since Hermes was the God of Boundaries and these were busts of the God which had been broken, will never be known. Suspicion fell strongly upon him. Though he did his best to have an immediate trial, his enemies would not consent. They probably had little evidence. In any case they distrusted their ability to convict him when he was about to sail as general of this expedition. So the preparation went on, and the ships were assembled.

Thucydides could not have seen the departure of the fleet, but he describes it with all the vividness of an eyewitness, the beautifully decked galleys, the people on the shore bidding farewell to their friends, the brilliance of the equipment of the soldiers, the officers in their uniforms, the elaborate figureheads of the galleys and the ominous forebodings that filled the hearts of those who remained behind. ". . . . and terrors which had never occurred to them when they were voting the expedition now entered into their souls."

When all was ready for the departure, the trumpet proclaimed silence, a single herald offered prayer, and the responses were given by the men of all the vessels. From gold and silver bowls the officers and men poured libations of wine into the sea. The crews raised the hymn of battle, and in single file the galleys passed out of Piraeus Harbor. Then they ranged themselves in

line and raced at full speed twenty miles across the bay
to Aegina. Rounding the island, they passed on to Corcyra, where they picked up their allied forces and
started for Sicily.

The fleet that sailed from Corcyra was an impressive one. It consisted of 134 triremes and two pente-
conters, with five thousand hoplites, besides more than
twelve hundred light-armed troops. They were refused admission to the harbor at Tarentum and at
Locris and passed on to Rhegium.

Here a council of war was held. Lamachus, a
straightforward, honest general who was under the impression that war meant fighting, was for an immediate attack upon Syracuse. Alcibiades was for making
a progress around Sicily. He hoped by the display of
the magnificent Athenian navy and by the persuasive
quality of his own eloquence to win over allies. Nicias,
as might be expected, proposed a course which was
as near as possible to no action at all. He would make
a demonstration against Selinus, insisting on help from
Egesta, and then would return home. He would jus-
tify his own course by explaining to the Athenian assembly that the ambassadors had been hoodwinked
and shamefully deceived by the people of Egesta,
whose clever trick had now been unmasked. Here
again fate intervened to wreck the Athenian plans.
If Lamachus' downright course had been followed
Syracuse might easily have been captured, for the
Athenian power was overwhelming, and in spite of the
eloquence of Hermocrates, who was destined to lead
his country to victory, the Syracusans were in a blue
funk. If Nicias' advice had been followed Athens
would at least have saved her navy and her army. If

Alcibiades' advice had been followed and he had remained with the fleet he could probably have won over a large number of the cities of Sicily to the support of Athens.

But just at this moment one of the state galleys arrived from Athens with orders for Alcibiades to return and stand trial for the desecration of the Hermae. The resentment at Athens over this outrage had not died down but had rather increased since the departure of the fleet. The Athenians had become persuaded that Alcibiades was aiming at tyranny. So strong was this suspicion in the minds of the Athenians that Thucydides digresses at this point to tell the story of the murder of Hipparchus, the tyrant, by Aristogeiton and Harmodius.

Many Athenians had been arrested on suspicion of complicity in the mutilation of the Hermae, and finally one of these prisoners turned state's evidence. He accused a large number of people, all of whom were condemned to death, and the sentence was executed upon such as happened to be in Athens.

When Alcibiades was notified that he must appear at Athens to defend himself, he was not arrested but was allowed to proceed in his own ship, accompanying the sacred trireme. Under these conditions Alcibiades naturally escaped. Probably the intention was that he should do so.

Robbed of his energetic direction, Lamachus, probably in awe of the wealthy, impressive Nicias, consented to divide the fleet with him. They sailed about Sicily, the army landed and took up its headquarters at Catana. In these futile gestures the seventeenth summer (415 B. C.) of the war was wasted. During the following winter preparations were made for an attack upon Syracuse. In a preliminary engagement the Syracusans were defeated, but Nicias failed to follow up his victory. The Syracusans retreated to their city and sent an embassy to Sparta asking for help.

With the coming of the next summer, the eighteenth of the war (414 B.C.), Nicias, who had meanwhile received some reinforcements from Athens, began the siege of Syracuse. This operation, the most important of all the war, is described by Thucydides with the greatest of care. There can be no question that he himself had visited Syracuse and had gone over the entire battlefield. Nothing else can account for the accurate topography of his descriptions.

The modern visitor to Syracuse finds only a much shrunken city occupying a small tongue of land which forms the eastern boundary of the great harbor. The ancient city, which was as populous and as large as Athens, extended over all of the territory north of the harbor and even stretched for a considerable distance toward the northwest. Beyond was the plateau of Epipolae, gradually rising to terminate in a promontory called Euryelus. Across this plateau, from the harbor on the south to the sea on the north, Nicias proposed to build a wall. With unerring lack of sagacity he selected probably the worst position for his camp, the low ground east of and facing the harbor, and started building his wall. He seized the strategic position of Euryelus and strongly garrisoned it. The Syracusans, noting the progress of the cross-wall and realizing that if it were completed their city would be entirely invested and communication with their friends on the island made impossible, started a counter wall running along the ridge of the plateau at right angles with the Athenian wall. The siege became a race in wall building.

As these walls approached each other, skirmishes became frequent. In one of these small engagements another of the disasters that dogged the Athenian expedition took place. The Athenians had gained an advantage, and three hundred of their troops were pursuing the Syracusans at full speed. The Syracusans suddenly rallied, supported by their cavalry, and threw back the Athenians in confusion. Lamachus, brave soldier that he was, seeing this disaster, hurried to the rescue. Leaping across a ditch in his eagerness to reach the front, he fell and was mortally wounded.

Although the Syracusans were defeated in this engagement, they succeeded in getting near enough to Fort Euryelus to demolish about a thousand feet of the wall. Nicias, who happened to be in the fort, saved the rest of the lines by setting fire to the scaffolding which was still in position along the wall. His absence from the battle was accounted for by the fact that he was ill. The fatal disease from which he was suffering was already sapping his physical strength, and this accentuated his natural tendency to inactivity.

The Syracusans were now in despair. They opened communications with Nicias, looking to a cessation of hostilities, but nothing came of it, and meanwhile deliverance in the person of a single Spartan was at hand.

The Spartans, with their usual caution, hearing the appeal of the Syracusans, had decided not to send an

army, but unwittingly they did even better, they sent
Gylippus. When he reached Tarentum and heard of
the situation at Syracuse, he gave up hope for the safety of Sicily but still determined to do what he could.
He might at least save the Dorian colonies in southern
Italy and so he pressed on. Nicias heard of his approach but because he was accompanied by so few ships
concluded that it was a mere privateering expedition
and made no effort to prevent his entering Syracuse,
another fatal mistake.

Meanwhile Alcibiades had made his way to Sparta.
He offered to assist the Spartans and in a speech before the ephors and the magistrates he outlined his position. Athens by her treatment of him had ceased to
be his country. In the most barefaced manner he announced, "He is the true patriot, not who, when unjustly exiled, abstains from attacking his country, but
who in the warmth of his affection seeks to recover her
without regard to the means." He urged that assistance be sent to the Syracusans, for Athenian success
would mean the ultimate overthrow of Sparta.

Alcibiades encouraged the Spartans to fortify Decelea and thus have a base of operations against Athens which the Lacedaemonians could use the entire
year. The Spartans adopted both of Alcibiades' pro-
posals. They dispatched Gylippus and they seized
Decelea, a point on the slopes of Parnes about fourteen miles from Athens and within sight of the city.
The idea of fortifying some position in Attica was not
an original idea of Alcibiades. Pericles had foreseen
the possibility of such an event, and the Spartans
themselves had considered it. It needed, however, the
energy of Alcibiades to overcome the natural lethargy

of the Lacedaemonians. The occupancy of this point and the establishment there of a permanent garrison did immense harm to the Athenians.

> Hitherto the invasions had been brief and did not prevent them from getting something from the soil in the interval; but now the Peloponnesians were continually on the spot; and sometimes they were reinforced by additional troops, but always the regular garrison, who were compelled to find their own supplies, overran and despoiled the country. The Lacedaemonian king, Agis, was present in person, and devoted his whole energies to the war. The sufferings of the Athenians were terrible. For they were dispossessed of their entire territory; more than twenty thousand slaves had deserted, most of them workmen; all their sheep and cattle had perished, and now that the cavalry had to go out every day and make descents upon Decelea or keep guard all over the country, their horses were either wounded by the enemy or lamed by the roughness of the ground and the incessant fatigue.

The entrance of Gylippus, with small reinforcements which he had picked up on the way, heartened the Syracusans. While he was by no means the equal of Brasidas in resourcefulness and displayed none of Brasidas' attractive qualities of spirit, he was a capable general; his advice on military matters was sound, and the mere fact that the Syracusans now had a general from Sparta at the head of their troops gave them additional courage. He was to the Syracusans what Marshal Ney was to the forces of Napoleon. He was himself worth a division.

The seventh book of Thucydides, which is devoted almost entirely to the siege of Syracuse, is the finest part of all his *History*. In fact, it is doubtful if any

historical narrative has ever reached so high a point
of perfection.

The arrival of Gylippus cast a gloom over the already somber spirit of Nicias. This gloom was increased by a defeat which the Athenians suffered in
a small action in which Gylippus' cavalry played an
important part and by the arrival of reinforcements
which Gylippus received from some of his Sicilian
allies. Every day Nicias felt more strongly that the
expedition was a mistake and so during the winter,
the eighteenth of the war (414 B. C.), he wrote a
letter to Athens suggesting that the expedition be recalled. Meanwhile he kept his army on the defensive,
apparently so that there might be no chance of a victory detaining him longer in Syracuse.

Thucydides gives Nicias' letter in full. It shows
that its author was entirely without spirit, that every
slight difficulty seemed to him a mountainous obstacle.
He regrets that he cannot write more cheerfully but
feels that the Athenians should know the exact situation. He closes his letter by speaking of his own
sickness, a disease of the kidneys, and pleads to be relieved.

The effect on the Athenians was exactly the opposite from that intended. They determined to continue
the expedition but to relieve Nicias by associating with
him their two best generals, Eurymedon and Demosthenes. Eurymedon sailed at once, and Demosthenes organized a relief expedition. Nicias had intimated in his letter that an army and fleet as large as
the original expedition and plenty of money would be
necessary. He apparently had intended by the very
size of his request to insure its refusal. But the Atheni-

ans took him at his word and sent a fleet of seventy-three sail with five thousand infantry and numerous light-armed troops.

Meanwhile, as might have been expected, things were going well with the Syracusans. Under the inspiration of Gylippus' leadership they had continued their crosswall, had beaten the Athenians to the point of intersection and in this way made it possible to keep open their communications with the interior of Sicily.

The investment of Syracuse now became impossible, but worse than this was in store. A battle in the harbor took place between the Syracusan galleys and the Athenian fleet. The great harbor at Syracuse is magnificent in its proportions and is almost entirely landlocked. The Syracusans had taken advantage of a Corinthian device—they strengthened the fore part of their ships with heavy beams so that they could resist the shock of head-on collision. Large as the harbor is, it was not large enough to give the Athenians room for their favorite maneuvers. They could not draw the Syracusans into a running fight and ram them. They had to meet them head-on. Under these conditions the Athenian navy was defeated, a defeat that was all the more humiliating because of the splendor and character of the Athenian equipment and their pride in their naval supremacy.

Almost immediately after this defeat Demosthenes arrived with his reinforcements:

> The Syracusans and their allies were in consternation. It seemed to them as if their perils would never have an end when they saw, notwithstanding the fortification of Decelea, another army arriving nearly equal to the former, and Athens displaying such varied and

exuberant strength; while the first Athenian army regained a certain degree of confidence after their disasters.

In spite of the Syracusan despondency, Demosthenes at a glance realized the seriousness of the situation. He determined that an immediate attack while the Syracusans were overawed by the magnificence of his armament would be best. He knew that if he waited he would make the same fatal blunder which Nicias had made.

> For Nicias was dreaded at his first arrival, but when, instead of at once laying siege to Syracuse, he passed the winter at Catana, he fell into contempt, and his delay gave Gylippus time to come with an army from Peloponnesus.

He saw that the Syracusan wall must be taken at all costs. An attempt to take it by frontal attack was thwarted. He now determined on the dangerous expedient of a night attack, the moon being full. This attack was launched with the greatest of care and at first was successful. But as the Athenians advanced they fell into confusion. A counterattack by some Boeotian allies of the Syracusans was successful, and the whole army fell back in disorder:

> But in a night engagement, like this in which two great armies fought—the only one of the kind which occurred during the war—who could be certain of anything? The moon was bright, and they saw before them, as men naturally would in the moonlight, the figures of one another, but were unable to distinguish with certainty who was friend or foe.

As they retreated the confusion became greater. Many were forced off the narrow path leading down from the height. Some of them fell to their death, and others, unacquainted with the ground even after they reached the level plain, missed their way and were cut off.

This failure at once made it clear to Demosthenes that the siege must be abandoned. A council of war was held. Demosthenes urged immediate departure. Nicias urged that they should remain and continue the siege. He apparently had some vague hope that treachery within the city would betray it into his hands. He had his eye as always on what the people would do to them when they reached Athens. He knew, he said, "the Athenian people would not forgive their departure if they left without an order from home." Demosthenes was equally positive that the siege could not go on. If they must wait for a vote of the assembly at Athens, they should retreat to Thapsus or Catana and harry the country from there. The navy could then operate from a friendly harbor in the open sea where space was available for their tactics. Eurymedon agreed with him.

This should have settled the matter, but Nicias still persisted. He gave the impression that he had secret information which he could not share with his colleagues, and in awe of this owl-eyed wisdom Eurymedon and Demosthenes gave way. Their refusal to enforce their opinion cost them their own lives.

After the council of war broke up, Gylippus, who had been absent from Syracuse on a recruiting expedition, returned to the city with reinforcements. This apparently shook Nicias' determination, and he consented to departure. Everything was ready when fate played the last and fatal card. The moon was eclipsed (August 27, 413 B.C.). Not only the generals but the army were moved by superstitious fears. Nicias was told he must remain either three days or thrice nine. To be on the safe side, he chose the latter alternative, and the fate of the army and navy was sealed. The Syracusans offered battle, which the Athenians accepted. Eurymedon took charge of the fleet. He was defeated, and himself slain. The courage of the Syracusans rose with their success, and they determined now not to allow their adversaries to escape. They blocked the entrance to the harbor with ships chained together.

On the eve of the final tragedy Thucydides pauses to give an enumeration of the allies on either side. Both sides prepared for the final struggle. The two fleets made ready for a final battle. Thucydides gives the address of Nicias to his troops, in which he did his best to hearten them. Then, when they were about to engage, feeling

> .... that all which he had done was nothing, and that he had not said half enough, again addressed the trierarchs, and calling each of them by his father's name, and his own name, and the name of his tribe, he entreated those who had made any reputation for themselves not to be false to it, and those whose ancestors were eminent not to tarnish their hereditary fame. He reminded them that they were the inhabitants of the freest country in the world, and how in Athens there was no interference with the daily life of any man. He spoke to them of their wives and children and their fathers' Gods, as men will at such a time; for then they do not care whether their commonplace phrases seem to be out of date or not, but loudly reiterate the old appeals, believing that they may be of some service at the awful moment.

The Athenians now began the fight. The noncombatants lined the shore and the walls of the city, and the great struggle took place before their eyes, like a combat in some huge arena. Thucydides surpasses himself in the vividness of his description of the emotions of the onlookers:

> Being quite close and having different points of view, they would some of them see their own ships victorious; their courage would then revive, and they would earnestly call upon the Gods not to take from them their hope of deliverance. But others, who saw their ships worsted, cried and shrieked aloud, and were by the sight alone more utterly unnerved than the defeated combatants themselves. Others again, who had fixed their gaze on some part of the struggle which was undecided, were in a state of excitement still more terrible; they kept swaying their bodies to and fro in an agony of hope and fear as the stubborn conflict went on and on; for at every instant they were all but saved or all but lost.

The result of the battle was long doubtful, but finally the Athenians were utterly defeated and driven back to their camp. Demosthenes proposed to Nicias that they take what vessels remained and try to cut their way out of the harbor at daybreak. Nicias consented, but, though they still outnumbered their foes, the sailors refused to embark.

It was determined then to break camp the next morning and to seek safety at Catana or some other friendly town.

A carefully worded, treacherous message from Syracuse caused them to put off their departure until the third day. Meanwhile, of course, the triumphant Syracusans were planning the pursuit. On the third day after the sea fight the Athenians began to move, abandoning their dead and their wounded.

> The dead were unburied, and when any one saw the body of a friend lying on the ground he was smitten with sorrow and dread, while the sick or wounded who still survived but had to be left were even a greater trial to the living, and more to be pitied than those who were gone. Their prayers and lamentations drove their companions to distraction; they would beg that they might be taken with them, and call by name any friend or relation whom they saw passing; they would hang upon their departing comrades and follow as far as they could, and, when their limbs and strength failed them, and they dropped behind, many were the imprecations and cries which they uttered. So that the whole army was in tears, and such was their despair that they could hardly make up their minds to stir, although they were leaving an enemy's country, having suffered calamities too great for tears already, and dreading miseries yet greater in the unknown future.

Nicias, sick as he was, marched with his soldiers. For them he did his best, and no one could say that he did not at the end play the courageous commander. He heartened them with his words of encouragement, raising his voice louder and louder, as he spoke, that more might hear him. For three days they advanced on the road to the interior of Sicily, harassed by the Syracusan light troops. On the fourth day they found the road blocked by a wall. After a futile assault on the wall they retired toward the plain. The fifth day was spent in a bitter retreat, constantly under fire. On the sixth day they started very early, changing their course toward the sea. They forced their way through an obstruction the Syracusans had raised and marched on.

The Syracusans pursued, and now Demosthenes' command, which was bringing up the rear, became separated from the rest of the troops. On that day, entirely surrounded by the Syracusans, without food, he surrendered (September 16, 413 B. C.). His force numbered six thousand. Nicias, with his division, reached and crossed the river Erineus. The next day, the seventh, Nicias was informed of the fate of Demosthenes. He endeavored to surrender to Gylippus on terms. Gylippus refused. That night they attempted in vain to escape. At dawn of the eighth day (September 18) Nicias resumed the hopeless flight and under heavy fire reached the ford of the Assinarus. Here the final tragedy took place:

> The Syracusans stood upon the further bank of the river, which was steep, and hurled missiles from above on the Athenians, who were huddled together in the deep bed of the stream and for the most part were drinking greedily. The Peloponnesians came down the bank and slaughtered them, falling chiefly upon those who were in the river. Whereupon the water at once became foul, but was drunk all the same, although muddy and dyed with blood, and the crowd fought for it.

Nicias surrendered to Gylippus, telling him that he might do what he "pleased with himself, but not to go on killing the men." All the prisoners were brought into the city. Demosthenes and Nicias were put to death, perhaps with torture. Thucydides says that Gylippus did not consent to the execution, for he wanted to take the generals home to exhibit them. It was Demosthenes who had captured the Spartans at Pylos, and it was Nicias who had let them go. But the Syracusans would not consent to have them spared. The Corinthians were especially eager for the execution of Nicias. They feared that by bribery he might escape, for he was rich, and so, the allies of the Syracusans consenting, he was executed.

> For these or the like reasons he suffered death. No one of the Hellenes in my time was less deserving of so miserable an end; for he lived in the practice of every virtue.

The prisoners were thrown into those stone quarries which are now such a romantic sight for the traveller at Syracuse. But there was no romance in that autumn of the nineteenth year of the war (413 B.C.):

> There were great numbers of them, and they were crowded in a deep and narrow place. At first the sun by day was still scorching and suffocating, for they had no roof over their heads, while the autumn nights were cold, and the extremes of temperature engendered violent disorders. Being cramped for room they had to do everything on the same spot. The corpses of those who died from their wounds, exposure to heat and cold, and the like, lay heaped one upon another. The smells were intolerable; and they were at the same time afflicted by hunger and thirst. During eight months they were allowed only about half a pint of water and a pint of food a day. Every kind of misery which could befall man in such a place befell them.

Thucydides sums up his campaign in these memorable words:

> Of all the Hellenic actions which took place in this war, or indeed, as I think, of all the Hellenic actions which are on record, this was the greatest—the most glorious to the victors, the most ruinous to the vanquished; for they were utterly and at all points defeated, and their sufferings were prodigious. Fleet and army perished

from the face of the earth; nothing was saved, and of
the many who went forth few returned home.

Thus ended the Sicilian expedition.

This narrative marks the highest point which Thucydides reaches in all his history. It is the inevitable
climax, and nothing that followed, until the final disaster, could compare with it. If Thucydides had lived
to complete his *History,* he might have surpassed even
this wonderful description with the story of the fall
of imperial Athens. That he was not allowed to do
so is one of the great tragedies of incomplete master-
pieces.

Thucydides' restraint is nowhere shown so well as
in the relation of this catastrophe. There were incidents of the siege which he omitted that might have
made it even more vivid. One in particular. The
commander of the Athenian cavalry, Callistratus, had
saved his troop. They had made their way through
the enemy's lines and were retreating southward to
safety. He sent them on, and himself turned back,
crossed the Assinarus and reached Nicias' last camp.
Here he found the enemy, rode straight at them and
cut down five of them before he and his horse both fell
dead. And Plutarch also tells us that when imperial
Athens had fallen so low that her citizens rotted in
the Syracusan stone quarries and she was powerless to
give them aid, one of her citizens by the magic of his
poetry reached across the sea and set them free. For
the authorities in Syracuse freed every Athenian pris-
oner who could repeat for them some of the choruses
from the plays of Euripides. Perhaps nowhere in history has the triumph of art over force been so well il-
lustrated.

Nothing was left to make the tragedy incomplete. The news of the disaster reached Athens only casually. The Athenians refused to believe it. There was a story (Thucydides does not tell it) that a sailor came into a barber shop in the Piraeus and while he was being served spoke casually of the disaster as a thing which everyone knew. The barber in terror abandoned him and ran up to the city to inform the magistrates. The magistrates returned with him to verify the report, only to find that the sailor, half-shaven, had departed. The barber was imprisoned for spreading false and terrifying rumors.

Thucydides' eighth and last book covers the next two years of the war. The narrative breaks off, incomplete, and there are signs that this book had not received the author's final touch. It is not only that the book contains no set speeches, but there is about it a lack of finish and a certain amount of confusion. This narrative was bound to be an anticlimax, after the Sicilian expedition, but if it could have had its author's final revision it might have been improved.

The Athenians, when they at last accepted the grim fact of their defeat, rose to the occasion in a manner that makes one proud of the imperial city. Thucydides remarks caustically, "After the manner of a democracy, they were very amenable to discipline while their fright lasted."

The story of this part of the war is concerned almost entirely with events in the Aegean. It was the story of the revolt of the Athenian allies, of negotiations with the Great King of Persia and of the machinations of Alcibiades.

When the news of the Sicilian disaster became generally known, the Athenian allies fell away. They ".... were everywhere willing even beyond their power to revolt; for they judged by their excited feelings, and would not admit a possibility that the Athenians could survive another summer." They did survive for eight more. One after another the islands and the cities along the coast of Asia Minor revolted from Athens. Chios, Teos, Miletus, Erythrae, Lesbos, Lebedus, Cyme, Phocaea, Ephesus, Clazomenae, Cnidus, the great Island of Rhodes. The list is almost as impressive as the list of states that abandoned Rome after Cannae. If Athens had only possessed statesmen with the cold, unyielding determination of the Roman senators she might, even so, have survived as did Rome.

Thucydides' strictly chronological account of these two years is sometimes difficult to follow. The revolt of Chios is related in Chapters 7, 8, 14, 19, 24 and so on at short intervals throughout the book. The Athenians were never able to regain Chios. Samos was granted its independence and became the Athenian base in the eastern Aegean. The Peloponnesians early sought the support of the King of Persia. They concluded with him in the summer of the twentieth year of the war (412 B.C.) a contemptible alliance acknowledging the sovereignty of the King over all the lands that he or his ancestors had possessed. This, broadly interpreted, would have given him claim to all of Greece down to the Isthmus of Corinth. So shameful was the treaty that it was later revised, and the acknowledged sovereignty of the King was limited to Asia.

Alcibiades left Sparta during the twentieth year

of the war. At Sparta he had adopted Lacedaemonian customs and had in his rigorous physical regime been more Spartan than the Spartans themselves. It is doubtful if he enjoyed this manner of life, and when he seduced the wife of King Agis, he seems to have been gratifying his love of adventure rather than his lust for pleasure.

This and other actions on his part led to a degree of unpopularity so great that the Spartans ordered his execution, and he prudently withdrew.

In Asia Alcibiades fell in with Tissaphernes, the Persian governor of Lydia and Caria, with whom he conducted, during the time occupied by the remainder of Thucydides' narrative, a series of interesting frustrations. Alcibiades was hampered by no restraints that required him to tell the truth, and Tissaphernes was also a gifted liar. In the contest of deceit that followed it is hard to say which was the winner.

Alcibiades advised Tissaphernes not to help the Spartans, with whom he was allied, with any enthusiasm but to play off one party against the other until both the Athenians and the Spartans should be worn out. He struck at the heart of the matter by getting Tissaphernes to reduce the pay of the sailors. He

> was instructed by him [Alcibiades] to tell the Peloponnesians that the Athenians, with their long experience of naval affairs, gave half a drachma only, not from poverty, but lest their sailors should be demoralized by high pay, and spend their money on pleasures which injured their health, and thereby impaired their efficiency; the payment too was made irregularly, that the arrears, which they would forfeit by desertion, might be a pledge of their continuance in the service.

Meanwhile Alcibiades was doing his best to secure his recall to Athens. He played on the gullibility of the Athenians by telling them that he was a great friend of Tissaphernes and that he would make the King their ally. He intimated, however, that the King was not friendly toward a democracy and that a change of government would be necessary. If this could be effected the King was willing, so Alcibiades said, to meet the arrears due the sailors and to continue to pay them. Thucydides remarks that Alcibiades had no more love for oligarchy than he had for democracy, that his entire interest was in securing his own return.

In Athens the movement for a change of government was on foot. This was finally brought about, mainly by the influence of Antiphon and Theramenes. The government was to be in the hands of five thousand whose executive board was to consist of four hundred. The four hundred were duly chosen and functioned. The five thousand was never an active unit.

When, however, the news of this revolt came to the army and navy at Samos, they took affairs into their own hands. They declared that they, not Athens, were the city; and that they with their ships and their military power would legislate for the Empire. The army voted to recall Alcibiades. They made him general and put him in charge of operations, and here Alcibiades rendered for once a conspicuous service to his city. When the army proposed to go to Athens and settle with the Oligarchs, Alcibiades dissuaded them. It would have been fatal to leave the Aegean to the Lacedaemonians. As Thucydides says, "Then Alcibia-

des appears to have done as eminent a service to the
state as any man ever did."

Alarmed by the action of the fleet, the Oligarchs
at Athens now endeavored to make peace with Sparta.
They were ready to betray the city to them and were
finally thwarted in their plan by the narrowest margin. The Four Hundred were overthrown. Antiphon
and others of the leaders were executed, and the government was placed in the hands of five thousand citizens.

It was then that there came to Athens news almost
as terrible as the destruction of their fleet at Syracuse.
The great Island of Euboea had revolted. "Nothing
which had happened before, not even the ruin of the
Sicilian expedition, however overwhelming at the
time, had so terrified them." If the Lacedaemonians
had at this time attacked Athens from Decelea and
from the sea, it is hard to see how the city could have
survived. The Lacedaemonians were, however, as
Thucydides remarks, the most convenient of enemies.

The government was now in the hands of five thousand citizens, a number which was supposed to include
all who could furnish themselves with arms. They
received no pay. This government, in the judgment
of Thucydides, "during its early days was the best
which the Athenians ever enjoyed within my memory."

They confirmed the recall of Alcibiades, who from
this point on was principally responsible for the
Athenian campaigns. The scene of combat shifted
now to the Hellespont, where the Peloponnesian fleet
had gone to secure the revolt of the Greek cities Abydos and Byzantium. Here the Athenians won a bril-

liant victory under the direction of Thrasybulus, who was now becoming one of the leading Athenian generals. He was to deserve well of his country. We would give much to have Thucydides' account of his later career and his estimate of his worth.

The *History* of Thucydides closes with an account of Alcibiades' visit to Tissaphernes, a visit from which he brought back the usual false reports. At the close of the narrative we see Tissaphernes going to Ephesus, where he offered sacrifice to Artemis. The account of the twenty-first summer of the war (411 B. C.) was nearly complete. Six more years remained.

The rest of the story of the Peloponnesian War is told by Xenophon. This is much as if the last volume of *The Decline and Fall of the Roman Empire* had been written by Mark Sullivan.

Xenophon begins bravely enough; he has the tune but, alas, he hasn't the words. He imitates Thucydides' method, his mind he can in no way match. Even the method soon breaks down. With the greatest care Thucydides had marked the beginning of each summer and winter. His chronology was painfully exact. At first Xenophon notes the difference between the summer and winter campaigns but he soon tires of this rigorous exactness, and the narrative assumes that vague commonplaceness which is sometimes mistaken for lucid simplicity. It is not so much that his account is less complete—Xenophon devotes an average of nine pages to a year where Thucydides had been writing thirty-five to fifty; it is the banally pedestrian character of the narrative that makes the transition from the *History* of the Peloponnesian War to the *Hellenica* so maddening. The opening paragraph may serve as an example:

> After this, not many days later, Thymochares came from Athens with a few ships; and thereupon the Lacedaemonians and the Athenians fought another naval battle and the Lacedaemonians were victorious, under the leadership of Asesandridas.

The locality of the battle, the number of ships involved and the losses on either side are left to the imagination.

For the sake of completeness it may be worth while to summarize here the events of the closing years of the war. In the first summer (the twenty-second, 410 B.C.) after the close of Thucydides' *History,* the Athenians, led by Alcibiades, Theramenes and Thrasybulus, defeated the Peloponnesian fleet under Mindarus at Cyzicus. The dispatch sent to Sparta was intercepted by the Athenians, "Our success is over, Mindarus is slain; the men are starving; we know not what to do." Peace on the basis of *uti possidetis* was offered by Sparta and refused by Athens.

At Athens the Five Thousand were deposed, and the old democracy was reinstated. Under the energetic and able leadership of Alcibiades, Athens slowly began to regain her possessions. The control of the Hellespont, the indispensable avenue of supply, was regained, but Pylos was lost to the Lacedaemonians and Nisaea to the Megarians.

Three years after the victory at Cyzicus, in the twenty-fifth year of the war (407 B.C.), an event occurred which had far-reaching effects. Cyrus, the brother of Artaxerxes, the Great King, replaced Tissaphernes as governor of Lydia. He met Lysander, the Spartan admiral, and conceived a great admira-

tion for him.   And Lysander was, in fact, something
of a phenomenon; he was a Spartan who was imper-
vious to bribes.   Cyrus, too, was entirely unlike his
predecessor, Tissaphernes.   Cyrus was open, straightforward, generous and honest, where Tissaphernes
had been devious, deceitful and dishonest.   Cyrus and
Lysander became close friends.

That summer (407 B.C.) Alcibiades returned to
Athens.   His victories had induced his chastened countrymen to forgive his past treachery to his city and all
the harm and suffering for which he was responsible.
He was acclaimed as a deliverer, and the direction of
the war was formally entrusted to him.   His triumph
was short-lived.   That very year the fleet was defeated at Notium, and though Alcibiades was not present at the battle he was held responsible.   He retired
to a castle which he had acquired near the Hellespont.
He never saw his native city again, though he was
still to render her one more service.   Another disaster
Athens was to suffer this year, the defeat of Admiral
Conon at Mytilene.

And still the spirit of the Athenian people was not
broken.   They melted down the gold and silver offerings in the temples and put to sea one hundred and
fifty ships.   It was the last effort of the proud and
resourceful people, and fortune smiled on them for
the last time.   At the Arginusae Islands, off the coast
of Lesbos, the next summer, the twenty-sixth (406
B.C.), they engaged the Peloponnesian fleet and utterly defeated it.

And then the Athenian assembly, running true to
form, enacted not only a stupid but a criminal decree.
They condemned to death, all together and without

trial, the captains of the fleet, because they had pursued the enemy and had neglected to rescue the wounded and retrieve the bodies of the slain.   Among the executed was Pericles, the son of Athens' great statesman.

Again Sparta offered peace on the same terms, and again the terms were rejected.   So serious was the financial situation at Sparta that their sailors were forced to leave their ships and work as day laborers on the estates of the wealthy Chian landowners.   Cyrus was apparently not financing the Peloponnesian campaign.

And the reason for that, too, was clear.   Lysander was no longer in command of the fleet, debarred by a silly Spartan rule which forbade an admiral to hold office for more than a year.   Cyrus refused to furnish funds unless Lysander was in charge of the fleet.   The difficulty had to be overcome, however, in view of Cyrus' attitude, and an arrangement was made by which Lysander, though nominally second in command, should actually control operations.

Thucydides says, ". . . . there was a common and often-repeated saying that it [the war] was to last thrice nine years."   That fatal year had now arrived.

Lysander, in charge of the Peloponnesian fleet at Ephesus, refused battle and took his ships to the Hellespont, where he seized Lampsacus.   He had two hundred ships.   The Athenian navy, one hundred and eighty strong, followed him and again offered battle. He again refused, and the Athenians beached their ships across the narrow strait at Aegospotami.   Each day they rowed across and challenged the Lacedaemonians, who each day refused.   Whereupon the

Athenians recrossed, drew up their ships on the sand, went up the beach to places convenient for cooking their meal or scattered to Sestos two miles away, to get provisions. So imprudent was this procedure that Alcibiades came down from his nearby castle and advised the admiral in charge, Adeimantus, to beware of a surprise attack. He was promptly sent about his business. Adeimantus clearly preferred no victory at all to one which he would owe to Alcibiades.

On the fifth day the blow fell. The Athenians made their usual demonstration, returned to Aegospotami, drew up their ships, left them and prepared to dine. A signal from a polished shield was flashed to Lysander. He rowed swiftly across and captured almost without a blow one hundred and sixty ships with their crews. Twenty escaped. All the Athenians, about three thousand, were put to death. Adeimantus alone was spared, and the suspicion was not wanting that mercy had been shown him because he was a traitor. Among the ships that escaped was the state trireme, the "Paralus." It was night when the "Paralus" reached Piraeus. As the news spread up the long walls from the harbor to the city, the "sound of wailing followed its progress, one man passing the news to another:—and that night no man slept."

Lysander did not hurry to Athens; he had no need to. He let it be known that all Athenians in the few remaining cities of the Athenian Empire would be given safe conduct to Athens and nowhere else. From the cities in Chalcidice, from Melos, Aegina, Lesbos, Naxos, they streamed into Athens, bringing more mouths to feed to a city that was already short of provisions. And the arrival of these fugitives from

Melos and the other cities recalled vividly to the
Athenians the fate which they had inflicted on these
towns, a fate which was now staring them all too plainly in the face.

When Lysander and his fleet did arrive and the
city was invested, there was still talk of resistance.
Only after starvation had begun to take an alarming
toll of the inhabitants would the Athenians surrender,
and when the terms were known, opposition to their
acceptance was voiced in the assembly.

The terms were moderate, considering the ruthless
treatment Melos and many another surrendered city
had received at the hands of Athens. Athens was to
lose all its empire and its fleet, the long walls and the
fortifications of Piraeus were to be torn down. Corinth and Thebes had advocated the ultimate penalty,
death to the men, slavery to the women and children,
but Sparta had refused to consent to the destruction
of the city that had shared with her the honor of sav-
ing Hellas from the Persians two generations before.
One would like to think that the pitiful but vain plea
of the Plataeans to be spared because of their heroic
resistance to the Persians still rang in the Spartan ears
and delivered them from the disgrace of sacrificing
Hellas' noblest city to Corinthian jealousy and Theban hate.

On these terms Athens surrendered (404 B.C.).
"The Peloponnesians with great enthusiasm began to
tear down the walls to the music of flutegirls, thinking that that day was the beginning of freedom for
Greece." As a memorial of his victory Lysander set
up at Delphi on the right of the Sacred Way, just
within the sacred enclosure, an elaborate monument—

statues of himself and his twenty captains. The boastful dedicatory inscription still exists, carved on a stone which lies near the museum.

Thucydides did not live to chronicle the fall of his imperial city but ere he died he had recorded for posterity the reason for its fall: they ". . . . were at last overthrown, not by their enemies, but by themselves and their own internal dissensions."

VII
THE HISTORY

IT IS abundantly clear that the interest of the Periclean circle in science had a strong influence on Thucydides. For not only does he sift his source material with rigorous scientific care, but throughout the *History* there are recurring evidences of his scientific interest.

This interest is best exemplified in his attitude toward historical writing. This is manifested in many ways. His critical treatment of his source material has already been noted (pages 67 ff.). The "fancies of the poets" and "the tales of chroniclers .... cannot be trusted .... and most of the facts in the lapse of ages have passed into the region of romance." Thus in his invaluable sketch of the history and colonization of Sicily he says that the oldest inhabitants were the Cyclopes and the Laestrygones, "but who they were, whence they came, or whither they went, I cannot tell. We must be content with the legends of the poets, and everyone must be left to form his own opinion." Having paid his debt to Homer, he proceeds with the real history of the Sicanians, the Elymi and other tangible peoples.

Thucydides is willing to sacrifice interest to accuracy, especially chronological accuracy. How this interferes with the flow of the narrative has already been mentioned (pages 85 ff.). It may be this feature of his work that Thucydides has in mind when he deprecates the uninteresting historical character of his account. It is for this lack of chronological accuracy that he blames Hellanicus. He shows further how his method is the only one which will give accurate chronology in a civilization which lacked a universal day-to-day dating system:

> I would have a person reckon the actual periods of time, and not rely upon catalogues of the archons or other official personages whose names may be used in different cities to mark the dates of past events. For whether an event occurred in the beginning, or in the middle, or whatever might be the exact point, of a magistrate's term of office is left uncertain by such a mode of reckoning. But if he measure by summers and winters as they are here set down, and count each summer and winter as a half year, he will find that ten summers and ten winters passed in the first part of the war.

The cost of military operations is almost always given, as are the wages paid to soldiers and sailors. The number of opposing armies and navies is always stated, and the loss on both sides where it can be known. In one instance Thucydides omits the figures because he says they would seem incredible. At the Battle of Mantinea, where the Lacedaemonian government deliberately concealed the number of its forces, Thucydides proves that there were 4,184 by the simple process of multiplying the length of the lines by the number of ranks.

His geographic and topographic data are remarkably full and accurate. He very seldom mentions a town without giving its exact location. Often he gives details of the neighboring topography. When rivers are mentioned, their source and course are described.

Thucydides and Tacitus have often been compared.
But in one particular, at least—I mean in geographic
exactness—they are as far apart as the poles. The battles in Tacitus, except perhaps the encounter between
Otho and Vitellius in the entangling grapevines of
Lombardy, could occur in "Barrett Wendell's back
yard" or anywhere else. But Thucydides is most exact. Through all the narrative distances and direction
are most conscientiously given. One example may suffice.

> The empire of the Odrysae measured by the coast-
> line reaches from the city of Abdera to the mouth of the
> Ister in the Euxine. The voyage round can be made
> by a merchant vessel, if the wind is favorable the
> whole way, at the quickest in four days and as many
> nights. Or an expeditious traveller going by land from
> Abdera to the mouth of the Ister, if he takes the short-
> est route, will accomplish the journey in eleven days.
> Such was the extent of the Odrysian empire towards
> the sea: up the country the land journey from Byzan-
> tium to the Laeaeans and to the Strymon, this being
> the longest line which can be drawn from the sea into
> the interior, may be accomplished by an expeditious
> traveller in thirteen days.

His topographic account of the siege of Syracuse
is a model of precision. Freeman believed that Thucydides had been over every foot of the ground and
had made exact measurements.

Accurate geographical description is not Thucydides' only interest. In connection with Phormio's operations around Oeniadae, Thucydides explains that
an expedition against this town is impossible in winter
because of the marshy character of the terrain. It
lies near the river Achelous, whose source and course

he accurately describes. He then explains the formation of the Echinades Islands:

> Most of the islands called Echinades are situated
> opposite to Oeniadae and close to the mouth of the
> Achelous. The consequence is that the river, which is
> large, is always silting up : some of the islands have been
> already joined to the mainland, and very likely, at
> no distant period, they may all be joined to it. The
> stream is wide and strong and full of mud ; and the
> islands are close together and serve to connect the de-
> posits made by the river, not allowing them to dissolve
> in the water. For, lying irregularly and not one be-
> hind the other, they prevent the river from finding a
> straight channel into the sea. These islands are small
> and uninhabited.

Incidentally, it may be mentioned that Thucydides'
prophecy has been fulfilled, and those islands are now
part of the mainland.

For oracles and portents Thucydides has a proper
scientific contempt. He even blames Nicias, whom
he admires, because he was too ready to listen to
soothsayers. Concerning the prophecy that the war
would last thrice nine years he says, "this was the soli-
tary instance in which those who put their faith in
oracles were justified by the event." Where an oracle
given by Delphi influenced the actions of a state or an
individual, that is a historical event and as such it is
chronicled.

Eclipses and earthquakes are consistently recorded
for this reason : they were to Thucydides in themselves
interesting phenomena and they were chronological
landmarks. For him they have no portentous significance. How far in advance of the popular beliefs of
the time he was can be seen from his remarks on earth-

quakes that happened in the sixth year of the war
(426 B.C.). This series of earthquakes prevented the
Lacedaemonians from invading Attica, though they
had advanced as far as the Isthmus of Corinth (on a
later occasion they removed an admiral from his fleet
because of an earthquake). That military fact having
been recorded, Thucydides notes further that along
the coast of Euboea the sea receded, then returned in
a huge wave, wrecking parts of several cities (Thucydides gives exact details, as a scientist should). And he
adds a tentative explanation for the phenomenon:

> I conceive that, where the force of the earthquake
> was greatest, the sea was driven back, and the sudden-
> ness of the recoil made the inundation more violent;
> and I am of opinion that this was the cause of the
> phenomenon, which would never have taken place if
> there had been no earthquake.

In the winter of the fifth year of the war (427 B.
C.) the Athenians conducted a marauding expedition against the Lipari Islands. Nothing came of it, but
Thucydides conscientiously records it and in the brief
notice manages to add the following scientific facts:
the islands are four in number (the names are given),
they were colonized by the people of Cnidus, only one
is inhabited, water is so scarce as to make a raid in
summer impossible; one of the uninhabited islands,
Hiera, is an active volcano, and the inhabitants believe (but Thucydides does not) that here is located
the forge of Hephaestus.

The following year Thucydides notes a devastat-
ing eruption of Mount Aetna, "the highest mountain
in Sicily." He reports, but does not vouch for the
date, that the last eruption preceded this by fifty years

and that three eruptions have been recorded since the Greeks began to colonize Sicily.

Thucydides, of course, records the eclipse of the moon that occasioned the fatal delay in abandoning the siege of Syracuse, and it is not surprising that he should have mentioned two eclipses of the sun that occurred, one in the first year of the war (431 B.C.), and the other seven years later.   But it is an evidence of real scientific interest in such things that the earlier eclipse should have been described in these terms:

> During the same summer, at the beginning of the lunar month (apparently the only time when such an event is possible), and in the afternoon, there was an eclipse of the sun, which took the form of a crescent, and then became full again; during the eclipse a few stars were visible.

If sociology were a science Thucydides would have been more interested in sociological facts.   In passing he does give details of sociological interest, such as the fact that the largest tribe of the Aetolians speak an unintelligible dialect and are said to eat raw flesh, that Alcibiades is a Spartan name, that the nobles in Samos are forbidden to intermarry with the common people.

And to the science of penology Thucydides makes the earliest contribution.   He says that in early ages penalties were comparatively light, that more severe penalties were devised since the milder were found ineffectual.   Even the death penalty failed to check crime.   Death deters nobody.   "For poverty inspires necessity with daring."   The case against punishment as a device for restricting crime has never been more briefly and completely stated.

ECONOMICS

The statement is often made that Thucydides is not interested in economics; the Parthenon is nothing but a treasury and the Propylaea a debit item on Athens' balance sheet, that his *History* gives little or none of the economic background of the war. Nothing could be further from the truth.

Thucydides definitely recognizes the fact that the cause of the war—the real, not the avowed, cause— was economic. It was "the growth of the Athenian power, which terrified the Lacedaemonians and forced them into war; . . . ." and he adds, "In arriving at this decision [to fight] . . . . the Lacedaemonians were influenced, not so much by the speeches of their allies, as by the fear of the Athenians and of their increasing power." These brief and comprehensive statements have already been noted.

In his sketch of the early history of Greece the economic foundation of society is constantly emphasized. Thus Corinth became an important center very early because early trade routes went by land, and her strategic situation on the Isthmus enabled her to take advantage of this fact. As early as Homer she was known as "wealthy Corinth." With the wealth she acquired a navy, put down piracy and so became a center for trade, both by land and by sea.

Thucydides shrewdly notes that Athens' prosperity was due to two causes. First, the soil of Attica was so poor that it was not an object of envy. Consequently Athens long evaded strife. And second, Athens increased her strength by extending her citizenship on liberal terms to refugees. Later he records the fact, now abundantly clear from archaeological researches, that Peisistratus adorned the city with temples and public buildings. Thucydides adds that this was done in spite of the fact that he imposed only a five per cent tax on the produce of the soil.

Athens' position of economic dependence on her empire is emphasized over and over again. "... . the fruits of the whole earth flow in upon" Athens, but this situation can be continued only if the allies are kept well in hand. Elsewhere the necessity of guarding the trade route to Egypt is made clear. The other side of this argument is developed by Nicias when he is trying to dissuade the Athenians from the expedition against Syracuse. He says that the people of Selinus and Syracuse have an advantage in the fact that they are self-sustaining; they raise their own grain and do not need to import it.

Thucydides devotes a brief paragraph to the revolt of Chios, one of the two independent allies of Athens. He speaks of its wealth, of its large number of slaves, larger in proportion to the free population than in any state in Greece except Lacedaemon, and notes the fact that except for Lacedaemon no state had maintained so stable a government nor had so wisely used its growing powers.

In describing the Odrysian Empire in Thrace, Thucydides gives the amount of tribute collected by Seuthes, "under whom the amount was greatest," as four hundred thousand dollars "of coined money, reckoning only gold and silver," and adds to this a summary of the empire's other resources.

Among the interesting economic facts given by Thu-

cydides may be mentioned: the children of soldiers
who died in the service of Athens were supported by
a state pension. When Corinth was sending colonists
to Epidamnus, transportation was provided and land
allotted, but colonists who found it inconvenient to go
personally could secure a share in the enterprise for
twenty dollars each. When Mytilene surrendered,
the land was divided into three thousand portions;
three hundred were allotted to the gods and twenty-
seven hundred were assigned by lot to Athenian settlers, some of whom preferred to remain in Athens as
absentee landlords, renting their portions to the former owners at fifty dollars a year. The prisoners captured at Iasus brought about four dollars a head when
sold to Tissaphernes, who had cornered the market.

Thucydides is, above all, a military historian, but
no ancient historian has given us anything like as much
information about the economics of the war he is
chronicling.

At the beginning of the war he gives Pericles' detailed inventory of the resources of Athens; for military successes are "gained by a wise policy and
command of money." These resources include an annual revenue from the tribute of six hundred thousand
dollars; a reserve fund of six million dollars, uncoined
gold and silver in offerings dedicated in the temples on
the Acropolis, half a million dollars; a considerable
but unspecified amount of similar treasure in other
temples, and the gold plates on the statue of Athena in
the Parthenon, forty thousand dollars. These offerings could be borrowed only if the city were in straits
and must be replaced (a state bond issue). The reserve had been larger, but recently $1,700,000 had

been spent in erecting the Propylaea and other buildings, and two millions on the siege of Potidaea, after the first invasion of Attica (431 B.C.).

The siege of Potidaea had been especially costly because the soldiers and sailors had been receiving double pay, forty cents a day, a great "drain on the resources of the Athenians." The usual pay (a drachma, twenty cents) is frequently noted, and when Tissaphernes attempted (probably on Alcibiades' advice) to reduce it to ten cents a day, he had a strike on his hands at once and was forced to advance his rate to very near the union scale. When Athens made a treaty with Argos, Mantinea and Elis, in the twelfth year of the war (420 B.C.), Thucydides preserves for us in the fourth article of the treaty the exact scale of pay to be in force among the allies. A city furnishing troops on request shall be responsible for the first month's pay, after that the city requesting the force shall pay foot soldiers fifteen cents a day, horsemen thirty cents.

Much is said about the expense of the Sicilian expedition. The crews received extra pay; one hundred fifty thousand dollars was sent to Nicias after he reached Sicily for expenses. The Syracusans had spent two million dollars. In fact, in describing the equipping of the expedition and its departure from Athens, Thucydides insists quite as much on the expense involved and on the drain on Athenian economic resources as he does on the brilliant display the flotilla made when it sailed from Piraeus. He speaks of the various costly items on the program and adds, "If any one had reckoned up the whole expenditure, both of the state and of individual soldiers and others . . . . he would have found that altogether an immense sum amounting to many talents was withdrawn from the city."

Thucydides gives us the five sources of economic loss sustained by the Athenians through the fortification of Decelea: (1) desertion of slaves, (2) interruption of revenue from the silver mines of Laurium, (3) the land tax, (4) the law courts, (5) the tribute. The tax on property, he tells us, was first enacted in the fourth winter of the war (428 B.C.) after the revolt of Mytilene. It brought in two hundred thousand dollars. He also tells us that the tribute was assessed by Aristides, that it originally brought in four hundred sixty thousand dollars annually and at the outbreak of the war six hundred thousand dollars and that after the disaster in Sicily and the revolt of so many cities it seemed more lucrative to replace this tribute with a five per cent export and import tax. "For their expenses became heavier and heavier as the war grew in extent, and at the same time their sources of revenue were drying up."

After this disaster expenses were ruthlessly slashed. The oligarchical government of the Four Hundred abolished all salaries of officeholders, and the democracy, when it came into power, did not dare restore them. Thucydides even thinks it worth while to record the fact that when the senate of five hundred were evicted from office by the Four Hundred, they were paid in full for their unexpired term of office. There is, perhaps, irony in Thucydides' remark that the senators thus "retired without offering any remonstrance."

One small economy had a tragic outcome. A contingent of mercenary troops from Thrace arrived too late to join the Sicilian expedition. They were receiving the attractive pay of twenty cents a day. This being more than the Athenians could afford to pay them for any service they could now render, they were sent home under the command of an Athenian general who was told to get what service he could out of them en route. He attacked the village of Mycalessus at dawn. The Thracians went berserk, killing not only the villagers without respect to age or sex, but even the livestock, horses, donkeys, chickens. They fell upon a boys' school, the largest in the place, where the children had just assembled, and massacred every one. The poor boys did not perish wholly in vain, for the professors of education, who are driven to glean their scanty harvest among thorns and in stony places, are able to extract at least three facts from this tragedy: a small fifth-century Greek village had more than one boys' school, education was not coeducational, and school "took up" soon after dawn.

These illustrations will be sufficient to show that Thucydides' *History* is far from neglecting the economic background of the war. In fact, from the very beginning of the work till the narrative is cut off in the twenty-first summer, the reader is never allowed to forget the fact that ".... wars are supported out of accumulated wealth, and not out of forced contributions."

Both in the speeches and in the narrative the necessity for providing funds for the war on the part of both the Athenians and the allies is consistently kept before the reader. The device which enables one generation to hand on the burden of a war's expense to posterity in the form of government bonds and pen-sions had not yet been invented. Thucydides was writing the history of a war and he knew well that ". . . . war is not a matter of arms, but of money which gives to arms their use. . . ."

The critics who complain that Thucydides does not emphasize the economic background of the war should read the *History*. They have merely mistaken an absence of footnotes for an absence of facts.

DIGRESSIONS

Thucydides' digressions serve several purposes. There are two long digressions in Book I, the first giving the history of Greece during the fifty years between the Persian and the Peloponnesian Wars, the second relating the tragic careers of Pausanias, the Spartan, and Themistocles, the Athenian. These have already been considered.

During the other seven books relating the events of the twenty-one years of war there are many digressions. Some of them are very short and give facts that would in modern practice be relegated to brief footnotes. Such are the notes on eclipses of the sun and the Spartan practice of liquidating the Helots, notably a secret massacre of two thousand.

Usually these brief digressions grow naturally out of the narrative. They do not interrupt its flow, though they are not always strictly required by Thucydides' plan to tell only the story of the war, a plan to which he adheres with unusual pertinacity. Thus, before describing the discomforts of the population of Athens after they had been forced into the narrow confines of the city, he digresses on Theseus, the early history of Athens and the happy life in the rural communities. In a similar way he describes the sufferings occasioned by the occupation of Decelea immediately after an account of how the Athenians seized and fortified a post in Laconia opposite Cythera. The short digression on the size and cost of the Athenian navy follows naturally after an account of the display of the fleet in force against the Lacedaemonians.

One of these brief digressions deserves special attention. Thucydides is describing the alliance made between Sitalces, ruler of Odrysia, and Athens. He is later to give a sketch of this Thracian empire, but here he digresses as follows.

Sitalces' father was Teres. He must not be confused with Tereus, who married Procne, the daughter of Pandion, King of Athens. Tereus did indeed come from a Thracian town, but it is now Daulia, a Phocian village not far from Delphi. Pandion would not have given his daughter to a remote Thracian but would have been likely to strengthen his border by a Phocian alliance. In any case, the names are different, Tereus and Teres. Sophocles had recently produced a tragedy, *Tereus,* in which he had made just this error, locating Procne's husband, Tereus, in Thrace. The reason for Thucydides' digression is without doubt a desire to correct the mistake and set the dramatist right.

In two places, at least, the effects of military actions are described in what might be regarded as digressions from the strict sequence of events. In connection with the account of the bloody civil strife in Corcyra, Thucydides pauses to explain in vivid detail just how the corroding virus of factional hatred affected the spirits of men in all parts of Hellas until "The meaning of words had no longer the same relation to things . . . ."; "The seal of good faith was not divine law, but fellowship in crime" and "Revenge was dearer than self-preservation." The amazement caused by the surrender of the Lacedaemonians at Pylos is also elaborated in a chapter that contains the only jest in the *History*.

But these digressions are brief and scarcely interrupt the train of thought. Most of them would, as has been said, appear as footnotes in a modern history, others would remain as they stand here in the text.

The long and terrifying account of the plague in the second year of the war is not really a digression, it is a narrative of an event of major importance in a military history, for it cost the lives of forty-four hundred of the soldiers on the Athenian rolls.

There are, however, two other types of digression that are used for quite different purposes.

Thucydides uses the first of these two types to state specifically his own views, once on the conduct and once on the historical nature of the war.

In the first instance he desires not only to state Pericles' policy for the conduct of the war but to record formally and positively his belief that Pericles was right and that Athens would have won if his policy had been consistently followed. This he does in the digression that occupies most of Chapter 65 in Book II. He concludes, "So that at the time Pericles was more than justified in the conviction at which his foresight had arrived, that the Athenians would win an easy victory over the unaided forces of the Peloponnesians."

In the second instance Thucydides is demonstrating the unity of the twenty-seven-year struggle as a single war in spite of the nominal peace of Nicias. Both these digressions give the historian an opportunity to foretell the outcome of the struggle, ". . . . the destruction of the Athenian empire and the taking of Piraeus and the Long Walls by the Lacedaemonians and their allies."

The second, and more frequent, type of extended digression is devoted to bringing in historical facts that lie outside the regular course of events. There are six of these. They are all but one interjected into a narrative well under way. They might be handled as excursuses in a modern work.

The digression in which the early history of Sicily is told is introduced at the beginning of the account of the Athenian expedition against Syracuse. In the fewest possible words Thucydides gives a list of the different people who have inhabited Sicily, followed by a list of Greek colonies with the name of the city which established each colony and usually the date of its foundation. For the early history of Sicily this is a priceless document.

Two of the digressions give, respectively, the history of the Odrysian Empire in Thrace and the history of Macedonia. In both cases Thucydides begins his account of the compaign and then, having his narrative well in hand and the reader's interest aroused, pauses to fill in his background. Incidentally, it might be noted that Thucydides brings to the history of these two little-known places a certain amount of personal knowledge, for he was familiar with the region. For once he almost descends to Herodotus' level and gives a glimpse of ethnic customs. ". . . . they [the Odrysae] were more ready to receive than to give; and he who

asked and was refused was not so much discredited as
he who refused when he was asked."

In the sixth winter of the war (426 B.C.) the Athenians were induced by an oracle to purify Delos. Thucydides makes this the occasion for a digression of a
unique character. He tells how the purification was accomplished, notes briefly the connection of Polycrates,
tyrant of Samos, with Delos. He then states that the
Athenians now revived the old Delian festival, which
had fallen on evil days. He speaks of the ancient Ionian festival and proves its musical and athletic character by two quotations in verse from the Homeric
hymns. To these events the Athenians added horse
racing. Nowhere is Thucydides so mildly human. Perhaps the horse racing—no, that would be too much to
expect.

The other two, the tale of the murder of Hipparchus by Harmodius and Aristogeiton, and the enumeration of the forces at Syracuse, call for special
comment.

The former is of considerable length and goes into
great detail, establishing the fact that Hippias was the
elder of the two sons of Peisistratus and giving in full
the epitaph in elegiac verse of Hippias' daughter, who
was married to the son of the tyrant of Lampsacus and
was buried in that city. This digression serves two
purposes. Just as in the introductory book the full
history of Hellas had been told in outline by inserting
digressions into the narrative, so this digression on the
history of Athens under the tyrants and the digression
on the merging of the Attic towns into the city of
Athens by Theseus and the easy life of the Athenian

citizens completes the history of Athens up to the Persian Wars. The reader now has before him, complete, the history of Hellas and the history of Athens.

Further, this digression has been introduced at a dramatic moment. It interrupts the account of the prosecutions for sacrilege connected with the mutilation of the Hermae. The state trireme had arrived in Sicily to bring back Alcibiades for trial. At Athens all was confusion. Men of high character were being arrested on the information of rascals. An oligarchical revolution and a tyranny were dreaded. The people think of their former tyrants; enter, the digression on the tyrannicides. The reader waits, all expectation, for the narrative to continue. It is the same postponement of a climax, the prolongation of suspense, that has already been noted in the use of digressions in Book I.

And this same device is used in the supreme narrative of the *History,* the tragedy at Syracuse. Demosthenes with his reinforcements has arrived, he has suffered defeat on land, the fleet has been defeated in the harbor, and Eurymedon has been slain, the Syracusans are closing the entrance of the harbor, and the Athenians are rallying for a final battle, on which their very existence depends; and Thucydides again pauses to give a complete catalogue of all the cities that took part on either side—the enumeration takes two long chapters (VII, 57, 58). Meanwhile we await the death struggle. This recurrent interruption of a narrative at a climactic point cannot be an accident. Thucydides believed that the Goddess of Chance controlled the ways of war, but he did not allow her to interfere with the austere progress of his narrative. A more potent goddess directed that.

THUCYDIDES' STYLE

There is no evidence that Thucydides' *History* had much influence on his contemporaries or those who immediately followed him. It has been seen that Xenophon tried to imitate his method when he began his *Hellenica,* but he soon wearied in welldoing. But in the first century B.C. Dionysius of Halicarnassus, in his works on rhetoric, has a great deal to say of Thucydides. Dionysius thought Thucydides had a grudge against Athens. He was fascinated, or rather irritated, by Thucydides' style; he discusses it in several of his essays, and finally devoted an entire book to the *History.* In general he finds that Thucydides' narrative passages are excellent but that the speeches will not serve as useful models for imitation. In which conclusion he was undoubtedly right. In a final burst of exasperation he concludes:

> [Thucydides] spent the whole twenty-seven years of the war in "upsetting" the style of those eight books and filing and polishing each one of his parts of speech; now expanding a word into a phrase and now condensing a phrase to a word, and at one time expressing a verbal idea by a substantive, and again turning the substantive into a verb; and perverting their use so as to make appellatives of names, and names of appellatives; active verbs of passive, and passive of active; and interchanging singular and plural, and predicating masculines, feminines and neuters of each other to the utter confounding of the natural sequence of the thought.

Whether or not Dionysius "discovered" Thucydides, there has never been a time since the pestered professor wrote those lines that Thucydides has not been regarded as a great historian, because of, or in spite of, his style.

Dionysius was the first critic, also, to point out the two styles in Thucydides, the narrative style and the oratorical style. For this Dionysius deserves no special credit, for they are clear to the most casual reader.

The style of the ordinary narrative is not especially puzzling, though the author's fondness for abstract terms often leads him to use awkward constructions. But the moment a set speech appears the reader's difficulties begin. No one who knows this author in translation only can have any idea of the difficulty of the language. Jebb says Thucydides, in his speeches, is so brief that a hearer could not follow his meaning and that the order of the words is intended for a reader, not a hearer. Grundy affirms that Thucydides' Greek was corrupted by his early life in Thrace, that he was dealing with a flexible language and that he twisted it till it cracked, and he quotes an enraged British scholar who prefers to remain anonymous but who in his wrath said, "Thucydides' Greek at its best was only good Thracian."

In fact, all those who have dealt intimately with Thucydides' style seem to emerge from the conflict in a state of vindictive gloom quite similar to that exhibited by Dionysius. Bury seriously thinks that self-expression for Thucydides was agony and that the more crabbed his style becomes the nearer we are to penetrating the cold reserve in which he enwraps himself. If this were really true, we could get at the man Thucydides by the simple process of assigning a series of sight translations from the *History* to competent Greek students. The passages most frequently mistranslated would be the real Thucydides.

Wilamowitz thinks that Thucydides had in him a

strain of northern barbarian blood, and Karl Blind, perhaps meaning the same thing, says that he was a German. Venizelos, the great Greek statesman, left at his death a translation of Thucydides into modern Greek. A recent reviewer has found fault with the translation—it is too easy for Thucydides. And the reader of Jowett's eloquent translation of the *History* must not be misled into believing that the Greek original is equally simple. A single example may suffice to illustrate this point. Pericles says, according to Jowett, that they may be deemed happy ". . . . whose days have been so ordered that the term of their happiness is likewise the term of their life." Mr. Bury's more literal translation gives a better idea of Thucydides' Greek: "For whom life was made commensurate to be happy in and to die in alike."

The following excerpt from a modern address in the Thucydidean style is not a caricature:

> And if now, as the hour of half-past two approaches [when my class in Thucydides meets] your audition detects in my admonition a Thucydidean inspissation of periphrastic antithesis, it is not counter to probability, look you, that by the habituation of five weeks, and at the same time laboriously exercising the tongue, even beyond its native capacity, it should gain the acquired faculty of expressing its own thoughts in alien idiom.
>
> In the immediate crisis of the present occasion you who sit there listening are as it were the soldiers of the classical army, and I who stand here speaking (unwillingly chosen to this office) am so to say (not to speak at length among you who know it all) the general who delivers to you no longer instruction but a reminder of encouragement, of all doing your duty as each possesses of celerity. . . . .

Two sources for this exhausting style have been

suggested. It has been pointed out that the early Greek thinkers were both philosophers and scientists, but that in the fifth century the two branches of thought separated. Celsus in his preface ascribes the rapid advance in medical science to the corpus of Hippocratic writing which was begun about the middle of the fifth century. Thucydides and Hippocrates were almost exactly contemporary, and it has been supposed by some that Thucydides, with his natural trend toward a scientific and realistic method, was influenced by the physician's writing. This seems unlikely. There is no evidence that the two men ever met; there is little likelihood that Hippocrates' treatise on *Airs, Waters, Places,* was put into circulation early enough to influence Thucydides' style, and there are no evidences of stylistic similarity between the *History* and the Hippocratic corpus.

The other source suggested is Antiphon. There is no evidence that Antiphon was Thucydides' teacher. But he was twenty years Thucydides' senior, they belonged to the same rhetorical school, and Thucydides greatly admired Antiphon's oratory. Still, the differences in style seem to me more significant than the similarities. If we were dealing with the speeches only, the similarity would be more significant, but it is well to remember that Thucydides' narrative style, while much simpler than his oratory, is still awkward and crabbed, and we have nothing in Antiphon with which to compare it.

It seems to me more likely that the explanation of this hampered style lies in the fact that we have here almost the earliest example of artistic Attic prose. Earlier histories had been written in Ionic. Thucydides was definitely antipathetic to Herodotus' easy, diffuse style, and the style of the logographers who preceded Herodotus was characterized by a disjunctive incoherence that knows no parallel save in the plot of a German opera.

Thucydides tried to create narrative prose in a new medium. That was no small task. How difficult it is to compose dignified prose in a language that has not been used for that purpose is shown by the fact that five of the very early histories of Rome, written by Romans for Romans, were written in Greek. To break a dialect to literary harness may not be so great a task as to elevate an entire language to a literary level, but it would involve much labor and much ingenuity, and the resulting product would be bound to have more than a trace of the odor of midnight oil. This I believe to be the explanation of Thucydides' extraordinary style—a heroic and only partially successful effort to create concise and artistic prose in a new medium. This is what Jebb means when he says of Thucydides, "a vigorous mind in the very act of struggling to mould a language of magnificent but immature capabilities."

Gildersleeve, however, dissents: "I would rather consider him [Thucydides] the great historian, a perverse genius as Dionysius has done than to look upon him as a Laocoon struggling with the twin serpents of diction and syntax which had not yet been tamed to the docility of nice Aesculapean snakes."

These defects in Thucydides' style, which have met with so much hostile criticism, are most evident in the speeches, which occupy between one-fifth and one-fourth of the whole *History*. The question may well be asked, then, are not the speeches a blemish on the *History?* And that question may at once be answered emphatically in the negative. In fact, the speeches are the most admirable feature of the whole work.

There are in all twenty-eight speeches and twelve addresses to troops by their commanders. Eight of the twenty-eight might have been, and probably were, heard by Thucydides. In these eight he seems to be giving the substance of what he actually heard. Of the others he says himself, "I have therefore put into the mouth of each speaker the sentiments proper to the occasion, expressed as I thought he would be likely to express them, while at the same time I endeavored, as nearly as I could, to give the general purport of what was actually said." That they are not actually correct reports in every case is shown by the fact that some of them contain references to events which occurred after the speech was delivered, "that unerring spirit of prophecy which follows the event." Jebb has acutely observed that this quality of the speaker is akin to the tragic irony of the drama.

In general the speeches are not "in character," though there are a few exceptions. The blunt, laconic speech of the Spartan general Sthenelaidas is one of these. So is the egotistical oration of Alcibiades in which he justifies his claim to leadership in the Syracusan expedition. The best example is the noble Funeral Oration of Pericles. Excellent as are the other speeches, this discourse has about it an elevation of thought and a dignity of expression that reflect the lofty character of the statesman. It must present largely what was said on that occasion.

The most important purpose that the speeches

serve is to indicate "what was proper to the occasion," that is, the motive from which the subsequent
actions spring. And it is this emphasis on motives
that is one of the new contributions that Thucydides
made to the writing of history. With him for the first
time the distinction is made between proximate and
ultimate causes. World wars are no longer caused by
the treacherous attack of the Thebans on Plataea or
the Japanese on Pearl Harbor but by deep-lying jeal-
ousies that find their expression for the Hellas of the
fifth century B.C. in these remarkable psychological
studies of Thucydides. The words may not be those
actually spoken, but the thoughts are those which fit
each of the critical situations which these formal orations invariably mark.

Thucydides terms this ultimate cause a "πρόφασις,"
using a medical term. And it has been said that he
probes and diagnoses like a surgeon. If he is indebted
to Hippocrates, it is not that his thought and termi-
nology are medical but that, regarding history as a
science, he dissects his characters and their actions
and chronicles his findings as would a surgeon and
finds no more need to comment on the moral quality
of the actions involved than a doctor does when he
diagnoses a case of appendicitis.

A second quality which is notable in Thucydides'
History is the arrangement of his material. His dramatic use of the digression has already been fully
noted (page 190). There is no need to repeat it here.

It has been sometimes said that the events of the
Peloponnesian War were dramatic in themselves.
That is true, but Thucydides has marshaled them in
such a dramatic way that one commentator has ac-

tually recast the *History* into a drama with five acts and a prologue. The juxtaposition of Pericles' eulogy of the glories of Athens and the terrible description of the plague is not accident. Immediately before the grandiose and tragic Sicilian expedition comes the heartless and haughty debate over the fate of Melos. Athens is there guilty of the most barefaced cruelty. In the immediately succeeding narrative she is punished by the entire loss of her army and navy. "He hath put down the mighty from their seats."

There are, too, countless little references which bind the narrative together and serve as echoes to plague those in distress by waking the memory of former good fortune, the delights of Attic rural life in the midst of the miseries wrought by the concentration in the city; the thoughts of the glories of the departure from Athens that rise to haunt the soldiers in the stricken camp at Syracuse.

Thucydides does not garnish his narrative with anecdotes to hold his readers' attention. There are not a half-dozen in the whole *History*: the Lacedaemonian ambassador who paused at the frontier to prophesy the doom of Hellas, Brasidas' losing his shield at Pylos, the jibe at the captive Spartans, the Ambraciot herald's dismay at the catastrophe which had overtaken his city, these are all. The stream of the narrative brooks no delay; in its hurried course to the inevitable and foreshadowed disaster it sweeps aside all superfluous anecdotic detail.

Macaulay calls the narrative of the failure of the Sicilian expedition "the *ne plus ultra* of human art— no prose composition in the world is placed so high." Macaulay himself would have done it excellently but in an entirely different way. Take, for instance, his account of King James's detention in his own palace at Whitehall. Macaulay writes,

> In the evening news came that the Dutch had occupied Chelsea and Kensington. The King, however, prepared to go to rest as usual. The Coldstream Guards were on duty at the palace. They were commanded by William, Earl of Craven, an aged man, who, more than fifty years before, had been distinguished in war and love, who had led the forlorn hope at Creutznach with such courage that he had been patted on the shoulder by the great Gustavus, and he was believed to have won from a thousand rivals the heart of the unfortunate Queen of Bohemia. Craven was now in his eightieth year; yet time had not tamed his spirit. It was past ten o'clock when he was informed that three battalions of the Prince's foot, mingled with some troops of horse, were pouring down the long avenue of St. James's Park, with matches lighted, and in full readiness for action. Count Solmes, who commanded the foreigners, said that his orders were to take military possession of the posts round Whitehall, and exhorted Craven to retire peaceably. Craven swore that he would rather be cut to pieces; but when the King, who was undressing himself, learned what was passing, he forbade the stout old soldier to attempt a resistance which must have been ineffectual.

Consider the wealth of knowledge of past history involved in this simple description. That is one of the things that gives charm to every page of Macaulay's *History*. Beneath the surface of the narrative lie hidden reminiscences of former events or allusions to other times that intrigue but do not distract the reader.

This Thucydides does not do. His narrative of the disaster at Syracuse is made vivid by the accumulation of details, not of facts or items of physical woe, though these are not wanting, but by a heaping-up of psychological reactions, fear, surprise at the disaster, regret, failure, despair; these are the emotions that fall on the army and the mental states that are, one after the other, ruthlessly analyzed by Thucydides; that most pathetic of all the speeches, that speech of Nicias' that Thucydides could not trust himself to reproduce, in which regardless of the jibes that might be leveled at him for repeating hackneyed and threadbare phrases, Nicias spoke to his soldiers of their wives and their children and their fathers' gods, the vain appeal to jealous gods whose jealousy must now have been appeased. And at the last, frenzy that drove the soldiers down into the Assinarus, where the water was a bloody ooze "and the crowd fought for it." Thucydides has laid bare the very soul of the Athenian army. This is why it is a matter "beyond tears."

CHARACTER SKETCHES

One of the duties imposed on a modern historian is to give his readers pen pictures of the actors in his drama. Thucydides did little of this. It is not surprising that he does not tell us their physical characteristics; personal details were not thought to be a proper subject for ancient biography. It remained for the gossip, Suetonius, to tell us the color of Caesar's eyes. But most of Thucydides' characters play their parts through and leave the stage without praise or censure from the historian.

Occasionally a weighty word of praise or blame will be dropped. The old Spartan King, Archidamus, is "an able and a prudent man." Thrasybulus is a steadfast opponent of an oligarchical movement. Leon and Diomedon are "respected by the multitude." Phrynichus is a man of "extraordinary zeal . . . . Having once set his hand to the work he was deemed by the others to be the man upon whom they could best depend in the hour of danger."

But the number of important characters about whom Thucydides says nothing is extraordinarily large.

Among the Athenians of importance, Thucydides passes over in silence the generals Eurymedon and Lamachus, who fell at Syracuse. He says nothing in characterization of the outstanding defender of Syracuse, Gylippus, though of Hermocrates, whose patriotism saved the city, he says, "a man of first-rate ability, of distinguished bravery, and also of great military experience. . . ." We are told nothing of the character of Phormio, Athens' greatest admiral, nor of Hippocrates, who was killed at Delium, and, most to be regretted of all, nothing in praise of the most able general who served Athens in the war, Demosthenes, who was executed by the patriots of Syracuse. It seems almost as if Thucydides were prejudiced against him, for he takes pains to mention the fact that the one hundred and twenty Athenians Demosthenes lost in the Aetolian campaign were "the very finest men whom the city of Athens lost during the war." Neither Perdiccas, whose rapid oscillations from one side of the war to the other leave the reader in a constant state of suspense, nor the eminent liar, Tissaphernes, is in any way described, except by his actions, which is perhaps enough.

The only Spartan whose character is delineated for us is Brasidas, whose successful raid on Amphipolis was responsible for Thucydides' banishment. No set description of him is given, but we are told that "for a Lacedaemonian he was not a bad speaker," that he favored war because it "brought him success and reputation," that "in all his actions [he] showed himself reasonable," and that "at a later period of the war, after the Sicilian expedition, the honesty and ability of Brasidas which some [of the cities in the Athenian Empire] had experienced, and of which others had heard the fame, mainly attracted the Athenian allies to the Lacedaemonians."   Two inferences may well be drawn from this praise of Brasidas. First, that though Brasidas was responsible for his disgrace, Thucydides had later come to like and admire him when he met him (while he was "associated with the Peloponnesians").   And, also, that Thucydides is here quietly telling the Athenians that reasonable honesty and ability in dealing with their subjects would have been requited by loyalty. His expressed appreciation of Hermocrates may lead us to conjecture that Thucydides had made his acquaintance at Syracuse.

To six Athenians, Thucydides pays the high compliment of more or less formal character sketches. And it is in these sketches that I believe it is possible to detect a certain amount of partiality on the part of this most reserved and aloof historian.

Antiphon was the arch-oligarch and was most instrumental in overthrowing the Athenian democracy, in "destroying the liberties of the Athenians," as Thucydides puts it. He may not have been Thucydides' teacher, but Thucydides' style shows some trace of his influence. To Thucydides he "is inferior in virtue to none of his contemporaries. . . ." The whole

passage shows an admiration for Antiphon quite un-
justified by ordinary standards. The complete passage is

> .... the real author and maturer of the whole scheme,
> who had been longest interested in it, was Antiphon, a
> man inferior in virtue to none of his contemporaries,
> and possessed of remarkable powers of thought and
> gifts of speech. He did not like to come forward in the
> assembly, or in any other public arena. To the multi-
> tude, who were suspicious of his great abilities, he was
> an object of dislike; but there was no man who could do
> more for any who consulted him, whether their busi-
> ness lay in the courts of justice or in the assembly. And
> when the government of the Four Hundred was over-
> thrown and became exposed to the vengeance of the
> people, and he being accused of taking part in the plot
> had to speak in his own case, his defence was undoubt-
> edly the best ever made by any man tried on a capital
> charge down to my time.

Alcibiades and Nicias, those two characters so dia-
metrically opposed to each other, yet each equally fatal
to Athens, are contrasted. To each Thucydides con-
cedes a full sketch and in addition allows each to describe himself, Alcibiades in the speech advocating the
Sicilian expedition and Nicias in his address to his soldiers before the catastrophe at Syracuse:

> The most enthusiastic supporter of the expedition
> was Alcibiades, the son of Cleinias; he was determined
> to oppose Nicias, who was always his political enemy
> and had just now spoken of him in disparaging terms;
> but the desire to command was even a stronger motive
> with him. He was hoping that he might be the con-
> queror of Sicily and Carthage; and that success would
> repair his private fortunes, and gain him money as well
> as glory. He had a great position among the citizens
> and was devoted to horse-racing and other pleasures

which outran his means. And in the end his wild
courses went far to ruin the Athenian state. For the
people feared the extremes to which he carried the law-
lessness of his personal habits, and the far-reaching purposes which invariably animated him in all his actions.
They thought that he was aiming at a tyranny and set
themselves against him. And therefore, although his
talents as a military commander were unrivalled, they
entrusted the administration of the war to others, because they personally objected to his private habits; and
so they speedily shipwrecked the state.

This is the only case where Thucydides gives us details of a man's private life. They are only given here
because Alcibiades' private life had an effect on the
public action.

It is noteworthy here that though Thucydides says
Alcibiades went far toward ruining the state, he lays
the blame for the ultimate catastrophe squarely on
the people, who "shipwrecked the state" because they
objected to Alcibiades' private life. And later he adds
that by preventing the fleet from sailing from Samos to
Athens to put down the oligarchy, Alcibiades did "as
eminent a service to the state as any man ever did."
Thucydides would have "humored this lion the state
had unwittingly reared."

Nicias, whose conservative piety Thucydides so
skillfully uses as a foil to Alcibiades' reckless wanton-
ness, is more completely and more sympathetically
drawn. He appears in the early narrative as the conqueror of Minoa and Cythera and the opponent of
Cleon in the episode of Pylos. But when he comes forward after Cleon's death as the advocate of peace,
Thucydides describes his dreary and timid character at
length:

.... Nicias the son of Niceratus the Athenian, who
had been the most fortunate general of his day, became
more eager than ever to make an end of the war.
Nicias desired, whilst he was still successful and held
in repute, to preserve his good fortune; he would have
liked to rest from toil, and to give the people rest; and
he hoped to leave behind him to other ages the name of
a man who in all his life had never brought disaster on
the city. He thought that the way to gain his wish was
to trust as little as possible to fortune, and to keep out
of danger; and that danger would be best avoided by
peace.

In Nicias' desire to "leave behind him to other ages
the name of a man who in all his life had never brought
disaster on the city" we see that his ambition was to
emulate Pericles, whose greatest pride was that no
Athenian had, through his fault, put on mourning.
Both men were wealthy, humane and honorable, but
here the likeness ended.

To this Thucydides later adds the significant item
that he [Nicias] "was too much under the influence of
divination and such like ...." Yet when he was put to
death after his surrender, Thucydides could say of
him, "No one of the Hellenes in my time was less de-
serving of so miserable an end; for he lived in the
practice of every virtue."

In no other case in all the *History* does Thucydides
express such pity for the fate of a commander. Nowhere else does he complain that the just are forgotten of God. Nicias, who by Thucydides' own account
had been wrong in every decision, who had by his delay and hesitation bungled every operation, who was
solely responsible for the disaster, does "not deserve
so miserable an end," but no word is said of the gal-
lant Demosthenes, who had been right in every deci-

sion he had made, who had fought with equal valor, who had been brought to ruin only by Nicias' stupidity. This is partiality hard to understand.

Turning from these two men, Antiphon and Nicias, for whom Thucydides shows sympathy, to the popular leaders who followed Pericles, Cleon and Hyperbolus, we have still further evidence of political bias on Thucydides' part.

In the fifteenth year of the war (417 B.C.) Hyperbolus, on whom the mantle of the demagogue Cleon had fallen, had been ostracized. Thucydides does not mention this fact at that point in his narrative, for it had no military significance. It was the result of a "deal" between the pious Nicias and the brash Alcibiades. Both of them, each fearing that he would be ostracized, agreed to throw the votes of his followers against Hyperbolus. Hyperbolus went into exile, accompanied by howls of ribald laughter, but the Athenians were so disgusted with this perversion of the test of ostracism that it was never employed again.

In the twenty-first year of the war (411 B.C.) this Hyperbolus was murdered at Samos. He comes into Thucydides' picture here because of his connection with the events that led to the overthrow of the oligarchy at Athens. Thucydides says of him, "There was a certain Hyperbolus, an Athenian of no character, who, not for any fear of his power and influence, but for his villainy, and because the city was ashamed of him, had been ostracized." Hyperbolus may have been all of those things, but it was not because of any of them that he was ostracized.

Thucydides has not a good word for Cleon, though he is forced to admit that he had great influence with the people. Cleon is the most violent citizen, "an object of general mistrust." He favored war because his rogueries and slanders would be more easily detected in peace. His failure to make peace after Sphacteria was not to be expiated. He was conceited and a coward. These things are probably true, but no impartial historian could have said of Cleon's boast that he would bring the Lacedaemonians from Pylos alive or dead within twenty days, ".... the wiser sort of men were pleased when they reflected that of two good things they could not fail to obtain one— either there would be no more trouble with Cleon, which they would have greatly preferred, or, if they were disappointed, he would put the Lacedaemonians into their hands."

A still more serious charge can be brought against Thucydides in his treatment of Cleon. In narrating Cleon's campaign around Amphipolis in the tenth year of the war (422 B.C.), the campaign in which he met his death, Thucydides purports to give a complete account of the cities which Cleon restored to the Athenian Empire after they had been occupied by Brasidas and the Lacedaemonians. It has been pretty conclusively proved from the tribute lists that Cleon's operations had resulted in the Athenian reoccupation of all the towns on the Chalcidian peninsulas of Athos and Sithonia, an important success for Cleon of which Thucydides says nothing. This *suppressio veri* and the sarcastic allusions to Cleon go far toward relieving Thucydides of the charge of being an impartial historian. His sympathies were strongly conservative, and his character sketches of Antiphon, Nicias and Cleon reveal this partisan bias.

Thucydides' two heroes are Themistocles and Pericles. Of them he must be allowed to speak for himself:

> For Themistocles was a man whose natural force was unmistakeable; this was the quality for which he was distinguished above all other men; from his own native acuteness, and without any study either before or at the time, he was the ablest judge of the course to be pursued in a sudden emergency, and could best divine what was likely to happen in the remotest future. Whatever he had in hand he had the power of explaining to others, and even where he had no experience he was quite competent to form a sufficient judgment; no one could foresee with equal clearness the good or evil event which was hidden in the future. In a word, Themistocles, by natural power of mind and with the least preparation, was of all men the best able to extemporise the right thing to be done.

Of Pericles he says:

> During the peace while he was at the head of affairs he ruled with prudence; under his guidance Athens was safe, and reached the height of her greatness in his time. When the war began he showed that here too he had formed a true estimate of the Athenian power. He survived the commencement of hostilities two years and six months; and, after his death, his foresight was even better appreciated than during his life. For he had told the Athenians that if they would be patient and would attend to their navy, and not seek to enlarge their dominion while the war was going on, nor imperil the existence of the city, they would be victorious; but they did all that he told them not to do, and in matters which seemingly had nothing to do with the war, from motives of private ambition and private interest they adopted a policy which had disastrous effects in respect both of themselves and of their allies; their measures, had they been successful, would only

have brought honour and profit to individuals, and, when unsuccessful, crippled the city in the conduct of the war. The reason of the difference was that he, deriving authority from his capacity and acknowledged worth, being also a man of transparent integrity, was able to control the multitude in a free spirit; he led them rather than was led by them; for, not seeking power by dishonest arts, he had no need to say pleasant things, but, on the strength of his own high character, could venture to oppose and even to anger them. When he saw them unseasonably elated and arrogant, his words humbled and awed them; and, when they were depressed by groundless fears, he sought to reanimate their confidence. Thus Athens, though still in name a democracy, was in fact ruled by her greatest citizen. But his successors were more on an equality with one another, and, each one struggling to be first himself, they were ready to sacrifice the whole conduct of affairs to the whims of the people.

In Themistocles it was sheer native ability that aroused Thucydides' admiration. In Pericles it was incorruptible intellectual superiority. In both cases it was the quality that made its possessor an acknowledged master of men.

THE MIND OF THUCYDIDES

Thucydides was a realist—"for all things have their times of growth and decay"—even the Athenian state, and he was not fond of the common people. He says most of the Athenians know nothing about Sicily, which is, perhaps, not surprising, but he also affirms that they are ignorant of their own history, of Harmodius and Aristogeiton; in fact, they know no more than other Hellenes. He has no high opinion of the human race in general. "Not unintelligent" is his highest praise. He is under no illusions. "So little trouble do men take in the search after truth; so readily do they accept whatever comes first to hand." He admires the power of the Scythians, but they are not "at all on a level with other nations in sense." *Hybris* is usually an overweening pride that provokes the gods to jealousy and is punished. In Thucydides it is a passion that inspires the thoughtless mob to foolish adventure, notably the expedition against Syracuse. Most men prefer to be called clever knaves rather than honest simpletons; the worst insult is to be called stupid. "For such is the manner of men; what they like is always seen by them in the light of unreflecting hope, what they dislike they peremptorily set aside by an arbitrary conclusion." "You are always hankering after an ideal state," and paying no attention to immediate necessities. Every man thinks he knows as much as a physician about the causes of disease. Even Sophocles, the dramatist most acceptable to the conservative Athenians, can make a stupid mistake which must be corrected.

Thucydides condescends only once in his *History* to relate a ludicrous anecdote:

> There is a story of a reply made by a captive taken in the island [of Sphacteria] to one of the Athenian allies who had sneeringly asked "Where were their brave men—all killed?" He answered that "The spindle" (meaning the arrow) "would be indeed a valuable weapon if it picked out the brave." He meant to say that the destruction caused by the arrows and stones was indiscriminate.

To explain a joke with such painstaking care is the clearest way to show a profound contempt for the mental capacity of the reader.

Twice only does Thucydides express pity for misfortune, for the massacre at Mycalessus and for the fate of the Athenians at Syracuse. He uses the particle τοι only three times in his *History,* once in Pericles' appeal to the pride of the Athenians, once in Cleon's appeal to the passions of the Athenians in his effort to persuade them to execute the entire population of Mytilene, and once in Nicias' appeal to his soldiers when he speaks of the disease of which he was slowly dying. These three times only; "A quiver in the face of Thucydides is always worth noticing."

The common people cannot be trusted to govern a state wisely. Pericles could rule, in fact did so, though Athens was nominally a democracy, but when death wrenched his hands from the helm there was found no one who could grasp it firmly and guide the ship safely to the haven of a secure peace.

The two persons who might have done so were not lowborn men of the people, like Cleon and Hyperbolus. They were aristocrats, the wealthy Nicias, who "lived in the practice of every virtue," and the playboy Alcibiades, nephew and ward of Pericles, whose character is revealed in one of his own speeches: ". . . . I must begin by praising myself; and I consider that I am worthy." Thucydides could not approve of him entirely, but he has high praise for Alcibiades' advice to the army not to leave Samos to go to Athens to restore the democracy, and he believes Athens was ruined by not trusting him. The ablest of generals, Phormio and Demosthenes, are not of the great ruling families and are allowed to play their parts and pass from the scene without a word of commendation.

Thucydides did not believe in unlimited democracy.

He had seen too clearly how it ruined Athens. Democracies are amenable to discipline only as long as the people are in fear of a disaster. He thought the limited democracy of the Five Thousand, at least during its early days, the best government Athens had had within his memory. His views of the functions of the state are those of Machiavelli and Treitschke. Gildersleeve thinks Thucydides inspired Treitschke. "In Thucydides we have what is fundamentally the conception of the state as embodied power. It was not till Plato that the conception of the state as embodying justice came into view."

He believed that the rule of Athens over her allies was a tyranny. Naxos was the first of the allied cities to be "enslaved contrary to Hellenic right; the turn of the others came later." ". . . . to an imperial city nothing is inconsistent which is expedient. . . ." Yet it was a better rule than the Lacedaemonians had given or could give. The Athens of Pericles had done more for the allied cities than they had done or could possibly do for Athens. Nicias was right in saying that to be taken for an Athenian was a compliment to any Greek. Athens was really "the School of Hellas," even though she might seem nothing but the schoolmistress.

The sympathies of the Hellenic world were with Sparta and her allies, but Athens should have won the war, for her resources were greater. It was only the stupidity of her leaders that lost the cause, that "contemptuous wisdom which has so often brought man to ruin that in the end it is pronounced contemptible folly."

Yet for all his contempt of the Athenian leaders and

of the mental processes of the average Athenian, Thucydides is proud of the unbreakable spirit of the imperial city.   Over and over again disaster falls on Athens, and we think that this is the end.   Yet over and over again the city rises, new sacrifices are made, and the war goes on.   "For in the hour of trial Athens alone among her contemporaries is superior to the report of her."

Thucydides does not pass judgment on the morals of the characters in his drama, be they men or cities. He relates without a tremor of voice the most contemptible tricks.   At Notium, Paches, the Athenian commander, invited Hippias to come out to a conference, promising to ". . . put him back in the fort, safe and sound."   During the conference the Athenians entered the citadel and slew the garrison.   Whereupon Paches "conducted Hippias into the fort" and then shot him full of arrows.   Many instances of successful barefaced infamy of this kind, passed over without condemnation, could be cited.

It is hard to avoid the conclusion that Thucydides believed in success.   It is possibly more true to say that he believed in ability, that great capacity for achievement aroused his admiration and that he cared not so much for the character of the deed wrought or the method of its accomplishment.   When Athens was in a frenzy over the mutilation of the Hermae, one of those arrested on suspicion made a confession in the hope of pardon, ". . . . whether true or false I cannot say; opinions are divided, and no one knew at the time, or to this day knows, who the offenders were."   The confession was accepted, and all those accused in it were condemned to death.   Thucydides says, "No one could say whether the sufferers were justly punished; but the beneficial effect on the city at the time was undeniable." This comment, while doubtless true, savors too much of cynicism to commend it to the gentle reader.

Again, though Thucydides did not favor the rule of the four hundred aristocrats, he looks with admiration on the ability displayed in the overthrow of the democracy. Antiphon, the chief conspirator (an ancient quisling who tried later to betray his city to Sparta), was "inferior in virtue to none of his contemporaries," and "For an easy thing it certainly was not, about one hundred years after the fall of the tyrants, to destroy the liberties of the Athenians, who not only were a free, but during more than one half of this time had been an imperial people."

These are words of admiration, but the "virtue" that enabled Antiphon to succeed was virtue only because it was successful. It was the same type of virtue which distinguished Darlan and Hitler—ability.

It has already been noted that Thucydides' two heroes are Themistocles and Pericles. No one will deny that he has made a wise choice. It seems that in these two men again the quality that aroused Thucydides' admiration was their sheer mental power. In Themistocles this was demonstrated by the ease with which he met every emergency, that same natural foresight which Palmerston possessed, to the immense disgust of Prince Albert. In Pericles, too, it was his intellectual superiority that won Thucydides' admiration: "he derives his authority from his capacity." It was not Thucydides who told us that Pericles' proudest achievement was the fact that "because of me no Athenian has put on mourning." Thucydides does not emphasize in Pericles his "simplicity which is so large an element in a noble nature," but the domination of a master mind over a restless people.

If Thucydides thought his banishment unjust, he has well concealed his feelings. It is true that he emphasizes the haste with which he answered the call for help from Amphipolis, and the efforts he made to thwart Brasidas. He is not fair to Cleon, who probably favored the decree for his exile, but it would indeed be hard to be fair to that demagogue. He is more than fair to Brasidas, who was the cause of his misfortune, and if he criticises the conduct of the war by the Athenians, that criticism is certainly justified.

It is clear that Thucydides loved Athens passionately, the Athens of Pericles, that he admired intellectual ability above everything else, and that he was prejudiced in favor of high birth and respectability. If it had not been for the accident that caused his banishment, that chance which "belies our calculation," might he not have been the third statesman in a triad with Themistocles and Pericles? High birth was his, and an intellect unmatched for profundity among his contemporaries, and an unsurpassed ability at least to write, if not to deliver, speeches. So equipped by nature and by laborious training, what might he not have accomplished if he had returned from Thrace a successful admiral? These thoughts must have entered his mind, but they throw no shadow on the pages of his *History*. Great political distinction was denied him, but the mental ability which he worshipped has left to the world his *History*, "an everlasting possession."

CONCLUSION

Thucydides' pre-eminence as a historian rests on several elements. He is the first scientific and the first philosophic historian. The story that as a lad he heard Herodotus read portions of his history may well be true. But in his conception of what is required of a writer of history he is nearer to the twentieth century A.D. than he is to the fifth century B.C.

Not only does he give an accurate chronology to his narrative, but all his facts are scrutinized with the painstaking care of a modern scientist. No effort is too great to ascertain the truth.

But mere facts are not enough. The meaning of the facts, their import in the scheme of things, is revealed. Not the proximate but the ultimate cause of events is sought.

And in the speeches, by giving to the principal actor on each occasion the thoughts appropriate to the occasion Thucydides has laid bare the motives that led to treachery and murder, to honor and heroism. And all the motives alike are presented without praise or blame, *neque amore et sine odio,* with a cold aloofness that inspires both dread and admiration.

Thucydides' passion for chronological accuracy imposed severe limitations on the arrangement of his material. Yet he has, with consummate skill, so used his digressions to postpone the crises of his story, so placed in close juxtaposition the contrasting incidents of his narrative that the reader passes swiftly from breathless admiration to breathless depression, from shuddering pity to trembling elevation, from the rapt wonder of Pericles' panegyric on the glories of Imperial

Athens to the terrors of the plague, from the murder
of the wretched Melians to the splendor of the Athenian fleet streaming out of Piraeus toward Aegina—
and ruin.   No historian, ancient or modern, has handled his material with more artistic skill.

The inadequacies in Thucydides' style have been
noted.   Yet no historian has made his characters more
living human beings or has been more successful in
bringing his readers into the very presence of the
drama he is describing.   He may be aloof, his style
may be crabbed, but no one can read his description of
the siege of Syracuse without feeling that he is personally present on the heights of Epipolae, on the shore
of the Great Harbor, witnessing the disaster that is
"beyond tears."

And not only is the reader an eyewitness but he has
become a partisan.   Though his reason tells him, and
Thucydides plainly says that the Syracusans are patriots fighting in a righteous cause, that the Athenians are
perpetrating an act of the most outrageous and unprovoked aggression, his sympathies are with Athens.   By
the potent magic of his art Thucydides has corrupted
us all.   Impartiality, that stillborn offspring of the judicial temperament, has vanished, and we are all
Athenians stretching out our arms to our sailors in the
fleet, imploring our Gods to give them victory.   This
is, in my opinion, consummately great historical narrative.

But Thucydides' pre-eminence lies not alone, nor
even chiefly, in the qualities I have mentioned.   It depends on the fact, already noted, that Thucydides' intellect was of the very highest order.

In the speeches he gives the thoughts that were "appropriate to the occasion." But it is to be doubted if many of his characters could have expressed their opinions as well as Thucydides has done it for them. Whether it be the Corcyraean envoy or Cleon appealing to expediency, we have in Thucydides that abominable doctrine set forth in its most compelling form: the three failings most fatal to empire are pity, sentiment, indulgence. "But if, right or wrong, you are resolved to rule, then rightly or wrongly they must be chastised for your good. Otherwise you must give up your empire, and, when virtue is no longer dangerous, you may be as virtuous as you please." The appeal for mercy because of past services to Hellenic freedom addressed by the Plataeans to the Lacedaemonians becomes in the language of Thucydides irresistible to anyone save a Spartan or a Theban:

> We kneel at your fathers' tombs, and we call upon the dead not to let us be betrayed into the hands of the Thebans, their dearest friends to their bitterest enemies. We remind you of the day on which we shared in their glorious deeds—we who on this day are in danger of meeting a fearful doom. And now we say no more; to men in our case, though we must, there is nothing harder than to make an end; for with the end comes the decisive hour.

And these speeches are not remarkable for their eloquence in the usual meaning of that term. They are not Bryanesque nor even Ciceronian. It is not silver-tongued oratory. It is the accurate and cogent expression of human thought. It is motive revealed without disguise. It is the utter and ruthless portrayal of human passion. Here are greed, jealousy, selfishness, hypocrisy stripped naked by one of the keenest observers who has ever contemplated the sordid spectacle of

human strife. His characters speak with an authority,
with an insight, that few of them can have possessed.
Their enunciation of the fundamental principles of human action are not their own but the product of Thucydides' observation and reflection. ". . . . the two
things most adverse to good counsel are haste and passion; the former is generally a mark of folly, the latter
of vulgarity and narrowness of mind." "Dullness and
modesty are a more useful combination than cleverness and licence." ". . . . I speak only with the eagerness of an exile; . . . . the true enemies of my country
are not those who, like you, have injured her in open
war, but those who have compelled her friends to become her enemies." ". . . . the powerful exact what
they can, and the weak grant what they must."

Every subject that Thucydides touches is illumined
by the brilliance of his intellect. The prehistoric period of Greek history becomes a reasoned progress
from savagery to civilization instead of a jumble of
mythological tales. Superstitions clinging to oracular
prophecies are swept away like so many cobwebs.
Counsels are darkened neither by priest nor by prophet. He saw clearly that it was not the Gods, not
even *Ate* that was destroying Athens. It was the blind
discord of faction. "[The Athenians] were at last
overthrown, not by their enemies, but by themselves
and their own internal dissensions."

Thucydides is not one of those who is heard for his
much speaking. He all too seldom pronounces an
opinion. But when he does speak it "is as one having
authority." "For such is the manner of men; what they
like is always seen by them in the light of unreflecting
hope. . . ." "For party associations are not based upon

any established law, nor do they seek the public good; they are formed in defiance of the laws and from self-interest." ".... simplicity .... so large an element in a noble nature."

Thucydides' *History* is an everlasting possession because in it he has transcended the role of a mere scientific chronicler concerned with telling the truth about the events of an insignificant war. He has (to go back to Aristotle) for one brief moment in two thousand years raised history to the level of poetry. The particular has given place to the universal. The individual has become a type. The war between Athens and Sparta has ceased to be a petty economic struggle for the domination of local trade, or a conflict of ideologies. It has become a vivid illustration of the immutable laws that govern human passions. It is war in a timeless setting waged in the presence of the eternal verities.

VIII
THUCYDIDES AND THE WORLD WAR
(Written in March, 1943)

A ND very likely the strictly historical character of
my narrative may be disappointing to the ear. But
if he who desires to have before his eyes a true picture
of the events which have happened, and of the like
events which may be expected to happen hereafter in
the order of human things, [if he] shall pronounce
what I have written to be useful, then I shall be satisfied. My history is an everlasting possession, not a
prize composition which is heard and forgotten." In
these memorable words Thucydides emphasizes the
reason which induced him to write his *History,* namely, that in the course of history events recur, and therefore an accurate record of the present may be used as a
guide for the future. His belief is that men's characters do not change from age to age, that physical laws
do not alter, and that, therefore, the same situations
in human history will produce like events. In other
words, history repeats itself. This proverb has apparently been derived from this passage in Thucydides.

It has been noted (page 21) that Aristotle thought
that poetry is a higher type of composition than history, because poetry is general, while history is specific.
Thucydides sought to make history general, that is, to
elevate it to the rank of poetry, "to reach political
knowledge by experience." This effort to reach political knowledge by experience was something new in
historical writing; it is one of Thucydides' greatest
contributions to the history of knowledge.

In passing it may be noted that his reflections on human behavior are often incorporated in the set speeches. One of the purposes which they serve is to afford the historian an opportunity to state principles which govern human action, principles which are as true today as they were when he wrote them.

While Thucydides believed that under similar conditions similar results would occur, he continually emphasizes the part played by fortune in human affairs: "The movement of events is often as wayward and incomprehensible as the course of human thought; . . . ." ". . . . the uncertainty of fortune, which may strike any one however innocent," ". . . . the inscrutable nature of war . . . . generally ends in becoming a mere matter of chance, ..." "war least of all things conforms to prescribed rules; it strikes out a path for itself when the moment comes." It is this "uncertainty of fortune" rather than the recurrence of a pattern in history which has impressed Sir Herbert Fisher. He says in the preface of his history of Europe:

> One intellectual excitement has, however, been denied me. Men wiser and more learned than I have discerned in history a plot, a rhythm, a pre-determined pattern. These harmonies are concealed from me. I can see only one emergency following upon another as wave follows upon wave, only one great fact with respect to which, since it is unique, there can be no generalization, only one safe rule for the historian; that he should recognize in the development of human destinies the play of the contingent and the unforeseen.

For Thucydides, however, history repeats itself subject to the action of "chance [that] belies our calculation." In foretelling future events from past historical experience, as Thucydides believes possible, the difficulty is to find situations so nearly parallel that what happened in one instance may be expected to happen again many years later. Gildersleeve remarks, "Historical parallel bars are usually set up for exhibiting feats of mental agility." The Peloponnesian War does, however, resemble the present global war in so many ways that the trial seems to me worth while, even at the risk of a fall.

The Peloponnesian War was, as Thucydides himself recognized, a world war. For the world at that time consisted of a very limited district, of which the eastern Mediterranean was the center. To the north of the Greek peninsula lay the great unknown territory of Europe, with its magnificent forests and its long wastes of steppes. This was an almost entirely unknown region. Amber filtered through from the shores of the Baltic Sea, and there were rumors of lands where the daylight lasted twenty-four hours, and a man who needed not to sleep could earn two wages. But of Europe and northern Asia the civilized dwellers of the south had only the vaguest ideas. Thrace was the boundary of their horizon, and Macedonia was so far away that Demosthenes, a century later, could speak of it as a country which no respectable gentleman would even mention. It was two hundred years after Thucydides' birth before Rome became important enough to make war with Carthage, and when the Peloponnesian War was at its height Rome was so insignificant that modern historians are still quarreling about what was happening on the Seven Hills.

Southern Italy and Sicily were Greek, and there was a Greek outpost at Marseilles, in southern France. Spain was indefinitely known, and the mariners who

ventured beyond the Pillars of Hercules were few.
They were mostly Phoenicians who had been to an
island far in the north, where the water was heavy and
thick, and the shore line changed twice every twenty-
four hours. Thence these daring adventurers brought
back a shiny white metal that hardened copper so that
it made passable weapons and lovely statues.

The Phoenicians themselves were part of the world
of the fifth century. They dwelt at Tyre and Sidon
and at Carthage, restless traders, builders of factories,
getters of money, thoroughly practical, realistic business men. They produced a great civilization that has
made one contribution, and one only, to the modern
world, the word "assassin."

To the south lay Egypt, but Egypt had long since
ceased to be a world power. Even in the days of the
Prophet Isaiah, Egypt was a "broken reed" and by
the fifth century it was as unimportant in the affairs of
the world of that day as is Spain in the twentieth century. Its future was behind it.

To the east lay the power of the Great King. Only
thirty years before Thucydides was born this great
power, this absolute monarchy, this ancient Russia,
was so powerful and aggressive that it threatened the
liberties of Greece. At the opening of the Peloponnesian War it was recognized that the power of Persia
was no longer a menace, but its wealth and resources
were such that its alliance with either of the combatants in this war might be decisive. The essential
rottenness of its civilization, the weakness of its gov-
ernmental system were to be proved to the world only
five years after the close of the war by a body of ten
thousand Greek mercenaries who made their way al-

most to Babylon and escaped in spite of all the Great King's efforts to capture them. But it was not until Philip II came to the throne of Macedon that he and his son Alexander were to take advantage of that weakness.

The Peloponnesian War thus involved all the known world. The great Persian Empire in the east and all the Greek cities participated in it. This meant that it swept from the coast of Asia Minor across Greece to Sicily and Italy. Only Egypt and Carthage held aloof. While Carthage and Sweden are radically different, the fact that each was not involved in the world struggle had much the same effect on them. Carthage was enriched by the activity of her traders, who monopolized a great deal of the commerce that ordinarily fell to the Greek mariners, just as Sweden in the present war has sold her iron ore and other products, at very lucrative prices, to Germany.

The world has shrunk in size during the last twenty centuries, and the great distances involved in the present war are offset by the swiftness of transportation. The time required to reach the most remote theater of war from either Athens or Sparta was roughly the same as the time now involved in reaching the Far East from New York or London. The present contest differs from the Peloponnesian War, as far as the distances involved are concerned, only in the speed with which news can now be transmitted. The Peloponnesian War, just like all wars previous to our Civil War, was affected by the fact that news traveled slowly. Thus the Spartan, Brasidas, refused to give up Scione, which he had captured after the Peace of Nicias had been made, because he had not heard of the peace at the time he attacked the city. This, of course, recalls the fighting of the Battle of New Orleans after peace with England had been declared in 1815.

The size of the forces involved in the battles of the Peloponnesian War seems to us often quite insignificant; for instance, at the Battle of Solygeia the Corinthians lost 212 men, and the Athenians less than fifty. But we must remember that it is only because of the great benefits that a scientific age has conferred on us quite recently that we are able now to have "bigger and better" wars. In the Boston Massacre three men were killed outright, and two died later of their wounds. Eight men fell in the Battle of Lexington, and Paul Revere was so unmoved by the carnage that he refused to allow it to distract his attention from the work at hand—rescuing from the inn a trunk belonging to John Hancock. At the Battle of Big Bethel, June 10, 1861, there were only three hundred Confederate soldiers involved. The Federal loss, which was the larger, was seventy-six, but the Confederate soldier who was in charge of the artillery was hailed as having "no superior as an artillerist in any country," and a Richmond newspaper said, "Big Bethel was one of the most extraordinary victories in the annals of war."

The Peloponnesian War, then, is a close parallel to the present war in one important respect: it involved practically all the known world.

The combatants arrayed on either side also bear a striking resemblance to the present alignment of forces. On one side we have a closely allied central power, Athens. She was supported by all the cities of

her empire, many of them cooperating with her un-
willingly, but Athens did have the advantage of a central position and immediate and definite command.
Any resolution taken by the Athenian Assembly was
at once put into effect without further debate or discussion.

Against this central power was opposed a confederacy headed by Sparta in the Peloponnesus. The two
most important members were Corinth, at the Isthmus, and Boeotia, lying northwest of Athens. These
allies were not closely united, a fact which Thucydides
recognizes: "The members of such a confederacy are
slow to meet, and when they do meet, they give little
time to the consideration of any common interest, and
a great deal to schemes which further the interest of
their particular state." Decisions could be arrived at
only after such conferences. This hampered efficient
action. The physical situation, therefore, in the Peloponnesian War is much like that of the present war:
a central, closely united core is opposed to a loosely
knit confederacy. The difference, of course, lies in
the fact that in the present war the central power is a
land power, whereas in the Peloponnesian War the
central power was naval. In this alignment the United
States corresponds to Persia, a country lying outside
the scene of the fighting, a little bit aloof and at first
undecided as to which side it should favor, and possessed of almost unlimited resources. Whichever side
could win the assistance of this aloof power might well
hope to gain the money and material necessary to complete the war successfully.

The Athenians belonged to the Ionic branch of the
Greek race, and the Spartans to the Dorian. The two

branches are quite different in character, and the contrast in their mental attitudes is not unlike the contrast between the German and British character. Thucydides characterizes the Athenians and the Peloponnesians at the outset of the war in a famous passage:

And you have never considered what manner of men are these Athenians with whom you will have to fight, and how utterly unlike yourselves. They are revolutionary, equally quick in the conception and in the execution of every new plan; while you are conservative —careful only to keep what you have, originating nothing, and not acting even when action is most urgent. They are bold beyond their strength; they run risks which prudence would condemn; and in the midst of misfortune they are full of hope. Whereas it is your nature, though strong, to act feebly; when your plans are most prudent, to distrust them; and when calamities come upon you, to think that you will never be delivered from them. They are impetuous, and you are dilatory; they are always abroad, and you are always at home. For they hope to gain something by leaving their homes; but you are afraid that any new enterprise may imperil what you have already. When conquerors, they pursue their victory to the utmost; when defeated, they fall back the least. Their bodies they devote to their country as though they belonged to other men; their true self is their mind, which is most truly their own when employed in her service. When they do not carry out an intention which they have formed, they seem to themselves to have sustained a personal bereavement; when an enterprise succeeds, they have gained a mere instalment of what is to come; but if they fail, they at once conceive new hopes and so fill up the void. With them alone to hope is to have, for they lose not a moment in the execution of an idea. This is the lifelong task, full of danger and toil, which they are always imposing upon themselves. None enjoy their good things less, because they are always seeking for more. To do their duty is their only holiday, and they deem the quiet of inaction to be as disagreeable as the most tiresome business. If a man should say of them, in a word, that they were born neither to have peace themselves nor to allow peace to other men, he would simply speak the truth.

Much as we regret to admit it, the Athenians seemed to the people of Greece, at the time the Peloponnesian War broke out, the embodiment of tyranny. They had treated their subject allies as if they themselves were absolute masters. Thucydides recurs to this statement over and over again. He says that "mutual fear is the only solid basis of alliance; for he who would break faith is deterred from aggression by the consciousness of inferiority." The Germans have frequently likened themselves to the Athenians, and, granting that the Athenians were as ruthless and unpopular as Thucydides says, the Germans may very well be right. On the other hand the Spartans, a Doric people, were slow to action and imperturbable. Their unwillingness to act often gave a false impression of timorousness. In this conflict they appear as the protectors of liberty and so they may, without a stretch of the imagination, be regarded as a parallel to the British people today. In fact, the Germans have made this comparison also. And it is worth while to insist on the validity of this comparison. While it is true that the Spartans, when they tried after the Persian War to assume the leadership of Greece, were more intolerable than the Athenians proved to be in the present league, they did not make tributaries of those who acknowledged their leadership, but took care that they should be governed by oligarchies in the exclusive interests of Sparta. The Athenians, on the other hand, exacted a tribute from all their allies except Chios and Lesbos, they openly affirmed that "the weaker must be kept down by the stronger," and Pericles himself says, "your empire has become a tyranny which in the opinion of mankind has been unjustly gained." Thucydides' remark about Naxos has already been quoted, "This was the first of the allied cities which was enslaved contrary to Hellenic right; the turn of the others came later."

Athens was a free city but she was also an imperial city. Her citizens were free men but they were also rulers; as free men they participated in the administration of the most perfect democracy that ever existed and created the most intellectual civilization humanity has known. As rulers they soon gave up their position as *primi inter pares* and became tyrants. In a debate recorded by Thucydides the Athenians argue with the inhabitants of the little Island of Melos that it is utterly hopeless for them, the Melians, to resist the Athenian aggression, because might makes right, and because they, the Athenians, have the power to subjugate the Melians and will consequently do so. They say bluntly, "For of the Gods we believe, and of men we know, that by a law of their nature wherever they can rule they will." The Melians appeal in vain to justice and suggest that they may be assisted by the Spartans. During the early months of 1914 this debate was read at the University of Toronto. Germany was substituted for Athens, Great Britain for Sparta and Belgium for Melos, whose people were later overwhelmed and butchered by the Athenians. The great difference, overlooked by the Germans, is that the

British did come to the rescue of Belgium, whereas the Spartans delayed till the Melians were massacred.

In making this comparison between the warring states of the fifth century B.C. and those of the twentieth century A.D.—in equating Athens with Germany and Sparta with Britain—I must make it clear that I am dealing with the foreign relations of the two Greek states, not with their domestic polity and the conditions under which their citizens lived. Here the similarity ends absolutely. The culture of Athens was the culture of a free people. Her citizens enjoyed all the privileges of an enlightened democracy. They were as free as are the citizens of Britain or of the United States. Sparta, on the other hand, was an armed camp. The lives of her citizens were regulated with more than Prussian precision. In internal affairs Sparta was Prussianism in its most highly developed form. But in their relations to the states and cities of their respective Confederacy and Empire, Sparta did play the role of Britain and Athens the role of Germany. The members of Sparta's confederacy followed her of their own accord, as the members of the British Commonwealth of Nations declared war on Germany, each in its own sovereign capacity. Athens compelled the unwilling members of her Empire to assist her as Germany today is retaining by force and fear the nations enslaved in her New Order. Athens never received—or deserved—from her subjects such a tribute to a just and enlightened rule as Britain won from the Boer Republic of South Africa, which in 1902 resisted with all its might incorporation into the British Empire and which in 1914 voluntarily chose to fight for that Empire against their German kin.

This general feeling of the Greek world at the opening of the Peloponnesian War is categorically affirmed by Thucydides:

> The feeling of mankind was strongly on the side of the Lacedaemonians; for they professed to be the liberators of Hellas. Cities and individuals were eager to assist them to the utmost, both by word and deed; and where a man could not hope to be present, there it seemed to him that all things were at a stand. For the general indignation against the Athenians was intense; some were longing to be delivered from them, others fearful of falling under their sway.

This corresponds very closely to the feeling against Germany in neutral countries in 1914 and 1939.

In addition to the similarity between the ancient and the modern conflict in the geographical position of the combatants involved and in their temperaments, there is a series of events in the present war that very closely parallels those of the Peloponnesian War.

Both wars began with a slight event remote from the central scene. The Peloponnesian War began with the quarrel between Corcyra and Epidamnus, much as the murder of the Austrian archduke at Serajevo in 1914 precipitated the present war. At the outset of the war the Athenians withdrew their citizens from the rural district of Athens into the city. So the Germans before this war withdrew the German families from the Baltic states of Latvia, Lithuania, and Estonia, at great cost of money and personal hardship, and resettled them in Prussia.

The feverish prelude to the Peloponnesian War, involving two conferences of the allies, one at Sparta and one at the Isthmus, reminds one of the twelve days of hectic diplomatic activity that reigned in Europe in the summer of 1914.

The Peloponnesian War, like the present war, was preceded by acts of treachery—the German attack on Belgium in 1914 and the Japanese attack on Pearl Harbor in 1941. In the Greek war, however, the treachery was perpetrated by an ally of Sparta, Thebes, which made the foul attack on Plataea, a Boeotian city in alliance with Athens, as Thucydides specifically says, because the Thebans thought that war was inevitable and they wished to seize Plataea before the Athenians could garrison it.

Until 1939 many people thought, especially the sleepwalkers in the British Government, that the World War was over and that "peace in our time" was assured. Since the autumn of 1939, however, all students of history have come to feel that the war of 1914-1918 and the war of 1939- are simply two phases of a single war, with an unquiet peace interposed between them. Just so, in the Peloponnesian War hostilities were actively waged for ten years, 431-421; there followed the so-called Peace of Nicias from 421 to 414; and then a renewal of the struggle from 414 to 404. Thucydides emphasizes in no uncertain terms that it was only one war and that the Peace of Nicias was no peace at all. He says, "If he have regard to the facts of the case, he will see that the term 'peace' can hardly be applied to a state of things in which neither party gave back or received all the places stipulated; . . . ." So, looking back over the 'twenties and early 'thirties of the twentieth century one can say that there was really no peace. There were the Japanese attack on Manchuria, the Italian attack on Abyssinia and the attacks by Germany on all her surrounding neighbors.

The mention of Nicias suggests an interesting parallel in the degeneracy of popular leadership in democratic Athens and democratic Britain during the first phase of the war. Pericles was succeeded by Nicias and Cleon, Asquith and Lloyd George by Baldwin and Chamberlain. I would not suggest that Lloyd George in every way resembles Pericles, although it was Lloyd George's driving energy that went far toward the winning of the first phase of the present World War, just as Pericles' wise counsels, as long as they prevailed, made Athens victorious. When Pericles was removed the government at Athens fell into the hands of the upright, religious and stupid Nicias. So, with the passing of Lloyd George's influence in Britain, we have the upright, honorable and ignorant Baldwin. Nicias, like Baldwin, never forgot that the soldiers were also voters, that the men in his army would also pass on his conduct when it was discussed in the assembly. In addressing the council of war at Syracuse, Nicias positively refused to withdraw the army; he knew, he said, that the Athenian people would not forgive their departure if they left without an order from home. The men upon whose votes their fate would depend would not, like themselves, have seen with their own eyes the state of affairs; they would have heard only the criticism of others, and would be convinced by any accusations which a clever speaker might bring forward. Indeed, many or most of the very soldiers who were now crying out that their case was desperate would raise the opposite cry when they reached home and would say that the generals were traitors and had been bribed to depart; and therefore he, knowing the tempers of the Athenians, would for his own part rather take his chance and fall, if he must, alone by the hands of the enemy, than die unjustly on a dishonorable charge at the hands of the Athenians. So Baldwin, in a burst of naïve truthfulness, said in the House of Commons, November 12, 1936, that if he had told the voters the truth, how unarmed Britain was and how much re-armament was necessary, his party could not possibly have been re-elected to power.

Cleon has been described by a competent authority as a hardheaded, middle-class, business politician. I would not suggest that Chamberlain is in every way like Cleon, for Cleon did have a good deal of ability and much energy, but at least the two are alike in tak-ing a hardheaded businessman's attitude toward poli-tics, and both men at a critical time utterly failed to fulfill the duty of a statesman.

The half-hearted, defeatist attitude which Nicias adopted in his conduct of the campaign against Syra-cuse, in which he did not believe, has been aptly com-pared to the pusillanimous leadership of the French forces in the present war by the "old men of Vichy." The aged Marshal Pétain's idea of patriotism is no higher than that of the youthful egotist, Alcibiades. "He is the true patriot, not who, when unjustly exiled, abstains from attacking his country, but who in the warmth of his affection seeks to recover her without regard to the means."

As the Peloponnesian War went on, the Athenians again and again removed entire populations of con-quered cities from their homes and either resettled

them elsewhere or enslaved the women and children
after killing the men.   Thus the inhabitants of Aegina
were ruthlessly deported, and the Melians extermi-
nated or enslaved.   I need not emphasize the parallel
here.

The Peloponnesian War was not, like the present
war, primarily a conflict of ideologies, but the two
leading states did see to it that friendly governments
should be set up in conquered cities.   The Athenians
erected and maintained a democracy on Samos, and
the Lacedaemonians changed it to an oligarchy immediately after the fall of Athens.   So Hitler has
erected Fascist governments in his satellite states, and
the United Nations are insisting, if not on democracies, at least on liberal governments in the reclaimed
areas of the globe.   So Brasidas promises to bestow
the blessings of freedom on Acanthus whether the citizens wished it or not:

> . . . . if you are of opinion that liberty is perilous
> and should not in justice be forced upon any one, but
> gently brought to those who are able to receive it,—I
> shall first call the Gods and heroes of the country to
> witness that I have come hither for your good, and that
> you would not be persuaded by me: I shall then use
> force and ravage your country without any more
> scruple.   I shall deem myself justified by two over-
> powering arguments. In the first place, I must not per-
> mit the Lacedaemonians to suffer by your friendship,
> and suffer they will through the revenues which the
> Athenians will continue to derive from you if you do
> not join me; and in the second place, the Hellenes
> must not lose their hope of liberation by your fault. On
> any other ground we should certainly be wrong in tak-
> ing such a step; it is only for the sake of the general
> weal that we Lacedaemonians have any right to be

forcing liberty upon those who would rather not have it. For ourselves, we are far from desiring empire, but we want to overthrow the empire of others. And having this end in view, we should do injustice to the majority if, while bringing independence to all, we tolerated opposition in you.

This is the very essence of the determination of both Hitler and Japan to give a "New Order" to reluctant peoples.

The Sicilian campaign, which sapped the resources of Athens and was one of the causes of her downfall, closely resembles Germany's campaign against Russia. The reasons, both real and alleged, for the Sicilian campaign in the fifth century B.C. and the Russian campaign in the twentieth century A.D. are exactly the same. Thucydides says, "Their chief argument was that, if the Syracusans were not punished . . . . but were allowed to . . . . get the whole of Sicily into their own hands, they would one day come with a great army, Dorians assisting Dorians . . . . and would unite in overthrowing Athens herself." Just so, the Germans tell us, the Russians were organizing a Pan-Slav Communism and were about to overrun the whole world. Thucydides punctures both pretensions when he says, "They [the Athenians] virtuously professed that they were going to assist their own kinsmen and their newly-acquired allies, but the simple truth was that they aspired to the empire of Sicily." Both were entirely unprovoked assaults on peaceful neighbors, and in both cases the cost to the attacking party was ruinous.

The Peloponnesian War was decided in favor of Sparta by the intervention of Persia, with its vast resources. That intervention was brought about by

Cyrus, who was an ardent admirer of the Spartan general, Lysander. To Lysander, Cyrus promised the taxes of his province, his own private fortune, and if that were not sufficient, he said that to secure revenue for the war he would melt down the gold and silver throne on which he sat. Mr. Roosevelt's admiration for Mr. Churchill is well known and though he has never offered his private fortune in support of Mr. Churchill's cause, the warm personal relation between the two men certainly facilitated American aid and intervention.

To recapitulate, then, the Peloponnesian War and the World War of 1914-1945 alike involve the whole world. They were both waged between a central power, united but with reluctant allies, and a loose confederacy. The central power, restless and aggressive, provoked the conflict against the complacent and inert outer alliance. The sympathies of the neutral states were with the allies. The proximate cause of both wars was a relatively insignificant incident. Before war began, in each case, outlying citizens were withdrawn within the boundaries of the central power. War was begun after a hectic period of negotiations and was preceded by a treacherous attack while the peace was still unbroken. Each war was interrupted by an armistice that was falsely called a peace. Both wars are marked by the deportation of the population of cities and nations and by a desire of the combatants to compel allies to adopt a form of government similar to their own. In each war the central power was fatally weakened by an ambitious predatory attack on a strong neutral nation, and both wars were decided in favor of the allies and against the central power by the intervention late in the war of a powerful nation lying outside the immediate theater of hostilities.

If, then, these parallel bars seem close enough together to allow one to perform upon them without being torn asunder, what events may be expected to happen in the present war, since it is so similar to the world war of the fifth century B.C.?

First, one or two economic consequences. As the Peloponnesian War progressed, more and more of the Athenian citizens came into the employment of the state. It has been estimated that at the close of the war one third or one half of all the adult male citizens of Athens were beneficiaries of public employment. In fact, Thucydides says that one reason why the Athenians were in favor of the Sicilian expedition was because it would furnish "an inexhaustible mine of pay for the future." It is not necessary to point out that this extraordinary employment of citizens by the state has already happened in the present war. It might, however, be well to notice that both Plato and Aristotle, men whose opinions deserve consideration, thought that this large employment of civilians by the state was one of the causes of Athens' later degeneration. The implications and the warning for us should be clear.

Another conclusion that might be drawn from the situation in fifth-century Greece and the situation today is that as long as men's characters remain as they are, and governments are what they should not be, no weak city or state can maintain its independence unless it is protected from predatory empires like Athens, Germany and Japan by outside alliances. Witness Melos and Belgium. The free cities of Greece were free only at rare intervals. They have been enslaved by the King of Persia, by Athens, by Macedon, by Rome, by Turkey and by Germany. Independence in this world, whether it is the world of fifth-century Greece or the present global world, requires strength; or, if that is impossible, weakness must be supported by another's strength. We talk of freedom for India, and some of us go about with badges of "Free India Now," but no thoughtful person can believe that there can be any freedom for India unless that freedom is supported by the armed strength of Britain or the United States or China. The Irish hurl epithets at the British and proclaim their freedom, but the freedom of Ireland rests on the British Navy.

As the Peloponnesian War went on, and passions became more inflamed on either side, reprisals increased in number. For, Thucydides says,

> . . . . when men are retaliating upon others, they are reckless of the future, and do not hesitate to annul those common laws of humanity to which every individual trusts for his own hope of deliverance should he ever be overtaken by calamity; they forget that in their own hour of need they will look for them in vain.

In the massacre of the Jews by Germany and in the murder of the United States flyers by Japan we can see the beginning of this bestiality, and one may safely predict that the end is not yet.

A predatory empire will in the end be defeated by the hatred which it arouses. When Athens lost her fleets and her armies in Sicily, her subject allies were eager to revolt; they were, to use Thucydides' words, "everywhere willing even beyond their power to revolt," and without question that will be the attitude of the subject allies of Germany, once the power of the Reich really begins to crack.   They and the raped countries of Europe who have been basking in the sunshine of the "New Order" will help in tearing apart the empire that foisted that abortion of mediaevalism on the world.   When the Athenian Empire faced defeat, Thucydides says, "The states which had been neutral determined that the time had come when, invited or not, they could no longer stand aloof from the war; they must of their own accord attack the Athenians." So, when England was driven to the wall, Mussolini asked permission of Hitler to help bomb London and hastened to climb on the hearse which he mistook for a band wagon.   When the Reich is reduced only a little more, we may expect that Turkey and perhaps Sweden and the Argentine will feel that "invited or not, they can no longer stand aloof from the war."

Victory will come to the side which has the greater resources.   Thucydides says, ". . . . and war is not an affair of arms, but of money which gives to arms their use, and which is needed above all things when a continental is fighting against a martime power: . . . ." The correct understanding of that single sentence would have prevented Germany in 1914 and in 1939 from embarking on a conquest of the world.   The addition of the resources of the United States to the side of the allies, like the addition of Persian gold to the revenues of Sparta, will be found to be the deciding factor in this world war.

The false peace that interrupted the Peloponnesian War was brought about by war weariness and by the appeasers who in Athens and Sparta were able to take advantage of it.   In our world war the false peace of

1918 was the result of the partial defeat of the aggressor. In both cases appeasement brought forth its perfect fruit. In Greece the aggressor, Athens, took advantage of the peace to make an unprovoked and predatory attack on Sicily. Germany took advantage of the appeasers in Britain and France to attack Austria and Czechoslovakia. In both cases there will be no peace until Germany, like Athens, is completely defeated.

Of the Athenian navy's complete annihilation at Aegospotami, a recent historian says, "Thus with the suddenness and unexpectedness of a clap of thunder from a clear sky the great war was over." The long overstrained resources of Athens broke like a parting hawser, and the overinflated bubble of the super-racial myth may burst with equal suddenness.

To negotiate a peace between an alliance and an empire overthrown will not be an easy thing. This may be self-evident, but it is noted by Thucydides: "Charges brought by cities or persons against one another can be satisfactorily arranged; but when a great confederacy, in order to satisfy private grudges, undertakes a war of which no man can foresee the issue, it is not easy to terminate it with honour." Thucydides' narrative unfortunately does not come down to the end of the war. If we had his reflections on the final downfall of Athens and the victory of the allies, we should undoubtedly have more material with which to forecast the peace negotiations. One thing is clear from the outcome; it is that magnanimity will be found in the hearts of the great powers rather than in the smaller and more selfish allies. It was Sparta that, at the end, decided that Athens should not be destroyed, though the Corinthians and Thebans were clamorous for its destruction; so we can be sure that, when peace negotiations come at the close of this war, magnanimity, that alone can achieve a lasting peace, will be found in the hearts of the great democracies, not in the counsel of the less important allies.   The truth of this surmise is already proved by the wise advice of Madame Chiang Kai-shek against vindictive peace: "While it may be difficult for us not to feel bitterness for the injuries we have suffered at the hands of the aggressor, let us remember that recrimination and hatred will lead us nowhere."

When the central powers begin to fall and the inevitable revolt of the subject nations comes, with it will come civil war.   No better description of the horrors of this civil strife between quislings and the patriots of the enslaved nations of Europe will be found than Thucydides' description of the horrors of civil war in Corcyra and its effects on the morals of a people:

> And revolution brought upon the cities of Hellas many terrible calamities, such as have been and always will be while human nature remains the same, but which are more or less aggravated and differ in character with every new combination of circumstances.   In peace and prosperity both states and individuals are actuated by higher motives, because they do not fall under the dominion of imperious necessities; but war, which takes away the comfortable provision of daily life, is a hard master, and tends to assimilate men's characters to their conditions.
>
> When troubles had once begun in the cities, those who followed carried the revolutionary spirit further and further, and determined to outdo the report of all who had preceded them by the ingenuity of their en-

terprises and the atrocity of their revenges. The meaning of words had no longer the same relation to things,
but was changed by them as they thought proper. Reckless daring was held to be loyal courage; prudent delay
was the excuse of a coward; moderation was the disguise of unmanly weakness; . . . . The tie of party was
stronger than the tie of blood, because a partisan was
more ready to dare without asking why. (For party associations are not based upon any established law, nor
do they seek the public good; they are formed in defiance of the laws and from self-interest.) The seal of
good faith was not divine law, but fellowship in crime.
. . . . Revenge was dearer than self-preservation. . . . .
In general the dishonest more easily gain credit for
cleverness than the simple for goodness; men take a
pride in the one, but are ashamed of the other.

The cause of all these evils was the love of power,
originating in avarice and ambition, and the party-spirit
which is engendered by them when men are fairly em-
barked in a contest.

That is a picture of what will happen in Europe
when the dragon's teeth sown by the Nazis produce
their awful brood.

One conclusion that may be drawn from the Peloponnesian War derives not from the physical similarity of that conflict to the present world war nor from
the aggressive nature of the Athenians and their im-
perialistic ambition, but from their character as free
citizens of a free state. As such they present a marked
contrast to the subject soldiers of the oligarchies
against whom they fought. The Athenians found the
Syracusans, who were also democratic like themselves,
the bravest enemies against whom they fought. And
of the spirited resistance of the Athenians, Thucydides
says:

And yet after they [the Athenians] had lost in the Sicilian expedition the greater part of their fleet and army, and were now distracted by revolution, still they held out three years not only against their former enemies, but against the Sicilians who had combined with them, and against most of their own allies who had risen in revolt. Even when Cyrus the son of the King joined in the war and supplied the Peloponnesian fleet with money, they continued to resist, and were at last overthrown, not by their enemies, but by themselves and their own internal dissensions.

And the reverse of this may be seen in the discouragement of Sparta when misfortune began to come upon it.   Thucydides says:

> Fortune too was against them, and they were panic-stricken by the many startling reverses which had befallen them within so short a time. They feared lest some new calamity like that of the island [Sphacteria] might overtake them; and therefore they dared not venture on an engagement, but expected all their undertakings to fail; they had never hitherto known misfortune, and now they lost all confidence in their own powers.

A reasonable inference from these mental reactions may be that the citizens of a free state will show a far better morale under stress than those of a paternalistic, repressive government. Defeat will not daunt them. They will be like the Athenians, of whom Pericles says, ". . . . in the face of death they resolved to rely upon themselves alone. And when the moment came they were minded to resist and suffer, rather than to fly and save their lives; they ran away from the word of dishonour, but on the battlefield their feet stood fast, ..." And when the moment came for England, abandoned by her ally and stripped of her armor, she

too ran away from the word of dishonor, and even after Dunkerque the feet of her freemen stood fast. "We
shall fight on the beaches, we shall fight on the landing
grounds, we shall fight in the fields and in the streets,
we shall fight in the hills, we shall never surrender."
And here, too, Thucydides has anticipated our World
War and Churchill, for he says, "The greatest states
and the greatest men, when misfortunes come, are the
least depressed in spirit and the most resolute in action." "I would say to this house as I said to those
who have joined this government, I have nothing to
offer but blood, toil, tears and sweat."

To use, then, the experience of history to arrive at
political knowledge of what this war will bring: the
employment of vast numbers of voters by the government as a result of the war effort constitutes a real danger to our democratic institutions; it was fatal for Athens. There will be no freedom for small states except
in collective security. As the war goes on, even greater crimes against humanity will be perpetrated by the
central powers. But a predatory empire has in its nature the seeds of destruction, and when that destruction is imminent, nations now neutral will join the allies. Victory will go to the side with the greater resources. A complete victory, unconditional surrender,
will be necessary to a lasting peace. The soldiers of
the democracies will show greater stamina, better morale. The collapse of the central powers will be sudden. There will be no long fight to the death, for the
bully is not a good loser. Magnanimity will be shown
in the peace terms and will be extended to the defeated
by America, the British Commonwealth, China or Russia, but not by the lesser nations.

Perhaps no more disheartening pilgrimage can be undertaken at any shrine in Europe than the journey up the Sacred Way of Delphi. At this "earth's central shrine" the Greek states deposited trophies of their victories and offerings to their gods, and the trophies that line the Sacred Way mark, almost entirely, victories of Greek over Greek, of one city over another, of the Arcadians over the Lacedaemonians, of the Thebans over the Spartans, of the Tarentines over the Messapians. Chief among them is the insulting tribute which Lysander set up to himself for his victory over the Athenians at Aegospotami:

> Here in this trophy Lysander victorious set up his
>   own statue
> When with his swift moving ships, he crushed the
>   Cecropian power
> Crowning his native land, Lacedaemon, th' Acropolis
>   of Hellas
> Sparta unsacked by the foe, fatherland of the fair dance.

It is only when one reaches the end of the Sacred Way that he comes upon the stone where rested the entwined bronze serpents that supported the tripod that was dedicated in honor of the final victory of the free Greek cities over the Persian empire at Plataea.

When Adam and Eve were driven out of the Garden of Eden, the curse was laid upon woman that in sorrow she should bear her offspring. So it is with the human race. Not a single great idea has been born to humanity that has not been bought with the blood and suffering of countless people. It cost thirty years of hideous civil war in Germany to establish the principle that a man might worship God as he chose. It cost all the stained glass in England to establish the principle that government should be conducted by the people through their representatives in Parliament and not by an irresponsible king. It cost the lives of hundreds of thousands of Americans and the economic ruin of half our country to abolish human slavery and to establish the fact that "no man is good enough to rule another man without that other man's consent." It is costing untold millions of lives and billions of treasure today to establish, we hope, the principle that small civilized nations shall not be wantonly enslaved by powerful barbarous states, and it cost the blood and suffering of the Hellenic cities to establish the principle that free men might in their own cities and in their own states govern themselves without interference from an alien power. The monuments to fratricidal strife that line the Sacred Way at Delphi are memorials to the birth of this idea; they mark the birth pangs of civic freedom, they are the everlasting monuments to a people that has conferred many benefits upon mankind, but none greater than the idea that a free man "bows the knee to no other man, but to the gods alone."

NOTES

NOTES

All the quotations from Thucydides, unless otherwise noted, are from Jowett's translation (*Thucydides*. Translated into English. By Benjamin Jowett. 2nd ed., revised; Oxford: Oxford University Press, 1900). This translation has become a sort of King James version of Thucydides, and while it contains errors, as does the "authorized" version of the Scriptures, for simple dignity and clarity it remains unmatched.

References to Thucydides' *History* are given simply by book and chapter—e.g., II, 65. The following books are referred to simply by the name of the author—e.g., Bury, Jebb:

Bury, J. B. *The Greek Historians.* London: Macmillan Co., 1909.
Finley, John J., Jr. *Thucydides.* Cambridge, Massachusetts: Harvard University Press, 1942.
Gildersleeve. Miller, C. W. E. *Selections from Brief Mention of Gildersleeve.* Baltimore: The Johns Hopkins University Press, 1930.
Grundy, B. G. *Thucydides and the History of His Age.* London: John Murray, 1911.
Henderson, B. W. *The Great War between Athens and Sparta.* London: Macmillan Co., 1927.
Jebb, Sir Richard C. "The Speeches in Thucydides," *Essays and Addresses.* Cambridge, England: Cambridge University Press, 1907.
Shorey, Paul. "Implicit Ethics and Psychology of Thucydides," *Transactions and Proceedings of the American Philological Association,* XXIV (1893), 66-88.
Zimmern, Alfred E. "Thucydides the Imperialist," *Solon and Croesus.* Oxford: Oxford University Press, 1928.

In translating amounts of money mentioned by Thucydides the following very rough equivalents have been used with the full knowledge that they are inadequate: talent, $1,000; mina, $20; drachma, 20 cents.

NOTES TO CHAPTER I

P. 3   Thucydides states the purpose of his *History* after his Introduction, Book I, Chapter 22; Herodotus, at the beginning of his narrative. The information about the Egyptians' osculatory preferences is in II, 41.

P. 4.   Macaulay's remarks are quoted from his essay on *History.* His scorn for Xenophon is probably directed at Xenophon's picture of Socrates, which gives about as good an idea of the philosopher as one would have of Lincoln if he were to have received all his information from reading the pithy and often vulgar anecdotes that pass as "Lincoln stories."

P. 4. I mean seriously the criticism of Caesar's early writing. The remark of the centurion is in IV, 25.

P. 5. Livy's preface is recommended to students of the writing of history.

P. 6. Tacitus' account of Agricola's death is in Ch. 43. The translation is that of Maurice Hutton in the Loeb Series.

Pp. 8-18. The outline of the history of historical writing is based on H. E. Barnes's article, "History," in the *Encyclopedia Americana.* Barnes regards Polybius as superior to Thucydides because he produced more (which is true but irrelevant) and because he is more profound (which is not true). But it must be acknowledged, however reluctantly, that this article on "History" is a creditable performance.

P. 9. Hegel's identification of the Christian virtues with the various world religions is from the article on "History" in the *Encyclopedia Britannica.*

P. 11. The idea that prophecy is rationed is not mine: I owe it to Professor J. N. Brown, of the State Teachers' College, Denton, Texas.

P. 12. The quotations from Theodore Roosevelt are taken from his address as President of the American Historical Association, delivered at Boston, December 27, 1912, and published in *History as Literature* (New York: Scribner's, 1913). See pp. 10 and 19.

P. 13. Powers, H. H. *The Things Men Fight For.* New York: Macmillan Co., 1916. Of this book Earl Cromer says (*Yale Review,* VI, Jan. 1917, 283): "Nowhere has it (the question of an enduring peace after the first World War) been discussed with greater thoroughness and acumen than in a very able work entitled *The Things Men Fight For,* written by Professor Powers." It is a series of brilliant essays showing how its geographical location led each country of Europe to take one side or the other in the first World War.

P. 14 "The social privileges of the ancien regime . . . ." Langlos and Seignobos, *Introduction to the Study of History.* New York: Henry Holt & Co., 1925, p. 286.

If anyone doubts the statement that the sociologist is interested in generalities and oblivious to particular cases, let him try to secure a monetary contribution for any worthy charitable enterprise from a professional sociologist. I once extracted fifteen dollars from a very vocal sociologist, but it cost me twenty-five.

P. 15. Mr. Ellery Sedgwick pays his compliments to the new scientific historian in his review of G. M. Trevelyan's *Social History of England* in the *Atlantic Monthly,* Vol. 171 (1943), p. 147: "Now Trevelyan turns the flank of these professors of this bogus science. He reminds us that our ancestors were not abstractions. We are not children of want and plenty, or plotted curves of subsistence, but of men and women, bone of our bone."

Pp. 18-20. The drivel about the New History is taken from Barnes, H. E., *The New History and the Social Sciences* (New York: Century Company, 1925). Several of the quotations are from J. H. Robinson.

P. 20. The suggestion of setting-up exercises for the soul was made by G. Stanley Hall, none other.

Pp. 20, 21. The book on war guilt is H. E. Barnes's *Genesis of the World War* (New York: Alfred A. Knopf, 1927). The seven villains were Isvolski, Sazonov, Grand Duke Nicholas, Poincaré, Delcassé, Paul Cambon and Viviani.

It is, of course, rather idle at this time to show how wrong Barnes was in his attack on English foreign policy. Hitler has done that so completely that no further proof should be needed. This point is, however, worth making. Barnes says (*ibid.*, p. 499), "The German Ambassador asked Grey to formulate the conditions according to which England would remain neutral, but Grey refused point blank to do so, though he afterward falsely informed the House of Commons that he had stated those conditions." The German Ambassador says Grey refused to formulate the conditions; Grey says he did formulate them. Therefore Grey lied. In J. S. Ewart's *The Roots and Causes of the Wars*, Vol. I, p. 137, Grey is quoted as saying in the House of Commons that the German Ambassador, speaking on his own personal initiative and without authority, asked for conditions of neutrality. "We did go into that question, and those conditions were stated in the House and made known to the German Ambassador." Barnes, in his assignment of war guilt, finds no place for the statement of Bethmann-Hollweg in the Reichstag on August 4: "We have informed the British Government that as long as Great Britain remains neutral . . . . we will not violate the territorial integrity nor independence of Belgium." (*Op. cit.*, Vol. I, p. 136.)

P. 21. The Hindu fable of the blind man and the elephant is told in verse by J. G. Saxe.

P. 21. "History a fable that men have agreed upon . . . ." Fontenelle, quoted by Allen Johnson; *The Historian and Historical Evidence* (New York: Scribner's, 1926), p. 42.

P. 21. "History an hypothesis to account for things as they are . . . ." G. Crump, *Logic of History* (London: The Society for the Promotion of Christian Knowledge, 1919), p. 11.

P. 21. Dr. Johnson on history, quoted by Macaulay in his *Essay on History*.

P. 21. Tolstoy, in *War and Peace,* Part II, has a long discussion of what history is. It is abundantly clear that he does not hold to the "great-man" theory of history. He pours out the vials of his scorn on that. He indicates in no uncertain terms what history is not. But after long and careful reading I am unable to tell what he thinks it is. Decisions are not reached by individuals like Napoleon and Alexander I but by the soul of the peoples they commanded.

P. 21. Aristotle, *Poetics,* 1451 b.

P. 22. "Two men seem to me to tower above all others: Thucydides and Ranke. The first of these was an active statesman and soldier . . . . the second a scholar and teacher by profession. . . . . Both represent the greatest progress made in their age toward a critical study of history and modern historical research and writing rest on the foundations which they have laid." Hajo Holborn, "The Science of History," *Interpretation of History* (Princeton: Princeton University Press, 1943), p. 63.

P. 24.   Mark Twain's aspersions on geology are contained in *Life on the Mississippi*, Author's National Edition (New York: Harper and Brothers, 1903), p. 151.

Pp. 24, 25.   Droysen on historical criticism, quoted by Allen Johnson, *op. cit.*, p. 133.

P. 25.   Lincoln to "bind up the nation's wounds," Second Inaugural Address, 1865.

Pp. 25, 26.   Von Bülow's *Memoirs*, Vol. II, pp. 474 ff.; and regarding Friedjung, Vol. I, p. 448.

P. 26.   Euripides, Nauk's Edition, fragment 910.

P. 26.   Eduard Meyer, *Forschungen zur alten Geschichte*, II, p. 368.

P. 26.   "A mind devoid of all prepossession . . . ." Allen Johnson, *op. cit.*, p. 160.

P. 26.   The impartial historian may have no friends . . . . Quoted from Lord Acton by C. G. Crump, *op. cit.*, p. 50.

P. 26.   Churchill, who is anything but "mute" (*vide* his six volumes on Marlborough) called Lord Acton "that great mute student," *Marlborough, His Life and Times*, Vol. I, p. 119

P. 27.   Polybius on the duty of a historian, XII, 14.

P. 27.   Gildersleeve on Polybius, *Brief Mention*, p. 209.

P. 27.   The quotation from R. C. Jebb is from his address on Macaulay, delivered at Cambridge, August 10, 1900.

Pp. 28, 29.   Gibbon on John XXIII, *Decline and Fall* edited by Bury, London: Methuen and Co., Sixth Edition, 1912, Vol. VII, p. 289.

P. 29.   Lord Acton on historians' opinions of Macaulay, quoted by J. W. Thompson, *History of Historical Writing* (New York: Macmillan Co., 1942), II, 300. His own opinion of Gibbon, II, 74-90.

P. 29.   Churchill's idea of the value of political history is from his *Marlborough*, Vol. V, p. 433.

P. 29.   Roosevelt, *op. cit.*, p. 18.

P. 30.   "The Beginnings of the Manufacture of the Mousetrap" and "The Potato Crop in Maine" are not the products of my jaundiced fancy. The former is suggested as a subject for historical investigation by Sherman Kent in his *Writing History* (New York: F. S. Crofts and Co., 1941), p. 20. Some years ago a history student in Oberlin College was asked, "How are you getting on in American history?" The disillusioned victim replied, "Well, we've got as far as the potato crop in Maine."

P. 30.   Montaigne on "good histories," *Essays*, II.

P. 30.   A historian who deals with written historical data only may be a very poor judge of human character. One of the leading ancient historians of England told me in the spring of 1939 that there were two reasons why Churchill was not included in the Cabinet: (1) the English people did not trust him; (2) his health was so poor that he was physically unable to carry the responsibilities of office. How can I trust that historian's judgment of Julius Ceasar?

P. 31. Haskell's *Cicero.* H. J. Haskell, Editor of the *Kansas City Star; This Was Cicero* (New York: Alfred A. Knopf, 1942). Professor Alfred R. Bellinger, of Yale, says of it, ". . . . for the general intelligent reader this is likely to be the best life of Cicero, past, present or to come." (*Saturday Review of Literature,* Vol. XXVI, No. 3, Jan. 16, 1943, p. 9.)

P. 31. Mommsen was writing at his desk in the Reichstag while Bismarck was speaking. Mommsen worked on, oblivious of Bismarck's oratory, for some time. Finally the noise broke through Mommsen's absorption and annoyed him till at last he arose in wrath and cried out, "Will not that silly student stop his outrageous noise?" He was so humiliated by his mistake that he never again occupied his seat in the Reichstag.

P. 32. Introduction, I, 1. Real cause of the war, I, 23. Theramenes, VIII, 68. Nicias' hope, V, 16.

P. 33. Introduction, I, 1. War an affair of money, I, 83.

P. 34. Peace at any price, I, 124. The new prevails, I, 71. Simplicity, III, 83. Revenge, IV, 62. Love of honor, II, 44.

P. 34. Macaulay on Thucydides: Trevelyan, G. O., *The Life and Letters of Lord Macaulay,* Appendix to Vol. I. A second note is added: "I am still of the same mind. May 30, 1836." And in his diary, November 25, 1848: "He is the great historian. The others one may hope to match; him, never. . . ."

It would have been interesting to include biography in this survey, for that arch-biographer Dumas Malone, who has presided over the *Dictionary of American Biography,* says that biography is not a science, social, natural or biological, but an art (*Interpretation of History,* Princeton University Press, 1943, p. 144). But two pages later he speaks of Gildersleeve as a "serene Olympian" and says that Saint-Gaudens "immortalized Abraham Lincoln in stone." Gildersleeve was an Olympian, all right, but "serene" is hardly the appropriate adjective, and Saint-Gaudens' Lincoln is cast in bronze.

Autobiography is still further afield, and anyway one would have to consider *Across the Busy Years* (Nicholas Murray Butler, 2 vols., New York: Scribner's, 1939). In reading these volumes I was often impressed by the fact that our country could hardly have survived if it had not pleased an all-wise—albeit inscrutable—Providence to create Nicholas Murray Butler. I was moved to give thanks for our preservation till I remembered that he had not only frequently saved his country but had also created Teachers College. I then abated my thanksgiving for I judged we had just about broken even.

CHAPTER II

P. 37. Wilamowitz points out (*Hermes,* XII) that all knowledge about Thucydides' life is autobiographical.

P. 38. The fact that Thucydides does not mention the third eruption of Aetna while he is discussing that phenomenon (III, 116) is usually taken as evidence that he was not living when it happened (396 B.C.). (Diodorus, XIV, 49.)

P. 39.   Thucydides in exile, V, 26. Acarnania, II, 80-82; III, 105-113. Sparta, I, 10.

P. 40.   The Athenians lived in the country, not in crowded walled cities. In this they were not like the other Greek communities. Just so, the Tuscans alone in Italy lived in isolated villas and country houses. Any observant traveler in Italy as late as 1910 would have noticed this fact. Around Florence the countryside was dotted with houses much like the English or American rural country. It is only since the beginning of the twentieth century that the Italians outside Tuscany have felt it safe to build and live outside the cities. In Greece the isolated rural house is practically unknown today.

P. 40.   Sophocles in Hades, Aristophanes' *Frogs*, 82.

P. 41.   The parody on Christ's words is Zimmern's, p. 91.

P. 41.   The quotation from the Funeral Oration, II, 38.

P. 41.   "For all the Athenians . . . ." Acts, 17, 21.

P. 41.   "The heavens declare . . . ." Psalms, 19, 1.

P. 42.   "Be still . . . ." Psalms, 46, 10.

P. 42.   Herodotus VIII, 8.

P. 43.   Cicero on Socrates, *Tusc. Disp.* V, 4, 10, 11.

P. 43.   Greater devotion to religion in war time. The sales of the Bible reported by Harper have increased twenty-five per cent since Pearl Harbor. Charles M. Seldon's *In His Steps* is selling at the highest rate in twelve years. Harry Emerson Fosdick's *On Being a Real Person* is third as a nonfiction best-seller. *Daily Strength for Daily Needs* has doubled its peacetime sales, and *The Robe* and *The Song of Bernadette,* both long at the top of the list of best-sellers, are both religious novels.

P. 43.   "Wonders are many . . . ." Sophocles *Antigone,* Jebb's translation, 332 ff.

P. 44.   "And a thing there is . . . ." Sophocles *Oedipus Coloneus,* Jebb's translation, 694 ff.

P. 45.   "Surely ye are the people . . . ." Job XII, 2.

P. 46.   "Musty old Japhet," Aristophanes *Clouds,* 985.

P. 46.   The observation about Hermes on the Parthenon frieze is not mine. It belongs to Professor H. H. Powers. For this and many stimulating comments on Greek art see his *Message of Greek Art* (New York: Macmillan Co., 1913).

P. 46.   Zimmern says (p. 92) that the change in Athens between 432 B.C. and 404 B.C. was like the change in England from Elizabeth to Victoria. The comparison is inept. The change was rather more like the change from the England of Shakespeare to the England of Shaw, from spaciousness to littleness, from gaiety to cynicism, from laughter to sneers.

CHAPTER III

P. 51. Character of Themistocles, I, 138.

P. 52. "The most famous victory . . . ." Herodotus IX, 64.

P. 52. When the Delian Confederacy was formed in 477 B.C. it included practically all the islands in the central part of the Aegean except Scyros and perhaps Andros. Aegina and the city of Carystus in Euboea were not members. The islands along the coast of Asia Minor and most of the Greek cities on the mainland were members. So were the Chalcidicean cities and the Islands of Thasos and Samothrace. In the Hellespontine district a majority of the cities belonged. The total number of cities was probably not far from 150. The tribute assessed amounted to $460,000. By 450 B.C. the number of cities included had risen to at least 260, and the annual tribute to $600,000. For the amount of the tribute see I, 96, and II, 13. For a discussion of these amounts see *Cambridge Ancient History,* V, 44 ff.

P. 56. Xenophon *Anabasis,* III, 2, 13.

P. 59. Massacre of Helots, IV, 80.

P. 61. Pericles' strategy, I, 140-144.

P. 63. According to Plutarch (*Lysander* XV, 3) the Lacedaemonians were greatly moved by an actor who declaimed at a banquet the opening chorus from the *Electra* of Euripides (lines 167 ff.), "O daughter of Agamemnon, Electra, to thy rustic house I come." They refused to destroy a city which had produced so great a poet.

CHAPTER IV

Pp. 67-71. Thucydides' outline of early history is contained in I, 2-20.

P. 68. Inferiority of early times, I, 11.

P. 69. Size of ships in Trojan War, I, 10. Length of Trojan War, I, 11.

P. 70. Contrast between Sparta and Athens, I, 10.

P. 71.   Pre-eminent importance of the Peloponnesian War, I, 23.

P. 72. The speeches, I, 22. Thucydides' banishment, V, 26.

P. 73. Cause of the war, I, 23.

P. 75. Speeches of the Corcyraeans and Corinthians, I, 32-43. Inevitability of war, I, 44.

P. 76. Cost of the siege of Potidaea, II, 13. Speeches of the Corinthians and Athenians at Sparta, I, 68-78.

P. 77. Credit for victory at Salamis, I, 74. Inevitable hatred of Lacedaemonians, I, 76. Might makes right, I, 76. Injustice resented, I, 77.

P. 78. Speech of Archidamus, I, 80-85. Speech of Sthenelaidas, I, 86.

P. 79. Lacedaemonians' reasons for declaring war, I, 88. Thucydides' reason for digressions (inaccuracy of Hellanicus), I, 97. Digression on the *pentecontaetia,* I, 89-117.

P. 80. Real cause of the war, I, 118.

P. 81. Careers of Pausanias and Themistocles, I, 128-138.

P. 82.   Final demand of the Lacedaemonians, I, 139.

P. 83.   Pericles' speech, I, 140-144. Pericles says (I, 141), "The confederacy is made up of many races; all the representatives have equal votes, and press their several interests. There follows the usual result, that nothing is ever done properly."

P. 84.   Athenians refuse to submit to compulsion, I, 145. Alleged causes, I, 146.

P. 85.   Statement of historical method, II, 1.

P. 86.   Opening of the war, II, 2. Recurrent sentence, e.g., II, 103, and III, 116.

P. 87.   Incident of the herald, II, 12.

P. 88.   Discomforts of crowded Athens, II, 16, 17. In the present war it was the population of the English cities that was sent to the country, but the discomforts and dissatisfaction resulting were identical.

P. 89.   Dissatisfaction with Pericles, II, 21. Brasidas, II, 25.

Pp. 89 ff.   Pericles' Funeral Oration, II, 35-46.

P. 92.   The plague, II, 47-53.

P. 93.   Effect of the plague, II, 53.

P. 94.   Pericles' characterization of the Athenian Empire, II, 63.

P. 94.   Pericles described, Plutarch *Per.* 8, 5.

P. 96.   Charles XII "a monstrous irrelevancy," Churchill, *Marlborough and His Times,* Vol. III, p. 190.

P. 96.   Uncertainties of fortune, III, 59; VI, 78; I, 78.

P. 97.   Pericles' policy justified, II, 65.

P. 97.   Pericles' death, Plutarch *Pericles,* XXXVIII, 4.

CHAPTER V

P. 101.   Execution of Spartan envoys, II, 67.

Pp. 101 ff.   Siege of Plataea, II, 71-78; III, 20-24; 52-68.

P. 103.   Macan in the *Cambridge Ancient History* (Vol. V, p. 413) makes this curious statement: "His (Thucydides') didactic purpose, the sin which so easily besets him and with which as artist or analyst he should have had nothing to do makes us wonder whether, for example, the siege of Plataea has been featured for purposes of instruction." Of course it is featured because it was dramatically and historically important. And as for "the sin of his didactic purpose" for which Thucydides is here rebuked, if it is a fault at all it is much less of a sin in a historian than to dilate at length as does Macan on topography with which he is unfamiliar and to present his readers with an inaccurate map. See Macan's *Herodotus,* Books VII-IX, Vol. II, pp. 342 ff.

Pp. 103 f.   Operations of Phormio, II, 83-92; 102, 103.

P. 104.   Brasidas' attempt on Piraeus, II, 93. Revolt of Mytilene, III, 2-14; 35-50.

P. 105.   This tendency is noted by Grundy, p. 5. In the case of England, however, consider Baldwin and Chamberlain! Harrow certainly did not fit Baldwin to rule.

P. 106. Cleon's speech, III, 37-40. Diodotus' speech, III, 42-48.

P. 107. Close of Mytilene narrative, III, 49.

P. 108. Capture of Minoa, III, 51.

P. 108. Homer, *Odyssey* VI, 182-185.

Pp. 108 ff. Revolution in Corcyra, III, 81-85.

P. 110. Massacre of the survivors, IV, 46-48.

P. 111. Demosthenes' invasion of Aetolia, III, 98. Demosthenes' defence of Naupactus, III, 102.

Pp. 112 f. Demosthenes' campaign against Ambracia, III, 105-113.

Pp. 113-119. Pylos and Sphacteria, IV, 3-40.

P. 118. The shield found in the Athenian Agora, *Hesperia* VI (1937), p. 348. Pausanias saw these shields (I, 15, 4).

P. 119. Capture of Cythera, IV, 54.

Pp. 120 f.· Demosthenes' Boeotian campaign, IV, 76, 77, 89-100.

P. 121. Athens' failure to support Sitalces, II, 101. Brasidas marches across Thessaly, IV, 78.

P. 122. Brasidas captures Amphipolis, IV, 103-106.

P. 123. The truce, IV, 118.

P. 124. Brasidas and Perdiccas, IV, 125-128. Death of Brasidas and Cleon, V, 10.

P. 125. Later career of Perdiccas, V, 6, 80, 83; VI, 7; VII, 9. Brasidas and Cleon, V, 16.

P. 128. False application of the term "peace," V, 26.

CHAPTER VI

P. 132. Breaking the Peace of Nicias, VI, 105.

Pp. 133-135. Destruction of Melos, V, 84-116.

Pp. 135 f. First expedition to Sicily, III, 86-88, 90, 99, 103, 115, 116.

Pp. 135 ff. The Syracusan expedition is described in VI and VII.

P. 136. Reason for the first expedition to Sicily, III, 86. Second expedition to Sicily, IV, 2, 24, 25, 58-65. Sicilian conference, IV, 58-65.

P. 137. Early history of Sicily, VI, 1-5.

P. 138. Egestan deception of the Athenians, VI, 46. (There exists in Egypt a silk hat which is passed up and down the Nile whenever the King makes a royal progress, each joint owner wearing it in turn when he approaches the Royal Presence and then expediting it forward to precede the Monarch at his next stop. It is known as "THE hat.") Athenian assemblies debating the expedition to Sicily, VI, 8-26.

P. 138. Nicias' motto; Benjamin Franklin revised by Mark Twain.

P. 139. Athens longs for Alcibiades; Aristophanes, *Frogs,* 1425. Aeschylus on Alcibiades; Aristophanes, *Frogs,* 1431-2.

P. 139. Real reason for the Sicilian expedition, VI, 6.

P. 140. Mutilation of the Hermae, VI, 27, 28, 53, 60.

P. 140. Hope for those initiated into the Mysteries; Cicero, *De Legibus,* II, 14, 36.

P. 141. Departure of the fleet, VI, 30-32.

P. 142. Size of the Athenian force, VI, 43. Opinions of the three generals, VI, 47-49.

P. 143. Arrest of Alcibiades, VI, 53.

P. 144. The account of the siege of Syracuse begins, VI, 66.

P. 145. Death of Lamachus, VI, 101. Nicias' illness, VI, 102; VII, 15, 77.

P. 146. Arrival of Gylippus, VI, 104, 105; VII, 1, 2. Alcibiades goes to Sparta, VI, 88-92. Alcibiades' definition of a patriot, VI, 92. Alcibiades advises fortification of Decelea, VI, 91; VII, 18.

P. 147. Harm done by fortification of Decelea, VII, 27.

P. 148. Nicias' letter to the Athenians, VII, 11-15.

P. 149. Athenian naval defeat, VII, 41. Number of reinforcements, VII, 42. Dismay of Syracusans, VII, 42.

P. 150. Growing contempt for Nicias, VII, 42. The night attack, VII, 43, 44.

P. 151. First council of war, VII, 47-49. Eclipse of the moon, VII, 50.

P. 152. List of allies, VII, 57, 58. Speech of Nicias, VII, 69.

P. 153. The noncombatants look on, VII, 71. The false message, VII, 73.

P. 154. The abandoned soldiers, VII, 75.

Pp. 154 f. The days of the retreat are recorded in Book VII as follows: first, second and third days, 78; fourth day, 79; fifth day, 79, 80; sixth day, 80-82; seventh day, 83; eighth day, 84.

Pp. 154 ff. The retreat and surrender, VII, 75-87.

P. 155. Nicias asks mercy for his men but not for himself, VII, 85.

P. 156. Thucydides' judgment of Nicias, VII, 86. Suffering of the prisoners, VII, 87. Thucydides' summary, VII, 87.

P. 157. Incident of Callistratus, Pausanias VII, 16, 4, 5.

P. 157. Euripides' choruses, Plutarch *Nicias,* XXIX.

P. 158. The sailor, Plutarch *Nicias,* XXX.

P. 158. Effect of the disaster on Athens, VIII, 1.

P. 159. Allies revolt, VIII, 2. Alliance of the allies with Persia, VIII, 18; second treaty, VIII, 37; third treaty, VIII, 58.

P. 160. Alcibiades banished from Sparta, VIII, 45.

P. 160. Alcibiades seduces Agis' wife, Plutarch *Alcibiades,* XXIII, 7.

P. 160. Alcibiades' advice to Tissaphernes, VIII, 45.

P. 161. Overthrow of the democracy at Athens, VIII, 63 ff. The revolt of the army at Samos, VIII, 75.

P. 161 f. Thucydides' praise of Alcibiades, VIII, 86.

P. 162. Attempt to betray Athens, VIII, 90. Revolt of Euboea, VIII, 95, 96. Lacedaemonians most convenient enemies, VIII, 96. Government of the Five Thousand, VIII, 97.

P. 163. Thrasybulus' victory, VIII, 105, 106.

P. 164. Battle of Cyzicus, Xenophon *Hellenica,* I, 1, 11-18. Dolorous dispatch, *Hel.* I, 1, 23.

P. 165. Alcibiades returns to Athens, *Hel.* I, 4, 8-21. Battle of

Notium, *Hel.* I, 5, 12-14. Conon's defeat, *Hel.* I, 6, 15-38. Battle of Arginusae Islands, *Hel.* I, 6, 29-38.

P. 165 f. Trial of the generals, *Hel.* I, 7, 1-35.

P. 166. Length of the war, V, 26.

P. 167. Battle of Aegospotami, *Hel.* II, 1, 15-28.

P. 168. Surrender of Athens, *Hel.* II, 2, 1-23. Destruction of the walls, *Hel.* II, 2, 23.

P. 169. Reason for Athens' fall, II, 65.

CHAPTER VII

P. 173. Fancies of the poets etc., I, 21. Colonization of Sicily, VI, 2 ff.

P. 174. Censure of Hellanicus, I, 97. Advantages of the summer-winter chronology, V, 20. Incredible figures suppressed, III, 113. Numbers at the Battle of Mantinea, V, 68.

P. 175. Battle of Locus Castrorum (first battle of Bedriacum), April 19, 69 A.D., between Otho and Vitellius; Tacitus, *Histories,* II, 42.

P. 175. Professor Albert H. Libyer, of the University of Illinois, remarked in his wrath that the people of Boston knew of nothing in the United States west of Barrett Wendell's backyard.

P. 175. Description of the Empire of the Odrysae, II, 97.

P. 175. E. A. Freeman on Thucydides at Syracuse, *History of Sicily,* Vol. III, pp. 589 ff.

P. 176. The Echinades Islands, II, 102. Nicias' superstition, VII, 50. Oracle on the length of the war, V, 26.

P. 177. Earthquakes in 426 B.C., III, 89. Tidal wave at Euboea, III, 89. Lipari Islands, III, 88. Eruptions of Aetna, III, 116.

P. 178. Eclipse of the moon during Syracusan campaign, VII, 50; of the sun, II, 28; IV, 52. (Thucydides is correct in his supposition that a solar eclipse always occurs at the beginning of a lunar month.) Aetolians a primitive people, III, 94. Alcibiades a Spartan name, VIII, 6. Nobles in Samos do not marry commoners, VIII, 21. Futility of death penalty, III, 45.

P. 179. Real cause of the war, I, 23, 88. Cause of Corinth's wealth, I, 13.

P. 179. "Corinth the rich"; Homer, *Iliad* II, 570.

P. 179. Cause of Athens' greatness, I, 2.

P. 180. Peisistratus adorns Athens and imposes tax of five per cent, VI, 54. Fruits of the earth flow into Athens, II, 38. Trade route to Egypt, IV, 53. Selinus and Syracuse self-supporting, VI, 20. Description of Chios, VIII, 24. Resources of Seuthes, II, 97.

P. 181. Children of dead soldiers supported by state, II, 46. Shares in colony sold, II, 27. Rent of allotments in Mytilene, III, 50. Prisoners at Iasus, VIII, 54. Resources of Athens, II, 13. The Parthenon and the Propylaea, II, 13 (see Jebb, p. 440, note 1).

P. 182. Soldiers' pay at Potidaea, III, 17. Tissaphernes and sailors' pay, VIII, 29. Payment of troops requested by allied cities, V, 47.

Extra pay for crews, VI, 31. $150,000 sent to Nicias, VII, 16. $2,000,000 spent by Syracusans, VII, 48. Cost of Sicilian expedition, VI, 31.

P. 183. Loss by fortification of Decelea, VI, 91. Property tax, III, 19. Original tribute $460,000, I, 96; at beginning of war $600,000, II, 13. Five per cent tax, VII, 28, 29. Abolition of pay for officeholders, VIII, 65; arrangement continued, VIII, 97. Senators paid for unexpired term, VIII, 69, 70.

P. 183 f. Murder at Mycalessus, VII, 29, 30.

P. 184. Wars supported by accumulated wealth, I, 141.

P. 185. War a matter of money, I, 83. Eclipse of the sun, II, 28. Liquidation of Helots, IV, 80. Digression on Theseus, II, 15.

Pp. 185 f. Woes occasioned by occupation of Decelea, VII, 27.

P. 186. Size of Athenian navy, III, 17. Teres confused with Tereus, II, 29.

Pp. 186 f. Effects of civil strife, III, 82.

P. 187. Amazement at surrender of Spartans, IV, 40. The plague, II, 47-54. Justification of Pericles' policy, II, 65. Unity of the two wars, V, 26.

Pp. 188 ff. The six digressions: (1) p. 188, history of Sicily, VI, 2-5; (2) p. 188, history of the Odrysian Empire, II, 97; (3) p. 188, history of Macedonia, II, 99; (4) p. 189, Delian Festival, III, 104; (5) p. 189, Harmodius and Aristogeiton, VI, 54-59; (6) p. 190, forces fighting at Syracuse, VII, 57, 58.

P. 189. Homeric *Hymn to Apollo,* II, 146 ff., 165 ff.; III, 104.

P. 191. Dionysius on Thucydides; *Second Letter to Ammaeus, Letter to Pompeius,* ch. 3; *De Compositione,* ch. 22; *De Admiranda vi dicendi in Demosthene,* chs. 1, 9, 10; *De Thucydide* passim.

P. 191. Thucydides' grudge against Athens, *Letter to Pompeius,* 774.

P. 191. Dionysius on Thucydides, *De Thucydide* 24, Shorey's translation.

P. 192. Speeches too brief for hearer to understand, Jebb, p. 423.

P. 192. Grundy on Thucydides, pp. 51, 52.

P. 192 Bury on Thucydides, p. 113.

P. 192. Wilamowitz on Thucydides; Gildersleeve, p. 312.

P. 193. Karl Blind on Thucydides; Gildersleeve, p. 312.

P. 193. For a fine critique of stuff of this kind see Gildersleeve, pp. 253 ff.

P. 193. Venizelos' translation of Thucydides, reviewed by A. W. Gomme, *Classical Review,* LVI (1942), 29-31.

P. 193. Bury's translation of II, 44; see Bury, p. 112.

P. 193. Imitation of Thucydides' style, a speech by Paul Shorey before the Classical Association of the Middle West and South, "A Thucydidean Paraentic Discourse," *Classical Journal,* XXIII (1927-28), 485.

P. 194. Celsus, *De Medicina,* praef, 8.

P. 194. That Thucydides is one of Hippocrates' disciples, at least a patient, is the thesis of C. N. Cochrane, *Thucydides and the Science of History* (Oxford: Oxford University Press, 1929).

P. 194. Professor John H. Finley, Jr., is convinced (and convincing) that Thucydides owes much of his style to Antiphon; pp. 266, 280 ff.

P. 195. The five early Roman historians, all of whom wrote in Greek: Q. Fabius Pictor, L. Cincius Alimentus, A. Postumus Albinus, C. Acilius, P. Scipio (son of the elder Africanus).

P. 195. "A vigorous mind . . . ." Jebb, p. 424.

P. 195. Macaulay thought the speeches a blemish (*Essay on History*): "The speeches of Thucydides are neither preceded nor followed by anything with which they harmonize. They give to the whole book something of the grotesque character of those Chinese pleasure gardens in which perpendicular rocks of granite start up in the midst of a soft green plain. Invention is shocking where truth is in such close juxtaposition with it."

P. 195. Gildersleeve, p. 92.

P. 196. The eight speeches Thucydides may have heard are: (1) envoys of Corcyra at Athens, 433 B.C., I, 32-36; (2) envoys of Corinth at Athens, 433 B.C., I, 37-43; (3) Pericles to the Athenian Assembly, 432 B.C., I, 140-144; (4) Pericles' Funeral Oration, Athens, 431 B.C., II, 35-46; (5) Pericles to the Athenian Assembly, 430 B.C., II, 60-64; (6) Cleon to the Athenian Assembly, 427 B.C., III, 37-40; (7) Diodotus to the Athenian Assembly, 427 B.C., III, 42-48; (8) Lacedaemonian envoys at Athens, 425 B.C., IV, 17-20.

P. 196. Thucydides on the speeches, 1, 22.

P. 196. List of events anticipated in the speeches, Jebb, pp. 392 ff. Tragic irony, Jebb, p. 399.

P. 197. πρόφασις, 1, 23.

P. 197. The *History* arranged as a play by Ulrici, Jebb, p. 436, note 2.

P. 198. The Funeral Oration, II, 35-46. The plague, II, 47-54. The Melian episode, V, 84-116. The Sicilian expedition, VI, VII.

P. 198. "He hath put down . . . ." Luke I, 52.

P. 198. Delights of rural life, II, 15. Recollections of past splendor, VII, 75. Anecdotes: Spartan ambassador, 11, 12; Brasidas at Pylos, IV, 12; jibe at captives, VII, 40; Ambraciot's dismay, III, 113.

P. 198. Macaulay on Thucydides; Trevelyan, *Life of Macaulay*, Vol. I, p. 449.

P. 199. King James's detention quoted by Jebb in an address on Macaulay delivered at Cambridge, August 10, 1900. Published by the Cambridge University Press, 1900.

P. 200. The unwritten speech, VII, 69.

P. 200. Color of Caesar's eyes, *nigris vegetisque* (keen black), Suetonius, *Julius Caesar*, 45.

Pp. 200 f. Archidamus, I, 79; Thrasybulus, VIII, 73; Leon, VIII, 73; Theramenes, VIII, 68.

P. 201. Hermocrates, VI, 72. Men lost by Demosthenes, III, 98.

Pp. 201 f. Brasidas a good speaker, IV, 84; favored war, V, 16;

reasonable, IV, 108; his fame attracts allies, IV, 81.

Pp. 202 f.   Sketch of Antiphon, VIII, 68.

P. 203.   Alcibiades, VI, 15.

P. 204.   Alcibiades deserves well of the state, VIII, 86.

Pp. 204 f.   Character of Nicias, V, 16; influenced by omens, VII, 50; his epitaph, VII, 86; Bury thinks this is irony, p. 120.

P. 206.   Ostracism of Hyperbolus, VIII, 73.

Pp. 206 f.   Cleon, violent citizen, III, 36; "object of mistrust," IV, 27; favors war, V, 16; desire for his defeat, IV, 28.

P. 207.   Cleon's campaign in Chalcidice, V, 2 ff.

P. 207.   Discussion of Cleon's campaign and the tribute lists, *Cambridge Ancient History*, Vol. V, p. 248.

P. 208.   Character of Themistocles, I, 138.

Pp. 208 f.   Character of Pericles, II, 65. "All things decay. . . ." II, 64.

P. 209.   Athenians ignorant of Sicily, VI, 1; of their own history, I, 20.

P. 210.   Stupidity of Scythians, II, 97. Hybris, II, 65. Knaves preferred to fools, III, 82. Unreflecting hope, IV, 108. Hankering for ideal state, III, 38. Every man a judge of disease, II, 48. Sophocles' confusion of Teres and Tereus, II, 29 (see p. 186). Incident of the arrow, IV, 40.

P. 211.   Massacre at Mycalessus, VII, 30. Three uses of $\tau o \iota$: II, 41; III, 40; VII, 77.

P. 211.   "A quiver . . . ." Gildersleeve, p. 257.

P. 211.   Nicias practices every virtue, VII, 86. Alcibiades appreciates himself, VI, 16.

P. 212.   Democracies amenable to fear, VIII, 1. Approval of the Five Thousand, VIII, 97.

P. 212.   Thucydides inspired Treitschke; Gildersleeve, p. 315.

P. 212.   "Thucydides' state embodies power . . . ." Letter from Sir Richard Livingstone, May 25, 1943.

P. 212.   Athens' empire a tyranny, II, 63. Naxos enslaved, I, 98. ". . . . to an imperial city," VI, 85. To be taken for an Athenian a compliment, VII, 63. Athens, school of Hellas, II, 41. Sympathies of Hellas, I, 119; II, 8, 63. Contemptuous wisdom, I, 122.

P. 213.)   Unbreakable spirit of Athens, II, 65. Athens alone superior to her reputation, II, 41. Murder of Hippias, III, 34. Mutilators of the Hermae, VI, 60. Justice doubtful, benefits certain, VII, 60.

P. 214.   Antiphon, VIII, 68.

P. 214.   "Arete" (virtue) is efficiency, getting things done, Gildersleeve, p. 314.

P. 214.   ". . . . because of me no Athenian has put on mourning," Plutarch, *Pericles* XXXVIII.

P. 214.   Simplicity a large element of noble natures, III, 83.

P. 215.   Attempt to save Amphipolis, IV, 102-106. Chance belies calculations, I, 140. ". . . . an everlasting possession," I, 22.

P. 216.   Thucydides hears Herodotus, Marcellinus' *Life of Thucydides*, 54.

P. 216. Thucydides nearer the twentieth century, Bury, *History of Greece*, p. 399.

P. 216. Thucydides a scientific historian. Joseph Gavorse, in his introduction to Crawley's translation of the *History* (Modern Library edition, p. xv), refuses to regard Thucydides as a scientific historian because the printing press was not in use when he wrote. To make a historian's quality depend on mechanical inventions would discredit most of the nineteenth-century historians because they were denied the benefit of the phonograph and the radio.

P. 218. The three failings, III, 40. "If right or wrong . . . ." III, 40. The Plataeans' speech, III, 59.

P. 219. "The two things . . . ." III, 42. "Dullness and modesty . . . ." III, 37. The eagerness of an exile, VI, 92. "The true enemies . . . ." VI, 92. "The powerful exact . . . ." V, 89.

CHAPTER VIII

This chapter was written in March, 1943, and since it has not been altered it will not be characterized by "that unerring spirit of prophecy that follows the event." Since it was written Sir Richard Livingstone's edition of Thucydides has appeared in the *World's Classics* (see Bibliography). He compares ancient Greece to modern Europe, "tearing itself to pieces in wars that it did not desire but could not avoid." I regret that I could not have had the opportunity to read his excellent introduction before writing this chapter.

P. 223. Aristotle on history and poetry, *Poetics* 1451 b.

P. 224. Uncertainties of war, I, 140; III, 59; I, 78; I, 122. (In a speech May 19, 1943, Churchill said, "War is full of surprises. A false step, a wrong direction of strategic effort . . . . might give the common enemy the power to confront us with new and hideous facts." Karl von Klausewitz says, "War is the province of chance. In no other sphere of human activity has such a margin to be left for the intruder because war is in such constant contact with it. It increases the uncertainty of every circumstance and deranges the course of events.") Chance belies calculation, I, 140.

P. 225. Gildersleeve's "parallel bars," *Atlantic Monthly*, Vol. 80 (1897), p. 330.

P. 225. Long days in the north, Homer *Odyssey* X, 82-86.

P. 226. Water heavy in the north, Tacitus *Agricola* 10.

P. 226. Isaiah's Egypt, *Isaiah* 36, 6.

P. 227. Brasidas' refusal to surrender Scione, IV, 122.

P. 228. Loss of Solygeia, IV, 44.

P. 228. Losses at Boston and Lexington; Esther Forbes, *Paul Revere and the World He Lived In* (Boston: Houghton and Mifflin, 1942), pp. 151-163; 269.

P. 228. Big Bethel; D. S. Freeman, *Lee's Lieutenants* (New York: Scribner's, 1942), Vol. I, p. 18.

P. 229. Contrast of an empire and a league, I, 141.

P. 230. Contrast between Athenians and Lacedaemonians, I, 70.

P. 231.   Mutual fear, III, 11, 12.

P. 232.   Weaker and stronger, I, 76.   Athens a tyranny, II, 63. Naxos enslaved, I, 98.

P. 232.   The Melian debate, V, 86-112.   See Hutton's essay on "Thucydides and History" in his *Many Minds* (London: Hodder and Stoughton, undated), pp. 54 ff.

P. 234.   Feeling against Athens, II, 9.

P. 235.   Reason for Theban attack on Plataea, II, 2.   Peace of Nicias no peace, V, 26.

P. 236.   Nicias on soldiers' votes, VII, 48.

P. 237.   Baldwin's exact words were (*Official Reports,* Fifth Series, Parliamentary Debates, Commons, for November 12, 1936): "Suppose I had gone to the country and had said that Germany was re-arming and that we must re-arm, does anyone think that this pacific democracy would have rallied to that cry at that moment?   I cannot think of anything that would have made the loss of the election, from my point of view, more certain."

P. 237.   Cleon a hardheaded businessman, Zimmern, p. 94.

P. 237.   Comparison by E. J. Feigin, Chicago *Sun,* July 21, 1943.

P. 237.   Alcibiades and Pétain, VI, 92.

Pp. 237 f.   Deportation of Aeginetans, II, 27.   Murder of Melians, V, 116.

P. 238.   Forced liberty for Acanthus, IV, 87.

P. 239.   Alleged and real reasons for attack on Sicily, VI, 6.

P. 239.   Cyrus' promise of support to Lysander, Xenophon *Hellenica* I, 5, 3.

P. 241.   Estimates on state support vary considerably.   The matter is discussed by A. Zimmern, *The Greek Commonwealth,* pp. 170 ff. Following Wilamowitz, he gives these figures: male adults in Athens between 35,000 and 44,000; employed by the State, Soldiers, 6,000; civil servants 1,500; jurors, 6,000, a total of 13,500, or one out of every three or four citizens.

P. 241.   Sicily an inexhaustible mine, VI, 24.

P. 241.   Plato's ideas on state employment, *Gorgias* 515; Aristotle's ideas, *Constitution of Athens* 27, 3; *Politics* IV, 6; VI, 2.

P. 242.   Retaliation, III, 84.   Desire of Athens' allies to revolt, VIII, 2.

P. 243.   War decided by resources, I, 83.

P. 244.   Sudden end of war.   Adcock, *Cambridge Ancient History,* V, 361.

P. 244.   Difficulty of peace, I, 82.

P. 245.   Madame Chiang Kai-shek in an address at Madison Square Garden, New York, New York, March 2, 1943; see *The New York Times,* March 3, 1943, p. 12.

P. 245.   Horrors of civil strife, III, 82.

P. 246.   Thucydides' description of the effects of civil strife is parallelled by Betty Wason's description of conditions in occupied Greece: "Anarchy rules in occupied Greece.   Murder is praised so long as it is the murder of the enemy.   Theft may be an act of great courage. Lying about one's harvest is a matter of humanitarianism. Everything is reversed, for there is only one law—to make life as difficult as possible for the army of occupation." Betty Wason, *Miracle in Hellas* (New York: Macmillan Co., 1943), p. 122.

P. 246. Bravery of the Syracusans, VIII, 96.

P. 247. Stubborn resistance of Athens, II, 65. Discouragement of the Spartans, IV, 55. Heroism of Athenians, II, 42.

P. 248. W. S. Churchill, *Blood, Sweat and Tears* (London: Putnam, 1941): "We shall fight them . . . ." House of Commons, June 4, 1940 (p. 297); ". . . . blood, toil, tears and sweat," House of Commons, May 13, 1940 (p. 276).

P. 248. Greatest men least depressed, II, 64.

P. 249. Epigram of Lysander in Delphi; see *Fouilles de Delphes*, III, 1, pp. 24 ff. Pauly-Wissowa, Suppl. IV, 1209 ff. Translated by Frances P. Lord.

P. 249. "All the stained glass . . . ." Yes, I am aware of the Five Sisters at York and the Parish Church at Fairford.

P. 250. "No man good enough . . . ." Lincoln.

P. 250. "Bow the knee . . . ." Xenophon *Anabasis* III, 2, 13.

BIBLIOGRAPHY

BIBLIOGRAPHY

For a full bibliography of the Peloponnesian War the reader is referred to the *Cambridge Ancient History*, Vol. V, pp. 489-529. A well selected bibliography is contained in John H. Finley, Jr's., *Thucydides*, pp. 329-332.

TRANSLATIONS INTO ENGLISH

The best translation, in my opinion, is still that of Benjamin Jowett. A second edition, revised, was issued by the Oxford University Press in 1900. The index compiled by Matthew Knight for the edition of 1883 is exceedingly useful.

The translation by C. F. Smith, in the Loeb Library, 1919-1922, in spite of the able corrective work of the editors of the Series, is exasperatingly disappointing.

The Oxford University Press has just issued (1943), in the *World's Classics,* a translation of Thucydides edited by Sir Richard W. Livingstone. Crawley's translation forms the basis of this edition, but there are many minor changes; some passages are the work of Sir Richard himself, and the Funeral Speech (II, 35-46) is given in Sir Alfred Zimmern's version. Some unimportant passages and the entire eighth book are omitted. Brief notes are added which greatly help the reader who has no classical background. The brief introduction (twenty pages) is one of the best essays on Thucydides that I know. One who has read this introduction and the abridged translation has all the best of Thucydides.

BOOKS AND ESSAYS ON THUCYDIDES

IN GERMAN

Das Geschichtwerk des Thucydides, by E. Schwartz (Bonn, 1919), is in my opinion an example of how historical criticism should not be done. A historian should not be placed on a witness stand where every statement is examined not in the light of what it is obviously intended to mean but what it can, by violent distortion, be made to imply.

Aristoteles und Athen, by Ulrich von Wilamowitz-Moellendorf (Göttingen, 1893), contains two stimulating passages about Thucydides (I, pp. 99-120; II, pp. 289-303). His *ex cathedra* statements remind me of Gildersleeve's remark that "the century began with the imperial Boeck and closed with the imperious Wilamowitz."

Thucydides und die Entstehung der Wissenschaftlichen Geschichtsschreibung, by Eduard Meyer (Vienna and Leipsig, 1913), is a work that only he could have written. Whatever one may think of German critical methods, it is an undoubted fact that Eduard Meyer brings to the interpretation of ancient history a breadth of knowledge and a store of information truly appalling. He was a great scholar. When he speaks it is well to listen.

274 THUCYDIDES AND THE WORLD WAR

IN ENGLISH

The best commentary on the Peloponnesian War is Volume V of the *Cambridge Ancient History* (Cambridge University Press, 1927). The chapter on Herodotus and Thucydides is not so good as it should be, considering that it is the work of R. W. Macan.

The Great War between Athens and Sparta, by B. H. Henderson (London: Macmillan Co., 1927), is an excellent commentary.

Thucydides and the History of his Age, by G. B. Grundy (London: John Murray, 1911), is excellent for topographical details (in spite of the fact that I believe him mistaken about the topography of Pylos and Sphacteria). He is the one English writer who has made himself thoroughly familiar by autopsy with the sites of the Greek battlefields.

Thucydides Mythistoricus, by F. M. Cornford (London: Arnold, 1907) is probably the worst book on Thucydides in English.

Clio Enthroned, by W. R. M. Lamb (Cambridge University Press, 1914) is one of the protests provoked by Cornford's effort.

Thucydides and the Science of History, by C. N. Cochrane (Oxford University Press, 1929). Every phase of Thucydides' *History* has been examined by "simple interrogation and by torture" to prove the influence of medical science on the historian. The result, in my opinion, is an incorrect diagnosis greatly endangering the reputation of the physician in charge.

Thucydides, a Study in Historical Reality, by C. F. Abbott (London: Routledge, 1925). An appreciative study of the great author.

Thucydides, by John H. Finley, Jr. (Harvard University Press, 1942). An excellent book, clear and sane. I find it hard to forgive Professor Finley for saying better than I possibly could so many things I should like to have said. I am especially grateful to him for his essay on "The Unity of Thucydides' History," *Harvard Studies in Classical Philology,* Supplementary Volume I (1940), pp. 255-298. This has, I hope, put an end to the fruitless endeavor to demonstrate the patchwork composition of the *History.*

The Ancient Greek Historians, by J. B. Bury (London: Macmillan and Co., 1909). The essay on Thucydides is not one of Bury's best efforts. It gives the impression of being written under contract to fill a lecture appointment.

"Thucydides the Imperialist," by A. E. Zimmern, in *Solon and Croesus* (Oxford University Press, 1928). Suggestive.

Thucydides, Political Philosopher, by W. W. Jaeger, in *Paideia* I, Book 2, Chapter 6 (Oxford University Press, 1939). A very thoughtful and competent discussion of the subject.

The Greek Commonwealth, by A. E. Zimmern (Oxford University Press, fourth edition, 1924). A book of real genius. A discussion of Athenian civilization in the light of Pericles' Funeral Oration. No recent book on the subject is so stimulating or shows so fresh a point of view.

"Implicit Ethics and Psychology in Thucydides," by Paul Shorey,

Transactions of the American Philological Association (1893), pp. 66-68. A brilliant piece of work, remarkable for its insight and analysis.

"The Speeches in Thucydides," by Sir Richard C. Jebb, *Essays and Addresses* (Cambridge University Press, 1907). In my opinion this is the best article on the speeches yet written. It is characterized by Sir Richard's graceful style, masterful scholarship and a sanity and literary taste unmatched.

INDICES

INDEX I

Passages Referred to in Thucydides' *History*

BOOK I		BOOK II	
Chapters	*Page*	*Chapters*	*Page*
2	179	1	85
2-20	67-71	2	86, 235
10	38	8	212, 234
13	179		
20	209	11	212
21	173	12	87,198
22	3, 72, 197, 215	13	76, 181, 183
23	71, 73, 197	15	185, 198
24	32	16, 17	88
32-36	196	21	89
32-43	75	25	89
37-43	196	27	181, 237
67-78	76	28	178, 185
70	230	29	186, 210
71	34	35-46	90, 196, 198
76	232	38	41, 180
78	96, 224	41	211-213
79	200	42	247
80-85	78	44	34, 193
82	244	46	181
83	33, 185, 243	47-53	93, 187, 198
86	78	48	210
88	79	53	93
89-117	79	60-64	196
90	34	63	94, 212, 232
96	37, 183	64	209
97	79, 174	65	97, 167, 187, 208,
98	212, 232		210, 213, 247
112	212	67	101
118	80	70-78	101
119, 122	212	80	39
124	34	83-92	103
127-138	81	93	104
138	34, 51, 208	97	175, 180, 188, 210
139	82	99	188
140	215, 224, 229	101	121
140-144	83, 196	102	175
141	83, 184	102, 103	103

Book III

Chapters	Page
2-14	104
11, 12	231
17	182, 186
19	183
20-24	101
34	213
35-50	104
36	206
37	219
37-40	106, 196
39	210
40, 41	218
42	219
42-48	106, 196
45	178
49	107
50	181
51	108
52-68	101
59	96, 218, 224
81-85	108
82	186, 210, 245
83	34, 214
84	242
86	136
86-88	135
88, 89	177
90	135
94	178
98	111, 201
99	135
102	111
103	135
104	189
105	38
105-113	112
113	174, 198
115	135
116	38, 135, 177

Book IV

Chapters	Page
2	136
3-40	113-119
12	198
17-20	196
24, 25	136

Chapters	Page
27	206
28	207
40	187, 198, 210
44	228
46-48	110
52	178
53	180
54	119
55	247
58-65	136
62	34
76, 77	120
78	121
80	59, 185
81, 84	201
87	238
89-100	120, 121
102-106	122, 215
108	201, 210
118	123
122	227
125-128	124

Book V

Chapters	Page
2	207
6	125
10	124
16	125, 201, 204, 207
20	174
26	72, 165, 176, 187, 235
47	182
68	174
80, 83	125
84-116	133-135, 198, 232
89	219
116	237

Book VI

Chapters	Page
1	209
1-5	137
2	173
2-5	188
6	139, 239
7	125
8-26	138
12	203
13	33

Chapters	Page
15	203
16	211
20	180
24	241
27, 28	140
31	141, 182
32	141
43	142
46	138
47-49	142
53	140, 143
54	180
54-59	189
60	140, 213
66	144
72	201
78	96
85	212
88-92	146
91	146, 183
92	146, 219, 237
101, 102	145
104	146
105	131, 146

BOOK VII

Chapters	Page
1, 2	146
9	125
11-15	148
15	145
16	182
18	146
27	147, 186
28, 29	183
30	183, 211
41	149
42	149, 150
43, 44	150
47-49	151

Chapters	Page
48	182, 236
50	151, 176, 178, 204
57, 58	152, 189
63	212
68	34
69	152, 200
71	153
73	153, 246
75	154, 198
75-87	154
77	145, 211
78-81, 83, 84	154
86	156, 204, 211
87, 88	156

BOOK VIII

Chapters	Page
1	158, 212
2	159, 242
6	178
18	159
21	178
24	180
29	182
37	159
45	160
54	181
58	156
63	161
65	183
68	200, 214
69, 70	183
73	200, 206
75	161
86	161, 204
90	162, 202
95	162
96	162, 246
97	162, 183, 212
106	163

INDEX II

Other Classical References

Author   *Page*

ARISTOPHANES—
    Clouds 985 46
    Frogs 82 40
    967 32
    1425, 1431 139
    Peace 230 125
ARISTOTLE—
    Constitution of Athens 27, 3 241
    Poetics 1451b 21, 223
    Politics IV, 6; VI, 2 241
CAESAR, *Gallic War* IV, 25 4
CELSUS, Preface 8 194
CICERO—
    De Legibus II, 14, 36 140
    Tusc. Disp. V, 4, 10 43
DIODORUS, XIV, 49 38
DIONYSIUS—
    Letter to Pompeius 774 191
    De Thucydide 24 191
EURIPIDES, Fragment 910 26
HERODOTUS—
    I, 1; II, 41 4
    VIII, 8 42
    IX, 64 52
HOMER—
    Hymn to Apollo 189
    Iliad II, 570 179
    Odyssey VI, 182 108
    X, 82 225
LIVY, Preface 4
MARCELLINUS, 54 216
PAUSANIAS—
    I, 15, 4 118
    VII, 16, 4 157
PLATO, *Gorgias* 515 241
PLUTARCH—
    Alcibiades XXIII, 7 160
    Lysander XV, 3 63
    Nicias XXIX 157
    XXX 158
    Pericles XXXVIII 98, 214
POLYBIUS, XII, 14 27
SOPHOCLES—
    Antigone 332 43
    Oedipus Coloneus 694 44

Author	Page
SUETONIUS, *Julius Caesar* 45	200
TACITUS—	
Agricola 10	226
43	6
Histories II, 42	175
XENOPHON—	
Anabasis III, 2, 13	56, 250
Hellenica	
I, 1, 11-18, 23	164
I, 4, 8-21	165
I, 5, 3	240
I, 5, 12-14	165
I, 6, 15-38, 29-38	165
I, 7, 1-35	165
II, 1, 15-28	167
II, 2, 1-23	168

INDEX III

The references are to pages. When a geographical place name is followed by a figure and a letter (e.g., 2.A), these refer to its location on the map. T. stands for Thucydides, and Pel. for Peloponnesian.

Abdera, 2.O, Euripides' plays popular in, 39.

Abydos, 2.R, Pel. fleet goes to, 162.

Acanthus, 2.N, forcible freedom of, 238.

Acarnania, T.'s knowledge of topography of, 39; expedition against, 104; Athens' influence paramount, 119.

Achelous, 4.L, river of Acarnania, 175.

Acton, Lord, on impartial historians, 26; on the "greatest historian," 29.

Adeimantus, Athenian admiral defeated at Aegospotami, 167.

Aegean, Thasos most beautiful island of, 37; islands of, 52; north end of, 53; products of East came across, 56; Athenian merchant fleet sailed through, 56; Minos' empire large part of, 67; inhabitants largely Carians, 67; scene shifts to northwest Aegean, 75; race across, 107.

Aegina, 5.N, island of, 57; most active commercial rival, 57; theater of war, 62; coast lost to Athens, 62; conquest of, 80; relief of, 83; captured and held, 119; refugees from, 167.

Aegospotami, 2.R, defeat at, 63; admirals in command at, 96; ships beached at, 166.

Aeolus, 4.D, (Lipari Islands), troops land on island of, 135.

Aeschylus, on Alcibiades, 139.

Aetna, 5.D, eruptions of, 177.

Aetolia, northwestern Greece, 61; Demosthenes' expedition through, 111; language unintelligible, 178.

Agricola, Julius, Tacitus' account of his death, 6; economic account of death, 12; geographic account, 13; sociological account, 14; psychological account, 15; Freudian account, 17.

Alcibiades, a possible successor to Themistocles and Pericles, 127; efforts to form Pel. league, 131; general against Syracuse, 138; character, 139; persuades Athenians to attack Syracuse, 139; charged with profaning mysteries, 140; ideas for campaign against Syracuse, 142; recalled and banished, 143; goes to Sparta, 146; prominent in last phase of war, 158; seduces King Agis' wife, 160; leaves Sparta, 160; dealings with Tissaphernes, 160; efforts to secure return to Athens, 161; self-seeking, 161; conspicuous service to Athens, 161, 204; recalled, 161; visit to Tissaphernes, 163; victory at Cyzicus, 164; his success, 164; returns to Athens, 165; retires to Hellespont, 165; warns Athenians at Aegospotami, 167; a Spartan name, 178; T.'s estimate of him, 203.

Alexander of Macedon, sees weakness of Persia, 227.

Ambracia, Acarnanians not willing to destroy, 113; Athens' influence paramount in, 119.

Amphipolis, 1.N, T.'s descent upon, 37; Brasidas at gates of, 37, 122; Brasidas' terms of surrender, 38; capitulation of, 38; access to sea blocked, 38; T.'s command at, 72; important Athenian city, 122; T. sails for, 123; Cleon makes attack on, 124; almost takes it, 124; public funeral for Cleon at, 124; attempt to recapture, 125; Athens to have back, 126.

Anaxagoras, contemporary of T., 37; friend of Pericles, 45; exiled, 46.

Antiphon, Athenian orator, plots against democracy, 161; executed, 162; influence on T.'s style, 194; praised by T., 202; ability admired, 214.

Aphetae, Skyllias' leap into sea at, 42.

Archidamus, urges moderation, 78; praised by T., 201.

Arginusae Islands, 4.R, victory at, 63; admirals executed after, 96; defeat of Pel. fleet, 165.

Argos, 5.M, not in Pel. league, 60; engagements center around, 62; organizes confederacy with Athens, 62; in alliance with Corinth, 62; Themistocles hounded out of, 82; Chrysis high priestess of, 86; Perdiccas joins Argos against Athens, 125; truce with Spartans expires, 126, 131; Corinth attempts to replace Sparta with Argos, 131; war with Epidaurus, 131; assisted by Athens, 131.

Aristides, assesses Delian tribute, 183.

Aristophanes, opinion of Theramenes, 32; T.'s contemporary, 39; war in his plays, 40; praises "good old times," 43, 45; criticizes Euripides, 45; compares Brasidas and Cleon to pestles, 125; on Alcibiades, 139.

Aristotle, history inferior to poetry, 21, 223; discovers political character of human race, 56; T.'s *History* answers his definition of poetry, 220; condemns state employment, 241.

Artemisium, 3.N, 10 miles from Aphetae, 42; Herodotus' opinion of legend, 42.

Assinarus, 6.E, river near Syracuse where Nicias surrendered, 157.

Athena, on east pediment of Parthenon, 46; gold on statue worth $40,000, 181.

Athens, 5.N, and Athenians, Amphipolis outpost of, 37; T.'s absence from, 38; fall of, 38; height of her power, 38; T.'s banishment from, 39; literary activity, 39; intellectual life of, 40; life at, 40; cramped conditions of, 40; loses whole world, 41; of 424-404 B.C., 41; T. left behind, 41; of Pericles' Funeral Oration, 41; their curiosity, 41; people devoted to religion, 43; triremes of, 44; T. not remain here during whole war, 45; Sophocles won prizes at, 46; return of T. to, 46; their conservatism, 46; spirit of new generation, 46; Acropolis buildings gain immortality for, 46; freed by Euripides, 46; defenseless, 47; mistakes ruined, 47; accept Themistocles' advice, 51; Spartans leave field to, 51; leadership of, 52; in league, 52; money employed by, 53; treasury moved to, 54; in control of Greek cities, 54; islands paying no tribute to, 54; islands subject to, 54; at call of, 55; had everything, 55; legal questions referred to, 55; expense of going to, 55; treasury removed to, 56; empire controlled by, 56; people of, 56; markets, 56; islands subject to, 56; manufactures of, 57; forced to abandon Boeotia, 57; mistress of naval empire, 58; beautification of, 58; Lacedaemonians opposed to, 58; maritime empire, 60; like Corinth, 60; jealousy of Corinth, 60; mistress of empire, 60; Corcyra appeals to, 60; wins first round, 61; peace satisfactory to, 61; under Alcibiades, 62; begins expedition against Syracuse, 62; breaks peace, 62; revolution in, 63; Euboea revolts, 63; fights on, 63; capitulates, 63; spared, 63; recently given up custom of wearing arms, 68; belief about tyrannicides, 70; contrast between Sparta and, 70; ruin of, 71; Corcyra appeals to, 74, 75; Corinthians send embassy to, 75; Spartans threaten, 76; contravention of treaty between Sparta and, 76; cost of siege to, 76; dispute between Corinth and, 76; Corinth's grievances against, 76; unpopularity, 77, 87; service rendered to Hellas, 77; cases of law brought to, 77; might makes right, 77; loss of Boeotia to, 80; Spartans send embassies to, 81; demands on, 81; Pericles first man of his day at, 83; quick decisions of, 83; dispute between Corinth and, 84; negotiations between Sparta and, 84; irreconcilable conflict and wreck, 84; triumph of expediency, 85; Pythodorus' archonship at, 86; Plataea ally of, 86; hostile feeling toward, 87; Archidamus sends herald to, 87; early history of, 88; sends naval expedition to Pel. coast, 89; first expedition sent to Peloponnesus, 89; solemn ceremony at, 89; glorification of, 90; Funeral Oration at, 90; reason for greatness, 90; imperial city of, 90; school of Hellas, 91; memory of greatness, 91; illumination of, 92; plague in, 93; sympathies of mankind with, 95; treatment of allies justified, 95; plague at, 96; victory for, 96; disasters heaped on, 96; greatness of Periclean, 97; Phormio returns to, 104; Phormio most able admiral of, 104; delegation from Lesbos sent to, 105; Pericles most influential citizen of, 105; fate of Oligarchs decided by, 109; Demosthenes greatest general of, 111; Demosthenes' troops sent to, 111; controls Ambracia, 113; shield of Brasidas taken to, 115; Cleon returns to, 117; Spartans send emissaries to, 119; Perdiccas becomes ally of, 121; news of disaster reaches, 123; sentiment for peace at, 123; Perdiccas joins combination against, 125; retains Nisaea and Minoa on Megarean coast, 126; assists Argos, 132; Corinthians declare war on, 132; does not declare war on Sparta, 132; allies desert, 159; Alcibiades returns to, 165; loses empire, 168; prosperity due to poor soil and extension of citizenship, 179; dependent economically on empire, 180; soldiers' children state-supported, 181; resources at beginning of war, 181; T. proud of, 213; central position, 229; Ionic race, 229; contrast with Sparta, 230; aggressors, 231; like Germans, 231; imperial city, 232; treatment of Melians, 232; citizens free, 233; unpopular, 234; population withdraws to city, 234; employment of citizens by state, 241; predatory, 241; desire of allies to revolt, 242; brave in adversity, 246.

Athos, 2.O, great mountain, 76.
Attica, population of, 40; inhabitants of, 61; fortified area of, 61; poor soil of, 67; Spartans promise to invade, 76; Peloponnesus sends army to ravage, 89; annual invasion of, 89; second invasion of, 89; not ravaged by Spartans, 101; Plataeans resist, 102; Spartans delay at, 114.
Augustine, Saint, writer of "Christian epic," 8.
Baldwin, Stanley, like Nicias, 108, 236.
Baltic States, population withdrawn, 234.
Barnes, Harry E., selects himself to determine cause of World War I, 20; calls Sir Edward Grey a liar, 20.
Big Bethel, battle of, 228.
Blind, Karl, on T.'s style, 193.
Boeotia, people of, allies of Lacedaemonians, 60; refuses to join league, 62; rich lands of, 67; loss of, 80; preparations for subjugation of, 120; attacked from west, 120; Demosthenes marches through, 120; Boeotia and Corinth, Sparta's most powerful allies, 131.
Bosporus, 1.V, grain came through, 56.
Boston Massacre, carnage at, 228.
Brasidas, saves Methone, 89; threatens Piraeus, 104; raids Salamis, 104; wounded at Pylos, 115; in Thessaly and Macedonia, 121; takes Torone, refuses to observe truce, 123, 227; fails to take Potidaea, 124; killed at Amphipolis, 124; with Cleon, greatest enemy of peace, 125; praised by T., 202; forces freedom on Acanthus, 238.
British, like Spartans, 231.
British Commonwealth, tribute to, 233; sleepwalkers in, 235.
Bülow, Prince von, believes personalities influence history, 25.
Bury, J. B., on T.'s style, 192; sample of T.'s style, 193.
Byzantium, 1.T, Pel. fleet goes to, 162.
Caesar, C. J., as a historian, 4; use of indirect discourse, 4; date of birth, 28.
Calchis, 4.N, access to sea to be prevented, 120.

Callistratus, bravery at Syracuse, 157.

Cannae, battle of, 159.

Cardozo, Justice, justifies emphasis on crises, 30.

Caria, Alcibiades in, 160.

Carlyle, Thomas, romantic historian, 9.

Carthage, overthrown, 95.

Carystus, 4.O, city on Euboea, 53; exempt from contribution, 53; subject to Athens, 54.

Catholic Reaction, effect on historical writing, 8.

Chaeronea, 4.N, revolution at, 120; occupation of, 120; rising prevented, 120.

Chalcedon, 2.V, on Bosporus, 53.

Chalcidice, outpost in, 37; three peninsulas, 76; Cleon goes to, 124; refugees, 167.

Chamberlain, Neville, like Cleon, 236, 237.

Chateaubriand, François René, influence on romantic history, 9.

Chersonese, cultivation of, 69.

Chiang, Madame, advises mercy, 245.

Chios, 4.P.R, large island, 53; independent island, 54; subordinate state, 58; revolts, 159; large slave population, 180; stable government, 180.

Churchill, Winston S., effect of his personality on history, 25; on Lord Acton, 26; believes in historical importance of battles, 29; a "practical" historian, 31; on Charles XII, 95; admired by Roosevelt, 240; great courage of, 248.

Cimon, his splendid deeds, 80.

Clazomenae, 4.R, revolts, 159.

Clemens, Samuel (Mark Twain), definition of pessimist, 5; on falsity of geological "facts," 24.

Cleon, advocates destruction of Mytilene, 105; his character, 105; in command at Pylos, 116-119; responsible for failure to make peace, 120; sent to Amphipolis, 124; retakes Torone, 124; killed at Amphipolis, 124; with Brasidas, greatest enemy of peace, 125; T.'s opinion of him, 207; T.'s judgment not fair, 207; like Baldwin and Chamberlain, 236, 237.

Cnidus, 6.S, revolts, 159.

Codington, Sir Edward, British admiral defeats Turks at Navarino, 114.

Colonists, reimbursed, 181.

Conon, Athenian admiral defeated at Mytilene, 165.

Corcyra, 3.I, quarrel of, 60; appeal to Athens, 60; Oligarchs appeal to, 74; refuses to reinstate Oligarchs, 74; democratic element, 74; Corinth its mother city, 74; warnings sent to, 74; offers to submit to arbitration, 74; Corinthians attack, 74; appeals to Athens, 74; dispute between Corinth and, 84; alliance with, 85; civil war in, 108; murderous outburst in, 109; Oligarchs driven from, 109; attacked by force, 109; Oligarchs fear Athenians surrender them to, 110; Athens secures passage to, 113; fleet on its way to, 113;

allied fleet goes north to, 114; allied fleet recalled, 114; fleet returns from, 116; powerful ally of Athens, 119.

Corinth, 5.M, gulf of, 57; marauding rival, 57; commercial rival, 57; Isthmus of, 57; member of league, 60; jealousy of Athens, 60; appeals to Sparta, 60; dissatisfied, 62; reasons for wealth of, 70; Oligarchs appeal to, 74; colonies devastated, 74; begins preparations to punish Corcyra, 74; Potidaea colony of, 76; Potidaea in sympathy with, 76; dispute between Athens and, 76; dispute between Corcyra and, 84; communication to be cut off, 120; Corinth and Boeotia Sparta's most powerful allies, 131; dissatisfied with terms of peace, 131; different combinations, 132; early importance due to trade, 179.

Coronea, defeat at, 80.

Cos, 6.S, physician of, 38; not lost to Athens, 62.

Creighton, Mandell, calls Macaulay greatest historian, 29.

Crete, 7.O, Minos, King of, 67.

Cyclades, confederacy embraced, 53; Naxos largest of, 54.

Cyllene, 5.L, shipbuilding yards of, 74.

Cyme, 4.O, revolts, 159.

Cyrus (the Younger), Prince of Persia, replaces Tissaphernes, 164; meets Lysander, 164; refuses funds to Sparta, 166; help decide war, 239; compared with Roosevelt, 240.

Cythera, 6.M, seized by Athenians, 119; refuge for Helots, 119; peace after seizure, 125; Athens gives up, 126.

Cyzicus, 2.S, naval victory at, 63; defeat of Peloponnesians, 164.

Damonides, professor of music, friend of Pericles, 45.

Dardanelles, grain came through, 56.

Decelea, 4.N, seized by Sparta, 146; five sources of loss because of its seizure, 183.

Delium, 4.N, Hippocrates falls upon, 120; proposed occupation of, 120; severe reverse at, 125.

Delos, 5.P, confederacy of, 52; membership in, 52; contributions of ships or money, 53; cities forced to join, 53; not allowed to withdraw, 53; Naxos a test case, 54; treasury at Delos, 54; moved to Athens, 54; three classes of members, 54; the tribute a burden to members, 55; legal requirements galling, 55; supplanted by Athenian Empire, 56; revenue beautifies Athens, 58; graves opened at, 67; tribute assessed by Aristides, 183; purified, 189.

Delphi, 4.M, monuments at, 168; the Sacred Way, 248, 250.

Democracies, ruled by second-class men, 105.

Demosthenes, Athens' best general, 111; attempts to invade Boeotia, 111; defeated, 111; utterly defeats Ambraciots, 112; commands with Cleon at Pylos, 114; attack on Boeotia fails, 120; sent to Syracuse, 148; urges raising seige, 150; surrenders, 155; not commended by T., 201.

Digressions, in Book I, 67, 79, 82, 84; on ease of Athenian life, 88; on Theseus, 185; on Athenian navy, 186; on Teres, 186; on military matters, 186; account of plague not a digression, 187; to state personal views, 187; to bring in events outside war, 188; early history of Sicily, 188; Odrysian Empire, 188; Macedonia, 188; Delos, 189; murder of Hipparchus, 189; dramatic purpose, 190.

Diodotus, opposes Cleon on Mytilene's punishment, 106.

Diomedon, praised, 201.

Dionysius of Halicarnassus, discusses T., 191; distinguishes narrative and oratorical style, 192.

Droysen, Johann Gustav, nationalistic historian, 10; historical "facts" unattainable, 24.

Earthquakes, no portentous significance, 176; prevent invasion of Attica, 177; sea receded at Euboea, 177.

Echinades Island, 4.L, formation described, 176.

Eclipses, no portentous significance, 176; of sun, 178.

Egesta (Segesta), 5.C, plea from, 137; Athenian envoys tricked, 138.

Egypt, vessels sailed to, 57; squadron defeated in, 57; expedition to, 80; a "broken reed," 226; like Spain, 226; non-participant in Pel. War, 227.

Eion, 2.N, trireme in harbor of, 38; T.'s seizure of, 38.

Eleusis, 5.N, profanation of mysteries, 140; Alcibiades accused, 143.

Elis, coöperates with Athens, 62; refuses to ratify treaty, 127; with different combinations, 132.

Elymi, early inhabitants of Sicily, 173.

Ephesus, 5.S, products from, 56; revolts, 159; Tissaphernes goes to, 163; Pel. fleet at, 166.

Epidamnus, 1.I, colony of Corcyra, 60; appeals to Corinth, 60; situation in, 73; democrats in power in, 74; Corinth grandmother to, 74.

Epidaurus, war with Argos, 131.

Epipolae, plateau at Syracuse, 144.

Erechtheum, erected during war, 46.

Erythrae, 4.R, revolts, 159.

Euboea, 4.N, confederacy embraced, 53; large island on east coast of Attica, 53; cities of, 53; conquered, 57; revolts against Athens, 63; recapture of, 72; final subjugation of, 80; recovery of, 85; revolts, 162.

Euripides, denies history a science, 26; T.'s contemporary, 38; influence on T., 39; craze for Euripides at Abdera, 39; plays affected by war, 40; an "advanced thinker," 43; his interest in human problems, 45; Jebb's advice to, 45; frees Athenians at Syracuse, 46, 157.

Europe, Black Death, 92.

Eurotas, banks of, 71.

Euryelus, fort at Syracuse, 144.

Eurymedon, sent with reinforcements to Syracuse, 148; votes to raise siege, 151; overruled, 151; slain in naval battle, 152.

Eusebius, writer of "Christian epic," 8.

Fascist mottos, 60.

Fisher, Sir Herbert, author of *History of Europe*, 23; believes chance governs history, 224.

Five Thousand, limited Athenian democracy, 162; praised by T., 162; deposed, 164.

Fortune, plays large role in war, 96, 224; Fisher endorses this belief, 224.
Four Hundred, organized by Antiphon and Theramenes, 161; overthrown, 162.
France, defeat of, 95.
Frederick III, of Prussia, effect of his death on history, 25.
Freeman, Douglas S., *Life of Lee* displays practical knowledge of politics, 30.
Freeman, Edward A., believed T., measured forts at Syracuse, 175.
Friedjung, Heinrich, denies history a science, 26.
Fronde, James A., romantic historian, 9; nationalistic historian, 10.
Funeral Oration of Pericles, 89-92.
Games at Olympia and Delphi, more important to Greeks than war, 124.
Gay, Nelson, swamped by collection of historical material, 22.
Gela, 5.C, conference at, 136.
Geology, validity of its facts questioned, 23.
George, Lloyd, counterpart of Pericles, 236.
Germans, like Athenians, 231.
Gibbon, Edward, stigmatized because interesting, 11; not impartial, 28; called greatest historian, 29; member of House of Commons, 31; not a contemporary historian, 33.
Gildersleeve, B. L., on T.'s style, 195; notes rare use of τοί, 211; on historical parallel bars, 225.
Greece and Greeks, independent cities of, 51; freedom of, 51; land forces of, 51; Persians driven out of, 51; eastern coast of, 52; devotion to politics, love of independence, 56; northwestern, 61; early history of, 67; backward parts of, 58; no collective action among states of, 68; history of, 73; signal fires flashed to, 75; account of early Greece, 79, 84; feeling hostile to Athens throughout, 87; service rendered to Greece by Plataeans, 103; operations in northwest, 103; outrages swept Greece, 109; Demosthenes appears in northwest Greece, 111.
Grundy, G. B., condemns T.'s style, 192.
Guicciardini, Francesco, secularizes history, 8.
Gylippus, sent by Sparta to help Syracusans, 146; character, 147; receives surrender of Nicias, 155; tries to prevent execution of Demosthenes and Nicias, 155.
Hades, Sophocles refuses contest in, 40.
Halicarnassus, 6.S, not lost to Athens, 62.
Hancock, John, owner of trunk, 228.
Harnack, Adolf, calls Macaulay greatest historian, 29.
Haskell, H. J., *This Was Cicero* shows practical knowledge of politics, 31.
Hegel, George W. F., his *Philosophy of History,* 9.
Helen, runs beside Eurotas, (Theocritus XVIII.), 71.
Hellanicus, blamed for inaccuracy, 79, 174.
Hellas, T. spent twenty years here, 46; forces drawn from all Hellas, 69; numerous allies in, 70; ancient towns of, 71; calamities of, 71,

72; services Athens rendered to, 77; greater part subject to Athenians, 79.

Hellespont, 2.R, district of, 37; defeat of fleet in, 63; scene shifts, 162; control of, 164.

Helots, support Spartans, 59; hunted yearly, 59; rebellion of, 80; refuge for them at Pylos and Cythera, 119, 126.

Hermes, on Parthenon frieze, 46; mutilation of statues of, 140, 141; punishment of possible guilty approved, 213.

Hermocrates, "Sicily for Sicilians," 136; praised by T., 201.

Herodotus, purpose in writing history, 4; affected by Euripides, 45; praises Pausanias, 51; T. descends to his level, 188.

Hipparchus, murdered by Aristogeiton and Harmodius, 143, 189.

Hippias, daughter's epitaph, 189.

Hippocrates (the general), Athenian general killed at Delium, 120.

Hippocrates (the physician), contemporary of T., 38; influence on T., 44, 194; on Sophocles, 44.

History, Roman idea of, 4; ancient historians not impartial, 7; the "Christian epic," 8; Renaissance history, 8; influence of Machiavelli and Guicciardini, 8; the rationalists, Voltaire *et al.*, 9; Hume's insular history, 9; romanticism, Carlyle, Froude *et al.*, 9; Hegel's influence, 9; national historians, Ranke *et al.*, 10; "scientific" history, 10 ff.; scorn of Macaulay and Gibbon, 11; economic history, 12; economic history of Agricola's death, 12; geographic history, 13; geographic history of Agricola's death, 13; sociological history, 14; sociological history of Agricola's death, 14; psychological history, 15; psychological history of Agricola's death, 15; Freudian history, 16; Freudian account of Agricola's death, 17; value of histories of thought, 17; the "new history," 18; its contributions, 19; its amazing conceit, 20; Johnson's idea of, 21; Tolstoy's idea of, 21; inferior to poetry, according to Aristotle, 21; Ranke's idea of, 22; collection of material, 22; importance of causes, 22; future historians confined to brief periods, 23; cannot be exact science, 23; Droysen on scientific history, 24; must deal with personalities, 25; Von Bülow believes in personal influence on history, 26; Euripides on, 26; Eduard Meyer on, 26; Lord Acton on impartial historians, 26; Polybius believed in impartial history, 27; Jebb on impartial history, 27; impartial history impossible, 27; Tacitus not impartial, 28; Gibbon not impartial, 28; Motley and Macaulay not impartial, 29; political history not great, 29; political history most important, 29; Churchill on, 29; Roosevelt on, 29; Cardozo on, 30; great historians men of affairs, 30; Montaigne on, 30; Freeman on Lee, 31; characteristics of great historians, 31; T. a great historian, 32; contemporary history not great, 33; T. great contemporary historian, 33; reasons for T.'s greatness, 33.

Hitler, Adolf, forces Fascist governments, 238; Russian campaign, 239.

Hume, David, writer of rational history, 9; *History of England,* 9.

Hyperbolus, ostracized, 206; T.'s opinion of him, 206.

Independence, possible for small states only if protected, 241.

Ionian philosophers, rationalistic doctrines, 42; reaction against, 42.

Istone, oligarchs retreat to, 109; women sent into slavery, 110.

Italy and Italian, site of colony of Thurii, 45; Athens has designs on, 135; attack on Abyssinia, 235.

Japan, defeats Russia, 51; treacherous attack, 235; attack on Manchuria, 235.

Jebb, Sir Richard C., advice to Euripides, 45; on T.'s speeches, 192; on source of T.'s style, 195.

Jews, secure priority on prophecy, 11; massacres of, 242.

Johnson, Dr. Samuel, despises writing of history, 21.

Kingsley, Charles, criticized by "new historians," 20.

Laconia, Athenians not to land on shores of, 133.

Lamachus, general against Syracuse, 138; ideas for campaign against Syracuse, 142; death, 145.

Lambsdorff, Count Vladimir, consequences of snub to, 26.

Lampsacus, 2.R, where Hippias' son-in-law lived, 189.

Lebedus, 4.S, revolts, 159.

Leontini, 5.E, requests Athens' assistance, 135.

Lesbos, 3.R, large island, 53; independent island, 54; subordinate state, 57; not lost to Athens, 62; revolt of, 104; independent member of Empire, 105; execution of one thousand in, 108; revolts, 159; refugees, 167.

Leucas, 4.K, Acarnanians descend on, 111.

Lexington, battle of, 228.

Lincoln, Abraham, assassination "just a fact," 12; effect of his death on history, 25.

Lipari Islands, 4.D, (Isles of Aeolus), detailed description of, 177.

Livy, reason for writing history, 5; not a contemporary historian, 33.

Locris, Demosthenes' expedition through, 111.

Lodge, Henry Cabot, conflict with Wilson, 25.

London, cartoons of, 41; great plague of, 93.

Lydia, Alcibiades in, 160; Cyrus becomes governor of, 164.

Lysander, Spartan general, meets Cyrus, 164; denied command by Spartan rules, 166; given actual command, 166; refuses battle at Ephesus, 166; goes to Hellespont, 166; victories at Aegospotami, 167; allows Athenian citizens to return to Athens, 167; takes Athens 168; his dedication at Delphi, 169, 249; helped by Cyrus, 240.

Macaulay, T. B., opinion of Xenophon, 4; facts dross of history, 7, 28; nationalistic historian, 10; stigmatized because interesting, 11; criticized by "new historians," 18; not impartial, 29; "world's greatest historian," 29; "practical" historian, 31; not a contemporary historian, 33; estimate of T., 34, 198; example of his style, 199.

Macedonia, intended attack on king of, 121; history of, 188.

Machiavelli, Nicolo, secularizes history, 8.

Mantinea, 5.M, coöperates with Athens, 62; Battle of, 62, 132; troops from, 112; different combinations, 132; number of soldiers given, 174.

Mantua, town hall of, 59.

Marathon, 5.O, descendants of men who fought at, 45; heroes of, 46;

encroachments of King of Persia arrested at, 51; aid of Plataeans at, 86.

Marseilles, Greek outpost, 225.

Megara, 4.N, occupied, 57; Athens forced to give up, 57; revoke decree of, 82; rescind decree against, 83; Minoa port of, 108.

Melos, 6.O, descent on, 133; Athens determined to make it part of Athenian Empire, 133; inhabitants not believe in assembly, 133; surrenders, 135; refugees from Melos reach Athens, 167; ruthless treatment of, 168; like Belgium, 232.

Messenians, assist in capture of Spartans at Sphacteria, 117.

Metaurus, Hasdrubal's death at, 95.

Methone, 6.L, Athenians attack, 89.

Methymna, 3.R, did not revolt, 104.

Meyer, Eduard, denies history a science, 26.

Michelet, Jules, nationalistic historian, 10.

Miletus, 5.S, products came from, 56; revolts, 159.

Minoa, 6.N, Nicias led expedition against, 108; retained by Athens, 126.

Mommsen, Theodore, calls Macaulay greatest historian, 29; member of Reichstag, 31; not a contemporary historian, 33.

Montesquieu, Charles, writer of rational history, 9.

Motley, John L., not impartial, 29; a "practical" historian, 31.

Mycale, 5.R, Persian army at, 52.

Mycalessus, 4.M, massacres at, 184; T. expresses pity for this, 211.

Mytilene, 3.R, revolt of, 104; Athenians enraged by revolt of, 105; forced to capitulate, 105; Cleon advocates death of male citizens of, 105; people spared, 107; execution of delegates from, 107; defeat at, 165.

Naupactus, 4.L, allied city of, 57; Phormio's base at, 103; eleven ships fled to, 104; Messenians of, 111; Demosthenes escapes to, 111; Aetolians descend on, 111; Demosthenes not in, 112.

Nausicaa, lovely maiden of Corfu, 108.

Navarino, bay of, 114.

Naxos, 5.P, question of withdrawal from league, 53; largest of Cyclades, 53; subdued by force, 54; subject to Athens, 54; revolt and reduction of, 80; refugees, 167.

New Orleans, battle of after peace, 228.

Nicias, favorite general, a conservative, 43; Stanley Baldwin of Athens, 108, 236; takes Minoa, 108; advocates command at Pylos for Cleon, 116; Peace of, 126; broken by Athens, 132; general against Syracuse, 138; dilatory character, 138; ideas for campaign against Syracuse, 142; fatally ill, 145, 154; despondent, 148; asks reinforcements, 148; receives them, 149; refuses to raise siege, 151; surrenders, 155; "least deserved his fate," blamed for superstition, 176; described by T., 205; like Pétain, 237.

Nile, vessels went up, 57.

Nisaea, 4.N, retained by Athens, 126; Athens loses, 164.

Notium, 5.S, defeat at, 63, 165.

"Observing the Heavens," 41.

Odrysian Empire, alliance with Athens, 121; limits stated, 175; revenue of, 180; peculiar custom of, 188.

Odysseus, and Nausicaa at Corfu, 108.

Oeniadae, 4.L, accurately described, 175.

Olpae, 4.L, Ambraciots seize, 112.

Olympia, 5.L, Spartans go to, 124.

Otho, Roman Emperor defeated by Vitellius, 175.

Paches, general at Mytilene, 106; dastardly murder of Hippias, 213.

Palmerston, John H. T., native ability like that of Themistocles, 214.

Panactum, 4.N, Athenians lose, 125; restored to Athens, 126; Boeotians to give up, 126; fortress destroyed, 131.

Parnassus, Demosthenes passing north of, 111.

Parnes, Hippocrates leads force over, 120.

Paros, 5.P, pride of, 55.

Parthenon, begun in T.'s youth, 38; pediment and frieze, 46; treasury of Confederacy of Delos, 54; $6,000,000 reserve there, 58; no art object to T., 179.

Pausanias, defeats Persians, 51; praised by Herodotus, 52; his career, 81.

Peisistratus, adorns Athens, 180.

Peloponnesian War, outline of, 60-63; first phase, 61; second phase, 61; third phase, 62; Athens defeated, 63; Spartans own two fifths of Peloponnesus, 70; its causes, 73; events preceding hostilities, 73-86; revolt of Epidamnus, 74; appeal to Corinth, 74; Corinth defeated by Corcyra, 74; appeal to Athens, 75; Athens sides with Corcyra, 75; revolt of Potidaea, 76; Athenians at Spartan assembly, 76; war voted by Lacedaemonians, 79; real cause, 79,80; Spartans responsible, 80; embassies sent to Athens, 81; Pericles speaks against appeasement, 83; opening of war, 68, 88; Athenians brought into city, 88; first attack on Athens and in Peloponnesus, 88, 89; the plague, 92; Pericles' death, 95; war lost by chance, 95; second invasion of Attica, 101; siege of Plataea, 101; its surrender, 102; Phormio at Naupactus, 103; Brasidas' raids, 104; revolt of Mytilene, 104-108; capture of Minoa, 108; civil war at Corcyra, 108-111; Demosthenes defeated by Aetolians, 111; utterly defeats Ambraciots, 112; number of slain incredible, 112; Pylos and Sphacteria, 113-119; dismay of Spartans, 119; capture of Cythera, 119; conditions ripe for favorable peace, 119; attempted subjugation of Boeotia fails, 120; operations in northeast Greece, 121-123; truce for a year, 123; Cleon and Brasidas killed at Amphipolis, 124; Peace of Nicias, its terms, 126; Peace of Nicias a betrayal of Sparta's allies, 126; Athens and Sparta allied, 127; reason for failure of Peace of Nicias, 131; war shifts to Peloponnesus, 131; new Pel. league, 131; Athens assists Argos, 132; confused war in Peloponnesus, 132; Athens breaks peace, 132; reduction of Melos, 133-135; the Sicilian expedition, 135-158; victory of Thrasybulus, 163; Athenian victory at Cyzicus, 164; Athenian defeat at Notium and Mytilene, 165; victory at Arginusae Islands, 165; the generals condemned, 165; Sparta offers peace, 166; war

to last three times nine years, 166; Aegospotami, 166; Athens surrenders, 168; terms, 168; economic cause, 179; a world war, 225,
227, 228; affected by slowness of news, 227; like and unlike World
War, 229; treachery at start, 235; decided by Persian intervention,
239; bitterness increases as war lasts, 242.
Perdiccas, King of Macedonia, enemy, later ally of Athens, 121; fails
to help Cleon, 124; deserts Athens for Argos, 125; blockaded by
Athenians, 125; later rejoins Athens, 125.
Pericles, praises Athens, 41; sympathy for Anaxagoras and philosophers, 45; for Damonides and Protagoras, 45; Age of, 57; favors
war, 83; his policy for the war, 83; prevents sally from Athens,
88; the Funeral Oration, 90-92; loses his leadership, 94; regains it,
94; his policy justified, 94, 127, 187; death, 97; T.'s estimate of,
97; humanity of, 98; forces occupation of Decelea, 146; T.'s hero,
208; ability admired by T., 214; compared to Churchill, 248.
Pericles (the Younger), executed after Arginusae, 166.
Persia and Persians, King of, 51; Greek fear of, 52; last battle with,
55; new factor, 62; takes side of Sparta, 62; defeated in four
battles, 71; Themistocles settles in, 82; treaties with Sparta, 159;
no longer menace, 226; weakness demonstrated by Cyrus, 226;
weakness seen by Philip and Alexander, 227; intervention decides
Pel. War, 239.
Pétain, Marshal, like Nicias, 237.
Phaeacians, at Corfu, 108.
Phidias, statue of Athena, 46.
Philip II of Macedon, recognizes weakness of Persia, 227.
Philippi, 1.O, on shore of Aegean, 37.
Phocaea, 4.R, revolts, 159.
Phoenicians, traders, 226; contribute word "assassin," 226; stood aloof
in Pel. War, 227; Phoenicia like Sweden, 227.
Phormio, Athenian admiral defeats Spartans under Cnemus, 103; and
again at Naupactus, 104; successful against Acarnania, 104; Ath-
ens' most distinguished admiral, 104; besieges Oeniadae, 175.
Phrynichus, a man of extraordinary zeal, 201.
Piraeus, 5.N, walls of, 47; harbor city, 61; Themistocles buried in, 82;
Athenians to withdraw into, 83; people settle about, 88; plague in,
93; Brasidas' attempt to attack, 104; departure of Sicilian expedition from, 141; news of defeat reaches, 167; fortifications torn
down, 168.
Plague, account of (92, 93) not a digression, 187.
Plataea, T. familiar with, 39; encroachments of King of Persia arrested, 51; Pausanias commander of Spartans at, 51; fortunes of,
85; Thebans enter, 86; ally of Athens, 86; attack on, 86, 235;
treacherous attack on, 87; postpone siege of, 89; siege begun, 101;
all but defenders removed from, 101; Boeotians to restore, 127;
trophy for victory at, 249.
Plato, condemns state employment of citizens, 241.
Polybius, exceptional writer, 3; believes in impartial history, 27; Gildersleeve on, 27.

Potidaea, 2.N, on the isthmus, 76; in sympathy with Corinth, 76; Sparta warns Athens against attacking, 76; revolts, 76; surrenders, 76; demand to raise siege of, 82; demand relief of, 83; siege of, 84; campaign against, 85; six months after engagement at, 86; attempt to capture, 124; cost of siege, 182; double pay for soldiers at, 182.

Powers, H. H., author of *The Things Men Fight For,* 13.
Prescott, William H., A "practical" historian, 31.
Propylaea, incomplete, 127; not art object to T., 179; cost of, 182.
Protagoras, friend of Pericles, 45; draws constitution for Thurii, 45.
Pylos, 5.L, not visited by T., 39; modern town of, 56; notable event at, 113; fleet detained by adverse winds, 113; description of, 113; Demosthenes asks men to fortify, 114; further attack on, 115; siege of Pylos lifted, 116; Cleon arrives at, 117; refuge for Messenians, 119; Athens gives up, 126; Pylos refuses to surrender, 131; marauding expeditions from, 132; Demosthenes accompanies expedition to, 136; Athens loses, 164.

Ranke, Leopold von, nationalistic historian, 10; would write impartial history, 22; a contemporary historian, 33.
Reformation, effect on historical writing, 8.
Revere, Paul, at Lexington, 228.
Rhodes, 6.T, island of, 53; products come from, 56; revolts, 159.
Rome, its fall not a laboratory demonstration, 24; overthrow of Carthage, 95; states abandoned, 159; early history written in Greek, 195.
Roosevelt, Franklin D., effect of personality on history, 25; admires Churchill, 240.
Roosevelt, Theodore, condemns dull history, 12; justifies emphasis on crises in history, 29.
Russia, defeat by Japan, 51; rich fields of, 56; Napoleon's losses in, 95.
Salamis, 5.N, encroachments of King of Persia arrested at, 5; decisive victory of, 77; Persian power broken at, 82; Brasidas' raid on, 104.
Salaries, abolished by the Four Hundred, 183.
Samos, 5.R, large island, 53; independent island, 54; conquest, 57; naval development of, 70; subjugation of, 80; granted independence, 159.
Samothrace, 2.P, neighbor to Thasos, 37; ruggedness of, 37.
Santayana, George, the "Christian epic," 8.
Scione, 3.N, Brasidas enters, 123.
Scott, Sir Walter, influence on romantic history, 9.
Selinus, 5.C, appeals to Syracuse, 138; self-supporting, 180.
Sestos, 2.R, Athenian sailors get provisions from, 167.
Shear, T. Leslie, discovers Spartan shield, 118.
Sicanians, early inhabitants of Sicily, 173.
Sicily, death of Aeschylus reported from, 38; prisons in, 46; idea of subduing, 62; Athens secures passage to, 113; fleet on its way to, 113; Athens has designs on, 133; two expeditions had been sent,

135; grain from, 136; invasion of planned, 137; third expedition, 137-158; earliest inhabitants, 173.

Sicyon, 4.M, demonstration against, 120.

Siphae, 4.M, fleet lands at, 120; to be occupied, 120; Demosthenes arrives at, 120.

Sitalces, Thracian King allied to Athens, 121; father of Teres, 186.

Socrates, his new philosophy, 43; advanced thinker, 43.

Solygeia, 5.N, battle of, Corinthian victory over Athens, 228.

Sophocles, T.'s contemporary, 38; plays not affected by war, 40; his gentleness, 40; little affected by new speculative thinking, 43; not influenced by Hippocrates, 44; his admiration for Athens, 44; wins prizes, 46; corrected by T., 186.

Spain, as weak now as Egypt was, 226.

Sparta, 6.M, and the Spartans, architectural poverty of, 39; land forces led by, 51; armed camp, 58; supported by Helots, 59; use iron for money, 59; venal, 59; military pre-eminence, 60; head of confederacy, 60; appealed to by Corinth, 60; Nicias' peace satisfactory to, 61; unable to enforce peace, 61; truce with Argos expired, 62; sells out Corinth, 62; alliance wrecked by, 62; wins second round, 62; reason for supremacy, 70; contrast between Athens and, 70; deserted, 70; visitor at, 71; Potidaeans send embassy to, 76; contravention of treaty between Athens and, 76; meeting of allies at, 76; Athenian embassy at, 77; Athens threatening, 79; votes for war, 80; rebellion of Helots at, 80; Bronze House at, 81; cities subject to, 81; appeasement of, 83; negotiations between Athens and, 84; Aenesias Ephor at, 86; Brasidas thanked by, 89; overtures of peace made to, 94; scales tipped in favor of, 95; Sparta more tyrannical than Athens, 95; commissioners sail from, 102; shock caused by surrender of, 118; wants to discontinue hostilities, 123; Perdiccas joins Sparta against Athens, 125; sold out interests of allies, 131; does not fulfill conditions of peace, 131; truce with Argos, 131; haggles over peace terms, 131; attempt to crush, 131; prestige high, 132; war with Athens not declared, 132; send Gylippus to Syracuse, 146; fortify Decelea, 146; importance of this, 147; treats with King of Persia, 159; Alcibiades at, 160; convenient enemies, 162; retake Pylos, 164; serious financial state, 166; offers peace after Arginusae, 166; refuses to destroy Athens, 168, 244; head of confederacy, 229; Dorians, 229; contrasted with Athens, 229; like British, 231; unbearable, 231; despondent in adversity, 247.

Sphacteria, 5.L, not visited by T., 39; peace after, 96; situation of, 113; Spartans land force on, 115; siege of Sphacteria begun, 116; capture of soldiers at, 119; attempted recovery of prisoners, 123, 126.

Sthenelaidas, Spartan Ephor advocates war, 78.

Strongyle, 4.D, troops land on, 135.

Strymon, Amphipolis, city on, 37.

Stubbs, William, calls Macaulay greatest historian, 29.

Suetonius, gives color of Caesar's eyes, 200.

298 THUCYDIDES AND THE WORLD WAR

Sweden, collapse of empire, 95; like Carthage, 227.

Syracuse, 5.E, T. visited, 39; expedition against, 62; effort to subdue, 62; Gylippus prevented from entering, 96; Nicias' disaster at, 97; its economic background, 136; expedition against, 137-158; early history, 137; excuse for invasion of, 137; Alcibiades, Lamachus, Nicias elected to lead invasion, 138; real reason for invasion of, 139; departure from Piraeus, 141; details of Athenian force, 142; despair of Syracusans, 142; futile policy of Nicias, 143; siege of Syracuse begun, 144; walls begun, 145; Gylippus enters Syracuse, 146; Athenians reinforced, 149; Athenians defeated in Great Harbor, 149; Athenian surprise attack fails, 150; siege continued, 151; moon eclipsed, 151; sea fight, Athenians defeated, Eurymedon slain, 152; final naval battle, 152; departure further delayed, 153; the retreat begun, 154; Demosthenes surrenders, 155; and Nicias, 155; put to death, 155; fate of prisoners, 156; captives freed by Euripides, 157; news reaches Athens, 158; Syracuse self-sustaining, 180; expense of expedition, 182; like Hitler's Russian campaign, 239.

Tacitus, character of his history, 5; his telegraphic style, 5; account of Agricola's death, 6, 7; his *Histories*, 7; criticised by "new historians," 20; a "practical" historian, 31; a contemporary historian, 33; geographical details inaccurate, 175.

Tanagra, 4.N, defeat at, 80; Delian shrine in, 120.

Tax, levied by Peisistratus, 180; replaces Delian tribute, 183.

Taygetus, towering range of, 71.

Tegea, 5.M, alliance wrecked by, 62; refuses to join league, 131.

Teos, 4.R, revolts, 159.

Teres, not to be confused with Tereus, 186.

Thasos, 2.O, T.'s connection with, 37; T.'s large interests in, 37; description of, 37; subdued by force, 54; T. on guard at, 123.

Thebes, 4.N, not mastered, 57; center of Boeotia, 60; treacherous attack on Plataea, 80, 235; larger force following from, 87; supporting forces from, 87; advocates death, 168.

Themistocles, responsible for defeat of Persia, 51; admired by T., 51; outwits Spartans, 80; career, 81; T.'s hero, 208; compared to Palmerston, 214.

Theramenes, a dude according to Aristophanes, 32; plots against democracy at Athens, 161; victory at Cyzicus, 164.

Thermopylae, 4.M, Leonidas sent to, 124.

Thespiae, occupation of, 120.

Thessaly, rich lands of, 67; Brasidas marches across, 121.

Thompson, James W., calls Gibbon greatest historian, 29.

Thrace, T.'s connection with, 37; Abdera in, 39; gold mines in, 123.

Thrasybulus, Athenian general, victory of at Byzantium, 163; victory at Cyzicus, 164; praised, 200.

Thucydides, exceptional character of his writing, 3; purpose in writing history, 4; Tacitus imitates his style, 5; deals with fundamental problems, 31; vivid portraits of persons, 31; deals with

INDICES

motives, 31; not impartial, 31; a political historian, 32; limits *History* to Pel. War, 32; a "practical" historian, 33; a contemporary historian, 33; reasons for greatness as historian, 33; called "greatest historian" by Macaulay, 34; facts of his life, 37 ff.; visits Sparta, Acarnania, Plataea, Syracuse, 39; did not visit Pylos, 39; influenced by Euripides, 39; associated with Pericles, 40, 45; influenced by Hippocrates, 44; history scientific in spirit, 45; return to Athens, 46; his history a gift to posterity, 47; admires Themistocles, 51; remarkable summary of early Greek history, 67-72; his method, 72, 85; fails to save Amphipolis and is banished, 123; asserts unity of war with Peloponnesus, 127; gives economic reasons for Sicilian expedition, 136; excellence of description of Syracusan expedition, 139; seventh book unsurpassed, 147, 198; estimate of Athens' disaster at Syracuse, 156; opinion of Nicias, 156; eighth book incomplete, 158; history of revolt of Chios all through Book VIII, 159; praises the Five Thousand, 162; narrative closes 411 B.C., 163; gives reason for Athens' defeat, 169; distrust of legends, 173; interest sacrificed to accuracy, 173; interest in science, 173-178; annalistic method defended, 174; military statistics carefully given, 174; geographical data accurate, 174; unlike Tacitus, 175; exact description of Syracuse, 175; no faith in oracles, 176; eclipses and earthquakes—gives dates, 176; on penology, 178; interested in economics, 179-185; resources of Athens, 181; soldiers' pay, 182; digressions, 185-190; with digressions, complete history of Hellas and Athens, 190; style, 191-200; Xenophon fails to imitate it, 191; "T.'s Greek only good Thracian," 192; imitation of, 193; cause for T.'s style, 194; not due to Hippocrates, 194; nor probably to Antiphon, 194; T. antipathetic to Herodotus, 195; style due to unformed character of Greek language, 195; the speeches, 196-197; use of medical terms, 197; arrangement of material, 197; few anecdotes, 198; describes mental states, 200; character sketches, 200-209; Archidamus, 200; Thrasybulus, 200; Diomedon, 201; Theramenes, 201; Hermocrates, 201; prejudiced against Demosthenes, 201; praise of Brasidas, 202; Antiphon characterized, 202; Alcibiades, 203; Nicias, 205; Hyperbolus, 206; Cleon, 207; T.'s bias revealed, 207; *suppressio veri*, 207; praise of Themistocles, 208; and Pericles, 208; T. a realist, 209; not fond of common people, 209; nor Athenians, 209; "crooks better than fools," 210; explains joke, 210; emotionless, 211; aristocratic prejudice, 211; T. no believer in pure democracy, 212; T.'s view of state, 212; believed in Athens' tyranny, 212; proud of Athens, 213; does not judge morals, 213; believed in success, 213; approves punishment of accused whether guilty or not, 213; admires ability of traitor, Antiphon, 214; admires ability of Themistocles, 214; and Pericles, 214; T.'s fairness, 215; his possibilities as a statesman, 215; modernity of his work, 216; interprets facts, 216; presents motives, 216; consummate arrangement of material, 216; vivid portrayal of characters, 217; speeches better than the reality, 217; brilliant statements, 219; keen insight, 219; universal character of the *History,* 220; reasons for writing the *History,* 223; part played by chance, 224; history repeats itself, 224.

Thucydides (not the historian), opposes use of Delian League funds to beautify Athens, 58.

Thurii, 3.F, colony founded by Athenians, 45.

Tissaphernes, Persian satrap, deals with Alcibiades, 160; a gifted liar, 160; visit of Alcibiades to, 163; replaced by Cyrus, 164; pays four dollars each for prisoners, 181; attempt to cut soldiers' pay, 182.

Tolstoy, Nikolaevich, despises nineteenth-century historical writing, 21; does not believe in personal influence in history, 25.

Torone, 2.N, Brasidas takes, 123; Cleon retakes, 124.

Tournia, siege of, 102.

Treitschke, Heinrich von, nationalistic historian, 10.

United States, corresponds to Persia, 229.

Venizelos, Eleutherios, translates T., 193.

Vitellius, Roman Emperor, defeats Otho, 175.

Voltaire, François, writer of rational history, 9; age of Louis XIV, 9.

Wilamowitz, Ulrich, on T.'s style, 192.

William I of Prussia, snubs Lambsdorff, 26.

Wilson, Woodrow, conflict with Lodge, 25.

World War, one war, 235; leadership like Pel. War, 236 ff.; removal of population, 234, 238; change of governments forced, 238; Syracusan expedition like Hitler's Russian campaign, 239; decided by U. S., 239; summary of comparison to Pel. War, 240; economic consequences of, 241; defection of Germany's allies, 242; to be won by resources, 243; false peace, 243; sudden end, 244; "soft" peace, 244; civil war in Europe, 245.

Xenophon, a poor historian, continues T.'s narrative, 163; imitates T.'s method, 163, 191; specimen of style, 164.

Xerxes, defeated by Athenian navy, 51.

INDEX OF NAMES ON MAP

Abdera, 2 O
Abydos, 2 R
Acanthus, 2 N
Achelous, 4 L
Aegina, 5 N
Aegospotami, 2 R
Aetna, 5 D
Amphipolis, 1 N
Arginusae, 4 R
Argos, 5 M
Artemisium, 3 N
Assinarus, 6 E
Athens, 5 N
Athos, 2 O

Bosporos, 1 B
Byzantium, 1 T

Calcedon, 2 U
Calchis, 4 N
Carystus, 4 O
Chaeronea, 4 N
Chios, 4 P
Clazomene, 4 R
Cnidus, 6 S
Corcyra, 3 I
Corinth, 5 N
Cos, 6 S
Crete, 7 O
Cyllene, 5 L
Cyme, 4 O
Cythera, 6 M
Cyzicus, 2 S

Decelea, 4 N
Delium, 4 N
Delos, 5 P
Delphi, 4 M

Egesta, 5 C
Echinades, 4 L
Eion, 2 M
Eleusis, 5 N
Epheseus, 5 S
Epidamnus, 1 I
Erythrae, 4 R
Euboea, 4 N

Gela, 5 D

Halicarnassus, 6 S
Hellespont, 2 R

Lampsacus, 2 R
Lebedus, 4 S
Leontini, 5 E
Lesbos, 3 R
Leucas, 4 K
Lipari Islands, 4 D

Mantinea, 5 N
Marathon, 5 O
Megara, 4 N
Melos, 6 O
Methone, 6 L
Methymna, 3 R
Miletus, 5 S
Minoa, 6 M
Mycale, 5 R
Mycalessus, 4 N
Mytilene, 3 R

Naupactus, 4 L
Naxos, 5 P
Nisaea, 4 N
Notium, 5 S

Oeniadae, 4 L
Olpae, 4 L
Olympia, 5 L

Panactum, 4 N
Paros, 5 P
Philippi, 1 O
Phocaea, 4 R
Piraeus, 5 N
Plataea, 4 N
Potidaea, 2 N
Pylos, 5 L

Rhodes, 6 T

Salamis, 5 N
Samos, 5 R
Samothrace, 2 P
Scione, 3 N
Selinus, 5 C
Sestos, 2 R
Sicyon, 4 M
Siphae, 4 M
Solygeia, 5 N
Sparta, 6 M
Sphacteria, 5 L
Strongyle, 4 D
Syracuse, 5 E

Tanagra, 4 M
Tegea, 5 M
Teos, 4 R
Thasos, 2 O
Thebes, 4 M
Thermopylae, 4 M
Thurii, 3 F
Torone, 2 M
Troy, 2 R

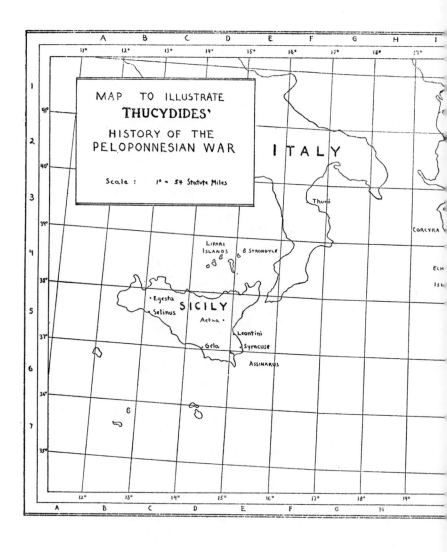

MAP TO ILLUSTRATE
THUCYDIDES'
HISTORY OF THE
PELOPONNESIAN WAR

Scale :   1° = 54 Statute Miles

ITALY

Thurii

CORCYRA

LIPARI
ISLANDS   B STRONGYLE

ECH

ISL

• Egesta   SICILY
Selinus

Aetna •

Gela   Leontini
          • Syracuse
      ASSINARUS

B